Innovation in Islam

Published in collaboration with the Center for International
and Regional Studies at Georgetown University's School
of Foreign Service in Qatar.

CIRS
CENTER FOR
INTERNATIONAL
AND REGIONAL
STUDIES

GEORGETOWN UNIVERSITY
SCHOOL OF FOREIGN SERVICE IN QATAR

# Innovation in Islam

*Traditions and Contributions*

EDITED BY
# Mehran Kamrava

UNIVERSITY OF CALIFORNIA PRESS
*Berkeley · Los Angeles · London*

University of California Press, one of the most distinguished university presses in the United States, enriches lives around the world by advancing scholarship in the humanities, social sciences, and natural sciences. Its activities are supported by the UC Press Foundation and by philanthropic contributions from individuals and institutions. For more information, visit www.ucpress.edu.

University of California Press
Berkeley and Los Angeles, California

University of California Press, Ltd.
London, England

© 2011 by The Regents of the University of California

Library of Congress Cataloging-in-Publication Data

Innovation in Islam : traditions and contributions / edited by Mehran Kamrava.
   p. cm.
Includes index.
ISBN 978-0-520-26694-0 (cloth : alk. paper)
ISBN 978-0-520-26695-7 (pbk. : alk. paper)
1. Islam—21st century.  2. Islamic renewal.
3. Islamic fundamentalism.
I. Kamrava, Mehran, 1964–.
BP60.I56  2011
297.2'609—dc22                    2010039651


19  18  17  16  15  14  13  12  11
10  9  8  7  6  5  4  3  2  1

*To Melisa,
Dilara, and Kendra*

# Contents

List of Illustrations ... ix
Acknowledgments ... xi

1. Contextualizing Innovation in Islam
   *Mehran Kamrava* ... 1

PART ONE. THE INTELLECTUAL PROCESS

2. Knowledge and Hermeneutics in Islam Today: Which Reform?
   *Tariq Ramadan* ... 23

3. Deconstructing *Epistēmē*(s)
   *Mohammed Arkoun* ... 39

4. Iranian Shi'ism at the Gates of Historic Change
   *Mehran Kamrava* ... 58

PART TWO. THE ARTS AND LETTERS

5. History from Below, Dictionary from Below
   *Nelly Hanna* ... 85

6. The Translation of the Qur'an: An Impossible Task: The Classical Linguistic-Theological Roots of the Debate
   *Nasr Abu-Zayd* — 98

7. Toward a New Understanding of Renewal in Islam
   *Adonis* — 111

8. Creation, Originality, and Innovation in Sufi Poetry
   *Patrick Laude* — 125

9. Innovation in the Visual Arts of Islam
   *Walter B. Denny* — 143

## PART THREE. ISLAM IN THE MODERN WORLD

10. Liberal/Progressive, Modern, and Modernized Islam: Muslim Americans and the American State
    *Sherman A. Jackson* — 167

11. *Hijab* and Choice: Between Politics and Theology
    *Ziba Mir-Hosseini* — 190

12. Modern Movements in Islam
    *John O. Voll* — 213

List of Contributors — 239
Index — 243

# Illustrations

1. Page in Kufic script from a Qur'an manuscript, ink on parchment, Iraq, ninth century C.E. / 146
2. Page of *shikasteh* calligraphy, ink on paper, Iran, eighteenth century C.E. / 147
3. *Shahada* (profession of faith), ink on paper, Kashgar, twenty-first century C.E. / 148
4. Advertising signage, Morocco, late twentieth century C.E. / 148
5. Plate with Kufic inscription, slip on earthenware, eastern Iran, tenth century C.E. / 150
6. Plate with figural decoration, luster on white ware, Iran, thirteenth century C.E. / 151
7. Bowl with figural decoration, *mina'i* colors on white ware, Iran, thirteenth century C.E. / 153
8. Jug with figural decoration, black line under turquoise glaze on reticulated white ware, Iran, thirteenth century C.E. / 154
9. Underglaze-painted tile panel made in Iznik, Mosque of Selim II, Edirne, Turkey, ca. 1572 C.E. / 155
10. Tomb of the Samanids, Bukhara, Uzbekistan, ca. 901 C.E. / 157
11. Glazed brick from the Great Mosque of Malatya, Turkey, thirteenth century C.E. / 158
12. Tile mosaic from the Attarin Madrasa, Fez, Morocco, late thirteenth century C.E. / 159

13. *Cuerda seca* ceramics from the tomb of Mehmed I, Bursa, Turkey, ca. 1421 C.E. / 160
14. Kocatepe Mosque, Ankara, Turkey, late twentieth century C.E. / 161

# Acknowledgments

In compiling this book, I was extremely fortunate to work with a highly dedicated group of scholars from across the world, all of whom shared a deep enthusiasm for the topic of innovation in Islam. I gratefully acknowledge their promptness, their dedication to the project, and their patience in putting up with unforeseen delays as the book made its journey from an intellectual brainstorming session in Doha, Qatar, to its present form.

Anyone who has suffered through the publishing process knows firsthand an author's need for Herculean perseverance and patience. Niels Hooper, my editor at the University of California Press, made the process of shepherding the project to its present form much less arduous than it might have been. My colleague Suzi Mirgani served as my eyes for fine detail and as a tactful negotiator when the contributors needed nudging with the paperwork. As the Publications Coordinator at Georgetown University's Center for International and Regional Studies (CIRS) in the School of Foreign Service in Qatar, where this project was conceived and worked on, Suzi meticulously oversaw all of the details of putting the book together. Natalie Prendergast joined CIRS toward the tail end of work on the project, spending many hours ensuring the volume's consistency in transliteration and style. I am deeply thankful to both.

The greatest thanks go to my wife Melisa and my daughters Kendra and Dilara. On a typical day, Melisa is the one who ensures that I have the peace and quiet needed to write. Suffice it to say here that I simply would not have been able to work on this, or on any other project, had it not been for the loving and nurturing atmosphere of our house, and for that, and much more, I am grateful to my wonderful family. It is to them that I dedicate this book.

CHAPTER I

# Contextualizing Innovation in Islam

MEHRAN KAMRAVA

Those of you who live after me will see great disagreement. You must then follow my Sunna and that of the rightly guided caliphs. Hold to it and stick fast to it. Avoid novelties, for every novelty is an innovation, and every innovation is an error.

—Abi Dawood Sulaiman bin Al-Aash'ath Al-Sijistani (202–275 A.H./ 817–888 C.E)

The above hadith, attributed to the Prophet Muhammad by the authoritative Abi Dawood, is often cited as evidence of Islam's innate conservatism and antithetical relationship with innovation. According to Bernard Lewis, "the gravamen of a charge of [innovation] against a doctrine was not, primarily, that it was false but that it was new—a breach of custom and tradition, respect for which is reinforced by the belief in the finality and perfection of the Muslim revelation."[1] As such, it is often assumed that Islam is fundamentally rigid and inflexible, more adept at waging wars against nonbelievers than at coming to terms with modernity.[2] Islamic theology, philosophy, and jurisprudence, based on a worldview articulated some fourteen hundred years ago, and lacking an experience akin to the Christian Reformation, are stuck in eras long gone by.[3] The underlying reason for this goes back to Islam's injunction against innovation, for innovation is to Islam, Lewis argues, what heresy is to Christianity.[4]

It cannot be denied that throughout Islamic history so far, "innovation" has been seen and treated as a slippery concept. The literal Arabic translation for "innovation" is *bid'a,* a concept that over time has come to acquire a highly negative connotation. After discussing the relationship between innovation and *bid'a,* and how the latter has come to acquire a negative, even dreaded connotation, this chapter will show, however, that innovation in Islam is neither new nor novel; nor, indeed, has it been that rare. Nevertheless, in the words of Michael Cook, for nearly a millennium a "conservative default" has characterized the Muslim world and the intellectual, artistic, economic, and scientific innovations produced within and under its umbrella.[5]

As with any other orthodoxy, discussions or manifestations of innovation are likely to provoke anger and rebuke when they are formulated and expressed within the context of Islamic orthodoxy. Naturally, reactions to innovation depend in large measure on exactly what is meant and understood by it, as well as the context within which this definition is produced and used. There is, nevertheless, more to the Muslim world's "conservative default" than the angry reactions of self-appointed bastions of traditionalism. Anti-innovationists operate within, and themselves are often products of, structural and environmental factors that shape and influence both their mind-sets and the mind-sets of their audience and their sympathizers. Why, then, the chapter asks, have the opponents of innovation found their message so resonant with the Muslim masses at large? The answer lies not so much in Islam itself or in anything intrinsically Islamic, but in the ways and means through which the teachings of Islam have been produced and perpetuated over time. As the chapters that follow show, in one form or another, innovation has historically been, and continues to be, present and persistent in Islam and the multiple facets of life that it engrosses. What have been absent, and ultimately what are urgently needed, are the institutions and the proper contexts that would facilitate its flowering.

## THE MEANING AND CONTEXT OF *BID'A*

*Bid'a* is "a belief or a practice for which there is no precedent in the time of the Prophet."[6] Though rarely mentioned in the Qur'an,[7] the notion became prevalent soon after the death of the Prophet to refer to beliefs and practices that appeared to counter those endorsed by the Sunna and the Holy Book. In fact, beginning in the third century of Islam, an entire genre of *bid'a* literature emerged, which, despite a lull between the fourteenth and twentieth centuries C.E., has lasted up to the present day.[8] On these grounds, there have been extreme cases in

Islamic history when innovations as various as tables, sieves, coffee, tobacco, the printing press, artillery, the telephone, the telegraph, and, more recently, voting rights for women have been rejected as *bid'a*, contrary to the Sunna of the Prophet and his Companions.[9] But inevitable changes in life and circumstances soon necessitated modification of strict interpretations of *bid'a*. Before long, distinctions began appearing between "good" or "praiseworthy" *bid'a*s and those that were to be avoided at all times.[10] Al-Shafii (b. 767 C.E.), after whom the Shafii school of jurisprudence is named, was one of the earliest jurists who presented nuanced interpretations of *bid'a*, dividing it into five categories: (1) those *bid'a*s that are necessary for and incumbent *(fard kifaya)* on the community, such as the study of grammar and rhetoric and investigations of the reliability of the men whose authority is cited for the Sunna; (2) forbidden *(muharrama) bid'a*s, which run contrary to the Sunna and the consensus and accepted beliefs of the community *(ijma')*; (3) recommended *(manduba) bid'a*s, such as the establishment of hospices and schools; (4) *bid'a*s that are disapproved but not prohibited *(makruha)*, such as decorating mosques and copies of the Qur'an; and, (5) those that are permitted *(mubaha)* because the law is silent in their regard, such as wearing clothes and eating pleasant food and drinks.[11]

Despite the efforts of Al-Shafii and others to distinguish between varieties of *bid'a*, over time the concept has become generally understood to mean "any modification of accepted religious belief or practice."[12] At the same time, more conservative Muslims have continued to label social practices of which they do not approve as *bid'a*.[13] This absence of a universally agreed-upon definition of *bid'a*, as well as the inevitability of the need for adaptation to new and emerging circumstances, no matter how reluctantly, have combined to result in a number of consequences for innovation in Islam. Most notably, there have been instances and episodes of profoundly consequential bursts of innovation either by renowned Muslims or under the banner and rubric of the religion, or both. Due partly to the inevitability of changes in life and circumstances, partly to the dogged determination of individual innovators, and partly to the rare combination of a hospitable environment and supportive institutions, there have been instances of innovation in Islam that have even found sanction and support among influential jurists of the faith. What is thus important for us to consider is *context*— the context within which something is defined as *bid'a*, or, more accurately, disparaged, rather than being seen in a positive and welcoming light.

There are countless examples that serve to illustrate the contextuality of *bid'a* at any given point in Islamic history. Here I shall briefly highlight two of the more interesting ones I have come across. In the early decades of the nineteenth century, when Sultan Mahmud II (r. 1808–1839 C.E.) was busy introducing modern reforms into the Ottoman state machinery and economy, a number of ulama (or mullahs) opposed the innovations on grounds that they both represented and facilitated *bid'a*. Some of these sentiments are reflected in an unattributed text from the time that denounces the evils of such modern innovations as steamships, factories, and the telegraph. In one of the passages, the text's anonymous author writes the following: "[Because of these innovations,] one's soul becomes insolent, because the soul is inclined to wicked deeds and most evil deeds are generally (committed) for money and valuables; and now if someone wishes to commit a deed in a far city, he can reach it quickly and do what he wishes."[14] He further goes on to denounce these innovations on grounds that they make one's soul "conceited," reduce one's reliance on and trust in the Almighty, and cause one's recompense to be diminished "because one attains one's goal easily without effort."[15]

While it is difficult to determine exactly how representative of the opinions of the traditional clergy this text might have been, it clearly does appear to reflect an overall sentiment of unease and even anger and fear directed at what are perceived as prime examples of *bid'a*. Mahmud II's reforms represented more than mere jurisprudential infractions. They threatened the financial and institutional interests of the ulama in areas such as education and law, where they had long had monopolistic control. Furthermore, the sultan's founding of a Ministry of Awqaf (religious endowment) seriously undermined the ulama's financial independence.[16] It is not unreasonable to conclude, therefore, that the charge of *bid'a* leveled against Mahmud II's reforms was motivated by concerns that were not based solely on religious considerations. At the same time, however, a number of the more senior ulama did not see the sultan's reforms in the same threatening light, or at least did not voice their opposition if they did, because of their proximity to the political establishment. Some, either out of prudence or out of conviction, even went so far as to join the ranks of the reformers.[17] Depending on their positions, ulama variously saw the identical reforms as *bid'a* or not *bid'a*.

A second, more pertinent example comes from the *adhan* (call to prayer) in Shi'ism. While performing this rite, Twelver Shi'as include Imam

Ali in the *wilaya* (spiritual and temporal authority) by reciting the phrase "I bear witness that Ali is the friend of God" after the *shahada* (bearing witness to Allah and the prophecy of Muhammad). Although in the minds of most Shi'as, the *wilaya* has been a permanent feature of the *adhan*, the *adhan* in fact did not include the *wilaya* during the lifetimes of either the Prophet Muhammad or any of the Shi'a imams.[18] Rather, the practice can be traced to the early sixteenth century. As part of a concerted effort by the Safavids to prop up a nascent state in Iran based on Shi'a identity, Shah Ismail (r. 1501–1524 C.E.) embarked on a determined campaign to encourage public expressions of Islam in a Shi'a form. One of his efforts to this end was to mandate that the *wilaya* be included in the *adhan*, a practice that had been seen as *bid'a* and thus prohibited, or at least discouraged, by earlier generations of Shi'a jurists.[19] By the time of Shah Tahmasp (r. 1524–1576 C.E.), the inclusion of the *wilaya* in the *adhan* formed only one part of a much larger menu of popular expressions of Shi'a religious identity that were meant to distinguish the Shi'ism of Iranians from the Sunni beliefs of Turks and Arabs. Other such identity-driven expressions included canonical cursing of the first three caliphs, visits to the shrines of imams or their descendants, and acts of self-mortification.[20] Although they initially viewed most of these innovations as *bid'a*, many of the non-Iranian Shi'a jurists brought into the country to propagate the new faith had no choice but to accept and endorse them. Before long, what had once been *bid'a* had, at least for the Shi'a of Iran, become part of the Sunna.

Both of the examples cited here point to the importance of the *political* context in shaping perceptions of an innovation as either acceptable or *bid'a*. But social, cultural, and economic contexts can be just as important in determining the fate of an innovation. Upon its introduction into the Cairo market by an especially enterprising merchant between 1580 and 1625, for example, drinking coffee—or "black water"—was seen as tantamount to *bid'a* and was therefore vehemently denounced by the ulama, who urged the faithful to attack and destroy coffeehouses.[21] "A half-millennium later, leaders of Saudi Arabia's puritanical Wahhabi sect proudly serve coffee to their guests, treating it as an ancient Arab delicacy, usually without an awareness of the history of the Arab and Islamic resistance to this custom."[22] The Saudi ulama's initial resistance to television in the early 1960s, on grounds that it contravened Islam's ban on graven images and encouraged idolatry, soon gave way to its endorsement. Once they learned of television's "immense potential as an instrument of religious indoctrination, they promptly discovered that it falls, after all, within the *sunna*," Timur Kuran notes.[23] "[N]umerous other innovations have gained Islamic legitimacy following a period of fervent resistance."[24] Often, jurists themselves, keenly aware of life's need for innovative change and adaptability, found ways around the prohibition of *bid'a* by manipulating the term. Such a manipulation, Vardit Rispler contends, "constructed another evaluative system outside of the Shari'a [Islamic law] which shares its terminology and general values but tackles phenomena not dealt with by the Shari'a."[25] By doing so, they would change the context within which *bid'a* was received and perceived. Perhaps more than any other factor, context determines whether an innovation indeed amounts to *bid'a* or is in accordance with the Sunna.

## OBSTACLES TO INNOVATION

Notwithstanding occasional bursts of innovation, the larger Islamic milieu has not on the whole been conducive to sustained innovative thoughts and ideas, practices, and institutions. Jonathan Berkey has argued that a "principled aversion to any innovation remained an important, if not universal, element in medieval Islamic discourse."[26] We see the same phenomenon, in one form or another, present at various other eras of Islamic history. An overarching conservative inertia overcame the Muslim world beginning in the tenth century C.E. A key aspect of Islam stricken by this inertia was *ijtihad*, independent reasoning, as opposed to *taqlid*, or accepting the opinions of the founders of *madhabs* (schools of jurisprudential thought). Beginning in the tenth century and lasting into the eighteenth and nineteenth centuries, a consensus emerged that *ijtihad* was forbidden and that *taqlid* was incumbent on all Muslims, both laymen and scholars.[27]

There were, to be certain, notable and highly consequential exceptions, among the most significant of which were the intellectual contributions of the likes of Ibn Sina (980–1037 C.E.) and Ibn Rushd (1126–1198 C.E.)—known in the West as Avicenna and Averroës respectively—both of whom shaped and influenced much of what we know today about science and philosophy.[28] Over the next few centuries, spectacular architectural glory was also achieved in such Muslim cities as Isfahan, Agra, and Istanbul.[29] But gone are the days when Islamic intellectual achievements—in mathematics and astronomy, artillery and industry, medicine, philosophy, and physics—paved the way and helped inform Europe's scientific revolution.[30] Islam's own internal scientific revolution was aborted, its spirit of discovery dampened, its contribution to world civilization now much smaller than that of Europe.[31]

What transpired to make Islam a bastion of conservatism? What was it that robbed it of its spirit of discovery and innovation? Why is it that Islam's most notable intellectually innovative movement of modern times—Wahhabism—calls for an aggressive regression into traditions, with its genesis not in Cairo, Isfahan, or Istanbul, once renowned for their intellectual vibrancy, but in the barren deserts of Arabia's backlands?[32]

The absence of spirit of innovation in Islam from about the tenth to the nineteenth centuries can be attributed to four interrelated and mutually reinforcing factors. Perhaps the most important of these has been what one scholar has called "Islam's self-image of timeless perfection."[33] With the Qur'an held to embody "the unaltered words of God," Islam is thought by the believers to outline the perfect way of life, which cannot possibly be improved upon. "In an already flawless social order, innovation cannot yield benefits and may well do harm."[34] Even to this day, there are articulate voices calling for the preservation of Islam's perfection and purity. "The protected knowledge of Islam is timeless and imperishable," writes one such voice. "It is handed down from one generation of Muslims to the next without innovations, alterations, or diminishment in value. Each generation uses this knowledge to protect and nurture a morally intelligent life."[35]

One important consequence of this denial of legitimacy to innovation is "institutional fixity." Islam, it is assumed, created the perfect social order, and along with it established all the institutions that society needs. If institutions are to change, the drag pulling them back makes the change halting and highly incremental at best, negligible or imperceptible at worst.

The institutional context within which Islam has found itself, or, more accurately, its lack thereof, has been a second important factor contributing to the Muslim world's "conservative default." On both the individual and collective levels, innovation depends on institutions. But the early institutions that were established, whether through religious or temporal authority, or both, became frozen in time and did not change with evolving needs and circumstances. In the economic domain, for example, by the time the fifteenth and sixteenth centuries arrived, the economic and financial institutions found in the Muslim world remained woefully inadequate to address the increasing volumes of trade with and competition from Europe. Whereas European economies rapidly developed institutions designed to facilitate their expansion in both depth and scope, much of the Muslim world lacked such basic economic instruments as impersonal contracts and financial exchange mechanisms, corporations, and record keeping.[36] As Timur Kuran explains, "No matter how motivated people are to experiment, take chances, or explore the unknown, if they cannot raise the necessary capital, or entrepreneurial rewards are vulnerable to predation, they will turn their energies elsewhere. To an outsider they will seem fatalistic or wedded to tradition. They will appear to lack the motivation to improve the workings of their society, solve problems, and raise living standards."[37]

Also consequential has been the absence of a mechanism in Islam whereby bodies of jurisprudential, theological, and philosophical knowledge can each be systematically collected, compiled, and, most important, built upon. Islam lacks a corporate body of jurist doctors, a church, either by whom or against whom cohesive bodies of religious doctrines could be collected and compiled over time. Islamic law saw its most remarkable growth in the first two hundred and fifty years of its existence, for example, driven by an *ijtihad* that was "open, bold, intellectually charged, and controversial."[38] But the subsequent closure of the "gates of *ijtihad*" by both *bid'a*-weary ulama and temporal authorities did much to abort what could have been a sustained expansion in Islamic legal thought and framework. Against a backdrop of Islam as the provider of the perfect social order, when it came to legal and jurisprudential issues, "neither innovative religious opinions nor the creative judgments of Islamic courts were treated as legal advances of broader relevance."[39] There were no legal precedents for judges to refer to, and they had instead to go back to the original sources to arrive at their opinions. The potential for evolution of Islamic legal and jurisprudential thought was undermined in the process.

A similar development characterized the practices of *ijtihad* and *tafsir* as well. Seldom were the conclusions and inferences derived from *ijtihad* and *tafsir* used as basis for further developing a progressively evolving doctrine or body of thought that built on previously acquired knowledge. Thus even like-minded jurists and ulama often operated in intellectual wildernesses, absent any nexus of solid, deeply rooted intellectual lineages. A "collective memory" of the innovativeness of the past and the dynamism of Islamic history never emerged.[40] Again, the prevailing "conservative default" served as an overarching backdrop against which innovative *ijtihad* in particular had to reinvent itself again and again, leading to dramatic reversals in the direction of thought from one time to another.⁴¹

The intellectual genealogy and subsequent career of Rashid Rida (1865–1935) best illustrates this point. Rida considered himself a great admirer and, perhaps undeservedly, the intellectual heir of the contemporary renowned reformist thinkers and activists Jamal al-Din Afghani and Muhammad Abduh.⁴² Both Afghani and Abduh sought to modernize and reform Islam by resurrecting its original spirit of *ijtihad*, scientific exegesis, rationality, and interpretation.⁴³ But Rida was more interested in Islamizing modernity than in modernizing Islam.⁴⁴ His approach to the Holy Book became increasingly literalist; he saw the West increasingly as a source of threat rather than scientific and technological inspiration, began advocating Shari'a as a suitable substitute for imported Western law, and preferred the caliphate to parliament.⁴⁵ In the end, the efforts of Rida and others like him turned the ostensibly progressive Salafism of Afghani and Abduh into "a backward-looking ideology ill-prepared to confront the challenges of the modern world."⁴⁶

Finally, stagnation and lack of innovativeness tend to be self-perpetuating. Innovation often creates disjunctures and opportunities for further innovation, whereas its absence makes society accustomed to inertness and stasis. A slow-changing society often develops an impulse to conserve and preserve its own and its surrounding environment. Conservative traditionalism can serve as a blanket stifling other potential sparks of innovation. As Kuran argues, "a society can stagnate because it was stagnant in the past. It can find itself trapped in a lethargic state characterized by low entrepreneurship, not because it lacks risk takers capable of innovation but simply because of its entrepreneurial history."⁴⁷

Together, these four factors—Islam's self-image of timeless perfection, the institutional context in which knowledge of Islam has been acquired and passed down, the absence of mechanisms for the accumulation of a collective memory of the dynamism and inventiveness of Islam, and the self-perpetuating nature of stagnation—have combined to reify popular and scholarly perceptions of *bid'a* as illegitimate tinkering with the Divine Will. Today *bid'a* is still seen as blasphemy, and the label is used, albeit seldom, against innovators perceived to be corrupting the purity and essence of the religion.⁴⁸ Needless to say, life in the normal sense as we know it today would not be possible, or at least would be exceptionally difficult, without some innovation. As J. Robson comments, "Only people of an ultra-conservative nature who live in an unreal world of their own ideas could insist that the practice of the Prophet and his Companions in al-Madīna may alone be followed, and that no allowance may be made for the development of knowledge and differing circumstances."[49]

Nevertheless, in an age when Islamic fundamentalism has, rightly or wrongly, become the public face of Islam for much of the world, and when the Muslim world is replete with dictatorships fearful of even innocuous smatterings of innovation, those advocating innovation in Islam face an uphill battle. The times and the circumstances may have changed, but the outlines of the arguments for and against innovation, and the threat of being accused of *bid'a*, have stayed the same.

None of this has succeeded in extinguishing the spirit of innovation in Islam altogether. As the present book attests, despite all the strikes against it, innovation has managed to find its way into Islamic literature and poetry, hermeneutics and knowledge accumulation, patterns of political rule and minority relations, perceptions of the modern world, and even the *adhan* and *ijtihad*. Collectively, the chapters argue that not every innovation has been seen as an error. Some innovations, in fact—indeed, many innovations—are perfectly compatible with and completely acceptable to Islam.

In working on the various chapters that comprise this book, the contributors were given a simple mandate. They were asked to highlight those innovative approaches, within the broader context of Islam, that have occurred in their areas of study and specialization. In a few instances, as the reader will quickly discover, the authors themselves make suggestions as to the changes needed to the context, perceptions, and hermeneutics of Islam—not to the sacred religion itself—that will enhance its resonance and its concordance with the modern world in which we live. The overriding objective here has been to demonstrate that Islam as both a worldview and as a comprehensive system of social and political organization is fundamentally adaptable, and therefore fundamentally applicable and relevant to today's modern world. As the authors here demonstrate, it is not Islam per se that needs to change in order for it to once again become a leading source of—or at least context for—innovative change and progress in fields such as scientific and intellectual production and social and political organization. There is nothing about Islam that is inherently inimical to adaptability and the essence of innovation. It is not in Islam itself that we must seek the answer to Bernard Lewis's rhetorical question "What went wrong?"[50] Instead, as argued above, the answer lies in the larger context within which Islam has historically found itself, in the ways in which knowledge about Islam has been acquired, accepted, and internalized, in perceptions about Islam that have developed and have become ingrained among both believers as well as non-Muslims, and in the reactive postures thus assumed worldwide in relation to Islam.

The chapters here, written by some of the contemporary pioneers of innovative thought and historiography in Islam, look at innovative approaches adopted by Muslims and in Muslim-majority societies in relation to literature and the visual arts, intellectual thought, debates and discourses revolving around gender issues, and Islam and perceptions of it in the modern world. Accordingly, the book is divided into three parts. Part I looks at the question of how knowledge of Islam is produced, accumulated, and given shape and direction, and what the current and future directions of Islamic thought, among both Sunni and Shi'a thinkers, are likely to be. In short, Part I examines the intellectual processes involved in formulating knowledge of Islam and moving it forward.

Tariq Ramadan's work leads the cluster of chapters in the first section of the book and offers a critical examination of the ways in which Islamic knowledge and hermeneutics are accumulated today. Ramadan also looks at those aspects of the religion's understanding and practice where reforms are needed, focusing specifically on the ways in which knowledge about and within Islam has been produced, accumulated, and transmitted. Ramadan rejects the proposition that the Qur'an itself needs to be reformed, a proposition that, he claims, is becoming increasingly prevalent among certain academic circles in the West. Instead, he maintains, it is the hermeneutics of Islam and, more specifically, the historical operationalization of certain key concepts—especially *tajdid* and *islah*, renewal and reform, and *ath-thabit* and *al-mutaghayyir*, the immutable and the changing—that need to be rethought and reformulated. "A dialogue has begun," Ramadan has written elsewhere. "An intense, constantly renewed dialogue between a Book that speaks the infinite simplicity of the adoration of the One, and the heart that makes the intense effort necessary to liberate itself, to meet him. At the heart of every heart's striving lies the Koran. It holds out peace and initiates liberty."[51] What is needed, Ramadan argues, is a changed *ijtihad*, a "critical reading of texts" under what Ramadan terms "very precise conditions."

Mohammed Arkoun's "Deconstructing Epistēmē(s)" takes these arguments one step further. Historically, Arkoun maintains, scholars have focused on the intellectual processes involved in the historical development of "Islam." With an intellectual career spanning decades, and a highly interconnected body of works and theoretical contributions that have yet to be systematized, Arkoun's contribution here goes to the heart of his larger project of developing a critique of Islamic reason.[52] We need to understand "Islam" as the intellectual productions of Islamic thought, he argues. Western scholarship on Islam has considered the history of Islamic thought in the cognitive frame of a linear history of ideas and schools of thinking in each discipline, focusing mainly on the major texts of the formative and classical periods. Despite sporadic scholastic reproduction, collection, and summaries by Muslim scholars over the past few centuries, in more recent times, up until the introduction of fragments of European modernity, Islam experienced what Arkoun calls "intellectual shrinking and epistemic regression."[53] To rectify this, Arkoun elaborates on the concept of historical epistemology and applies it to Islam's "closed official corpora."

An avid defender of postmodernist thought, Arkoun seeks first to deconstruct what he perceives as an ossified discourse of Islam and then to reconstruct a new one in its place. He has long decried "one-dimensional" approaches that "have exercised little or no intellectual caution in overgeneralization of the data concerning Islam."[54] Thus he sets out here—and elsewhere in his writings—to deconstruct and to open up the epistemic accumulation of knowledge on Islam. He does so by surveying four different discourses within Islam—the Qur'anic discourse, the hadith and *sira* (biographies of the Prophet Muhammad) discourse, the Shari'a-*fiqh* discourse, and the historiography discourse. Arkoun maintains that each of these discourses has a different linguistic and semiotic status, and must therefore be considered in its own historical epistemic environment without mixing any level of analysis with the traditional normative theological and exegetical approaches. Arkoun limits his inquiry to two basic epistemic systems: the deconstruction of the *Mushaf* and its epistemic environment, and the deconstruction of the foundational system of thought (*'ilm usul al-din* and *usul al-fiqh*). This, he believes, goes some ways toward a "radical revision of the concept of religion," eventually ending the erosion of its central message and making obsolete its polarization.

Ramadan and Arkoun, as well as Abu-Zayd and Mir-Hosseini in later chapters, call not so much for innovation *within* Islam as for innovative *approaches to* understanding Islam and its precepts. In chapter 4, I focus more specifically on the innovations that are currently taking place within Iranian Shi'a doctrine and jurisprudence. I chronicle the direction of Iranian Shi'ism after the country's 1978–79 revolution and the debates within it that have come to constitute what I label a "reformist religious discourse." Some of the most fundamental principles of Shi'a *fiqh* and theology have come into question as a result of this emerging discourse, I argue, the long-term consequences of which are bound to influence the overall nature and direction of Shi'ism in the future. This is despite political impulses emanating from the state to the contrary. I am reluctant to go so far as to maintain that the reformist religious discourse has sparked a religious "reformation" in Iran. But, I argue, it has indeed started a process that, *if given the right type of institutional support,* could result in a fundamental reformation of Iranian Shi'ism.

Part II concerns innovation in the literary and visual arts of Islam, beginning with Nelly Hanna's examination of Yusuf al-Maghribi's *Raf' al Isar fi Kalam Ahl Misr*, a seventeenth-century dictionary of the colloquial Arabic of Cairo. Hanna argues that the work is innovative because the author is more concerned with practice and words as they were used, rather than with the correct, or strict, dictionary meaning. He distinguishes between the ways in which a word was used by different sectors of the population.

Hanna approaches al-Maghribi's work in terms of the social, political, and cultural contexts of its time rather than in terms of the history of its genre. Thus it can be studied as a source for social history, or as a "dictionary from below," in the sense that the author includes the vocabulary used by women, by children, and by craftsmen. He also includes autobiographical information that sheds light on his life and his family. Hanna concludes that this approach to al-Maghribi's dictionary allows us to see links between the cultural history of the seventeenth and the nineteenth centuries.

Nasr Abu-Zayd tackles the question of translation of the Qur'an and the daily prayer, *salat*. This is a topic to which he has paid considerable scholarly attention over the years, and one that has caused him much discomfort and controversy.[55] In his contribution here, Abu-Zayd poses a simple but central question: is the prayer understood to be the word of God itself, or is it meant to represent the meaning of God's word? Put differently, can the Qur'an be read and understood in languages other than Arabic, especially in the today's world, when a majority of

Muslims around the globe happen to be non-Arabs? He explores this question from the three perspectives of theology, jurisprudence, and literary criticism, delving into the classic debate of whether the Qur'an is divinely created or man-made. Language, he maintains, is central to any understanding of religion—and especially of man's relationship to the Creator—and in ways that professions of faith are expressed. Ultimately, Abu-Zayd seems to reach ambiguous conclusions. For ritualistic purposes, he maintains, translation of the Holy Book cannot be allowed, but for learning and exploration, one can indeed resort to translation and interpretation. Innovate, but not too radically, seems to be the implied message.

Adonis and Laude turn their attention to poetry. Through examining the broader relationship between poetry and innovation in Islam, Adonis, one of the Muslim world's most celebrated contemporary poets, offers a frontal secularist assault on ossified conceptions of Islam. As the embodiment of perfection, he argues, Islam saw no need for literary and poetic innovation, instead associating poets with the supernatural *jinn*. "In Muslim religious life," he laments, "copying and imitation triumph over criticism and renewal." Islam today has become more of a "closed and ritualistic political system" rather than "one of learning and spirituality." What Islam lacks sorely, and what it needs urgently, is "renewal." Perhaps not coincidentally, Adonis prefers to use "renewal" *(tajaddud)* rather than "innovation" *(ibda')*. But, he concludes, there is a "deep theoretical revolution" inherent in Islam, which today has been hijacked by the forces of fundamentalism. Reclaiming the true essence of the religion, he argues, cannot take place in isolation from freedom, both of thought and action.

Patrick Laude focuses more specifically on Sufi poetry. In "Creation, Originality, and Innovation in Sufi Poetry," he explores the spiritual function of poetry in Sufism as a paradoxical, ever-shifting mediation between presence and absence. Beginning with a consideration of the Qur'anic understanding of poetry as a problematic human activity that may give rise to pretension and hypocrisy, he proceeds to define the requirements of what he considers to be "an authentically Islamic" poetry. Maintaining that Sufi poetry is in fact the epitome of Islamic poetry through its "cultivation of inner authenticity," Laude argues that poetic inspiration amounts to an originality flowing from the very source of the spiritual tradition.

Walter Denny focuses on innovation in Islamic visual arts. The commonly held vision of the visual arts holds that artistic innovation and artistic creation are virtually synonymous. The art of Islamic cultures, in common with all visual art traditions, also draws its distinctiveness in style, subject matter, genre, and aesthetics from its continuity with tradition. According to Denny, innovation within tradition has thus been encouraged, respected, admired, and emulated from the first centuries of Islam, when a distinctive Islamic style emerged in art and architecture, down to the present day, where we see new directions in contemporary visual arts from the Maghreb to Indonesia. What makes innovation in the Islamic artistic traditions distinctive, Denny argues, is the peculiar nature of interplay between innovation and tradition in different places and epochs. To examine how this interplay affects the creative process, Denny examines a number of specific cases: Islamic ceramics and the relationship between technical and artistic innovation; Islamic architecture and the relationship between engineering and spatial innovation; and the art of the Islamic carpet, deeply embedded in all social and economic levels of certain Islamic cultures, and often stereotyped as the most traditional of Islamic art forms.

Part III expands on the context and institutions through which innovation in Islam has been made possible, and the reactions to and consequences of the interplay between and Islam and the modern world. Regardless of what discourse and reality might be, *perceptions* of reality or discourses surrounding it are often something quite different. Perceptions of Islam, its role and place in modernity, and particularly its relationship with the generic "West" have been especially problematic in the post–9/11 world. Sherman Jackson draws our attention to the contemporary era and to realities as they currently affect Islam and Muslims in the West in general and in the United States in particular. In "Liberal/Progressive, Modern, and Modernized Islam: Muslim Americans and the American State," he looks at some of the most pressing issues related to perceptions, identity, and the self that Muslims in America face today. According to Jackson, even in the most learned circles of non-Muslim scholars and observers of Islam in the West, the notion that Muslims can fully indigenize their religion without compromising its fundamental constitution is challenged, if not rejected outright. This presumes, of course, that the West itself is an uncontested category to which Muslims, as newcomers, must simply accommodate themselves. It also assumes that liberalism is the only legitimate discourse in which such a conversation can proceed. Moreover, it also assumes that Muslims in the West are devoid of agency, and that "Islam" itself is a wholly fixed and unresponsive monad.

There is, Jackson argues, the ever-present danger that "predatory reason and rationality" will continue to perpetuate the gap between Muslims and non-Muslims in America. But both Islam as a religion, on the one hand, and American identity, on the other—or any other identity for that matter—are both heterogeneous and dynamic, and, in Jackson's view, adaptable and accommodating. Many of the habits, customs, and legal institutions attributed to Islam have been products of existing circumstances and predicaments rather than anything innately "Islamic." As such, there is nothing inherently contradictory between Islam and America, including especially American democracy and identity.

Questions of identity, symbolism, and theological justifications and discourses are further explored in chapter 11, in which Ziba Mir-Hosseini draws our attention to the issue of *hijab*—the covering of a Muslim woman's body—and the politics and theology of this most visible Islamic mandate in Islamic *fiqh* (jurisprudence). For more than a century, Mir-Hosseini claims, *hijab* has been a major site of ideological struggle between traditionalism and modernity, and a yardstick for measuring the emancipation or repression of Muslim women. In recent decades *hijab* has become an arena where Islamist and secular feminist rhetorics have clashed. For Islamists, *hijab* represents their distinct identity and their claim to religious authenticity: it is a divine mandate that protects women and defines their place in society. For secular feminists, *hijab* represents women's oppression: it is a patriarchal mandate that denies women the right to control their bodies and to choose what to wear. The clash has been particularly strident in Iran, according to Mir-Hosseini, where the state has twice intervened with legislation to an extent that no other Muslim country has experienced. Iran has also been a prime site for the emergence of "Islamic feminist" discourses that speak of *hijab* not as a "duty" but as a "right," and as a social rather than a religious mandate, and find juristic arguments to support this position. Mir-Hosseini—who herself is part of the generation of reformist Muslim intellectuals in Iran whom I discuss in chapter 4—traces the genealogy of this new juristic position from classical *fiqh*'s notions of *hijab*. She documents how jurisprudential positions and notions of *hijab* in Iran have evolved in response to sociopolitical factors. Her chapter concludes by highlighting wider implications of the new juristic position on *hijab* for establishing common ground between secular feminist and Islamic discourses.

In the book's final chapter, John Voll examines a different type of innovation in Islam, namely, that represented social movements. According to Voll, the broader patterns of the development of these movements reflect the dynamism of the interactions between Islam and modernity. It is important, he argues, to look at the broader historical dynamics of these developments as well as to examine the specific movements within their own unique contexts. Over the past two centuries, according to Voll, a wide range of innovative adaptations have taken place in the nature of both Islamic movements and also in modernity itself.

Voll's chapter reminds us once again of the importance of context for the extent to which adaptability and innovation may permeate Islam at a given time or place or, alternatively, may be divorced and distanced from it. The burdens accumulated by the hermeneutics and *epistēmē* of Islam over the course of their intellectual journey across the centuries have frequently overwhelmed and overshadowed its spirit of innovation and adaptability. As the works here and elsewhere by Ramadan, Arkoun, Abu-Zayd, and Mir-Hosseini demonstrate, there has also been a rich tradition within Islamic thought, both contemporary and classic, determined to rid Islamic hermeneutics of its historical barnacles and to free up its spirit of adaptability and innovation again. That innovative writers, thinkers, biographers, poets, and artists belonging to Muslim traditions have seldom met a receptive audience in their own surroundings, and that intellectuals and laypersons belonging to "the other," the West, have seemed reluctant to acknowledge and nurture the innovative stream within Islam, has made innovation in Islam appear even less of a reality, or possibility, than it really is.

Collectively, the chapters in this book give us insights into the complexity of the issues surrounding the notion and manifestations of innovation in Islam. As is amply evident in the following pages, "innovation" and all that it implies remain deeply contested in Islam in the fields of literature and the arts, hermeneutics and *epistēmē*, gender and race relations and representations, perceptions of "the other," and Islam's place in the modern world. What follows are far from definitive answers to questions that have long preoccupied observers and believers alike insofar as change and innovation within Islam are concerned. But this is nevertheless an important start to—or, more accurately, another effort to restart—the process of rethinking some of the propositions and perceptions that have come to characterize views of and views within Islam. For now, the contest continues.

NOTES

Epigraph: Abi Dawud Sulaiman bin Al-Aash'ath Al-Sijistani, *Sunan Abi Dawud,* vol. 3 (Beirut: Dar al-Kotob al-Ilmiyah, 1996), p. 206. The abbreviation A.H. stands for *anno hegirae,* "in the year of the Hegira," the Prophet Muhammad's move from Mecca to Medina in 622 C.E. (or A.D.), when the Muslim era begins.

1. Bernard Lewis, *The Middle East: A Brief History of the Last 2,000 Years* (New York: Touchstone, 1997), p. 227.
2. Bernard Lewis, *The Crisis of Islam: Holy War and Holy Terror* (New York: Random House, 2004), pp. 29–46.
3. Ernest Gellner, *Conditions of Liberty: Civil Society and Its Rivals* (London: Hamish Hamilton, 1994), p. 211, claims, for example, that Islam's "ideological monopoly" makes it inherently antithetical to such fruits of modernity as nationalism and civil society. For an elaboration of this point, see Dale Eickelman, "Islam and the Language of Modernity," *Dædalus* 129, 1 (Winter 2000): 119–135.
4. Bernard Lewis, "Some Observations on the Significance of Heresy in the History of Islam," *Studia Islamica* 1, 2 (1953): 53.
5. Michael Cook, "On Islam and Comparative Intellectual History," *Dædalus* 135, 4 (Fall 2006): 110.
6. J. Robson, "Bid'a," in *Encyclopaedia of Islam,* ed. P. Bearman et al. (Leiden: Brill, 2008), p. 1199.
7. The term *bid'a* itself is not mentioned in the Qur'an, but variations of its are (2:111–117; 6:101; 57:16; 57:27). Maribel Fierro, "The Treatise Against Innovations *(kutub al-bida'),*" *Der Islam* 69 (1992): 205.
8. Vardit Rispler, "Toward a New Understanding of the Term *bid'a,*" *Der Islam* 68 (1991): 321–322.
9. Lewis, "Some Observations on the Significance of Heresy in the History of Islam," p. 52.
10. For various legal classifications of *bid'a* by Muslim jurists between the second and twelfth centuries A.H., see, Rispler, "Toward a New Understanding of the Term *bid'a,*" p. 324.
11. Robson, "*Bid'a,*" p. 1199. Of course, Maliki, Hanbali, and Hanafi jurists were not without views about *bid'a,* brief summaries of which may be found in Rispler, "Toward a New Understanding of the Term *bid'a,*" p. 325.
12. *The Oxford Dictionary of Islam,* ed. John Esposito (Oxford: Oxford University Press, 2003), p. 138.
13. Ibid.
14. Rudolph Peters, "Religious Attitudes Towards Modernization in the Ottoman Empire: A Nineteenth Century Pious Text on Steamships, Factories and the Telegraph," *Die Welt des Islams* 26, 1–4 (1986): 95.
15. Ibid.
16. Ibid., p. 76.
17. Ibid., p. 77.
18. Liyakat A. Takim, "From *Bid'a* to *Sunna:* The *Wilaya* of Ali in the Shi'i *Adhan,*" *Journal of the American Oriental Society* 120, 2 (April–June 2000): 166.

19. Ibid., p. 169.
20. Ibid. p. 170.
21. Timur Kuran, "The Scale of Entrepreneurship in Middle Eastern History: Inhibitive Roles of Institutions" (MS, Department of Economics, Duke University, May 2007), p. 10.
22. Ibid. p. 17.
23. Ibid.
24. Ibid. For a discussion of the acceptance of parliamentary politics, once a *bid'a*, by Iranian clerics, see Abdul-Hadi Hairi, "Why Did the *Ulama* Participate in the Persian Constitutional Revolution of 1905–1909," *Die Welt des Islams* 17, 1–4 (1976–1977): 127–154.
25. Rispler, "Toward a New Understanding of the Term *bid'a*," p. 328.
26. Jonathan Berkey, "Tradition, Innovation, and the Social Construction of Knowledge in the Medieval Islamic Near East," *Past and Present* 146 (February 1995): 41.
27. Rudolph Peters, "*Ijtihad* and *Taqlid* in 18th and 19th Century Islam," *Die Welt des Islams* 20, 3–4 (1980): 135.
28. For concise discussions of both philosophers' contributions to science and philosophy, see Charles Van Doren, *A History of Knowledge: Past, Present, and Future* (New York: Ballantine Books, 1991), p. 115.
29. Michael Hamilton Morgan, *Lost Histories: The Enduring Legacies of Muslim Scientists, Thinkers, and Artists* (Washington, DC: National Geographic Society, 2007), pp. 233–236.
30. John Hobson, *The Eastern Origins of Western Civilisation* (Cambridge: Cambridge University Press, 2004), p. 180.
31. Ibid., p. 181.
32. Cook, "On Islam and Comparative Intellectual History," p. 111.
33. Kuran, "Scale of Entrepreneurship in Middle Eastern History," p. 20.
34. Ibid.
35. Ali Khan, "Islam as Intellectual Property," *Cumberland Law Review* 13 (2001): 635.
36. Kuran. "Scale of Entrepreneurship in Middle Eastern History," pp. 13–15.
37. Ibid.. p. 3.
38. Liaquat Ali Khan, "Free Markets of Islamic Jurisprudence," *Michigan State Law Review* 2006: 1496.
39. Kuran, "Scale of Entrepreneurship in Middle Eastern History," p. 22.
40. Ibid., p. 21.
41. For a recent attempt at compiling a comprehensive body of (progressive) Muslim thought, see Ghazi Bin Muhammad Bin Talal, *True Islam, and the Islamic Consensus on the Amman Message* (Amman: Amman Message, 2006).
42. Ana Belen Soage, "Rashid Rida's Legacy," *Muslim World* 98 (January 2008): 1.
43. Ibid., pp. 4–5.
44. Ibid., p. 3.
45. Ibid., pp. 6–10.
46. Ibid., p. 3.

47. Kuran, "Scale of Entrepreneurship in Middle Eastern History," p. 5.

48. C. A. O. van Nieuwenhuijze. "Islamism—A Defiant Utopia," *Die Welt des Islams* 35, 1 (April 1995): 21.

49. Robson, "Bid'a," p. 1199.

50. Bernard Lewis, *What Went Wrong? The Clash Between Islam and Modernity in the Middle East* (Oxford: Oxford University Press, 2002).

51. Tariq Ramadan, "Reading the Koran," *New York Times Book Review*, January 6, 2008, p. 6.

52. See esp. Ursula Gunther, "Mohammed Arkoun: Towards a Radical Rethinking of Islamic Thought," in *Modern Muslim Intellectuals and the Qur'an*, ed. Suha Taji-Farouki (Oxford: Oxford University Press, 2006), pp. 125–167.

53. Since the early 1970s, Arkoun has embarked on an ambitious critique of Islamic reason. During the past forty years, he has written extensively on this intellectual project, combined with a specific discipline he calls "applied Islamology," which he distinguishes from what he labels "classical Islamology and political sciences," See Mohammed Arkoun, *Rethinking Islam: Common Questions, Uncommon Answers,* trans. Robert D. Lee (Boulder, CO: Westview Press, 1994), pp. 86–88, and id., "Rethinking Islam Today," *Annals of the American Academy of Political and Social Science* 588 (July 2003): 18–39.

54. Mohammed Arkoun, "Islamic Studies: Methodologies," in *The Oxford Encyclopedia of the Modern Islamic World*, ed. John Esposito (Oxford: Oxford University Press, 1995), p. 332.

55. For a concise discussion of Abu Zayd's arguments concerning the Qur'an, see Navid Kermani, "Nasr Hamid Abu Zayd and the Literary Study of the Qur'an," in *Modern Muslim Intellectuals and the Qur'an*, ed. Suha Taji-Farouki (Oxford: Oxford University Press, 2006), pp. 169–192. On the controversy surrounding his writings, see Fauzi Najjar, "Islamic Fundamentalism and the Intellectuals: The Case of Nasr Hamid Abu Zayd," *British Journal of Middle Eastern Studies* 27, 2 (November 2000): 177–200.

PART I

# The Intellectual Process

CHAPTER 2

# Knowledge and Hermeneutics in Islam Today

*Which Reform?*

TARIQ RAMADAN

Many religious scholars *(ulama)*, as well as other thinkers and ordinary Muslims, oppose the use of the word "reform" in relation to Islam because they think it represents a threefold danger as far as faithfulness to the Islamic tradition is concerned. For some, "reforming" Islam thus means—or sounds as though it means—changing Islam, altering it in order to adapt it to modern times, which is not acceptable to a believing conscience. The second criticism comes from those who see in "reform" something foreign, an approach imported from the Christian tradition to cause Islam to undergo the same evolution as Christianity and thereby make it lose its substance and its soul. The third criticism is based on the universal and "timeless" character of Islam's teachings, which therefore, the argument goes, are in no need of "reform" and apply in all places and times.

Those criticisms, which are often set forth in very general terms, raise serious questions and require precise answers. The laudable and clearly stated intention of protecting Islam from deviation and betrayal can neither express nor impose itself, however, by rejecting any critical approach as to the nature of the necessary faithfulness to the universal message of Islam. In refusing the alienation caused by thinking about oneself through the categories of the Christian tradition, some people come to promote an even deeper alienation, identifying as "foreign" what in actuality is inherent in the Islamic tradition itself: such self-ignorance, nurtured by fear of change, of losing oneself, or more generally "fear of the other," is one of the major dangers that threaten the contemporary Muslim conscience.

## TAJDID AND ISLAH

In addition to the notion of *ihya'* (revival) associated with the philosopher and theologian al-Ghazālī (1058–1111 C.E.), the vocabulary of Islamic sciences contains two concepts directly drawn from scriptural sources and directly referring to the idea of "reform" and "renewal." The term *tajdid,* which literally means "renewal," or even "rebirth" and "regeneration,"[1] has always been frequent in Islamic literature, particularly for the past 150 years. The verb root of this noun can be found in a famous hadith of the Prophet: "God will send this [Muslim] community, every hundred years, someone [or some people] who[2] will renew [*yujaddidu*] its religion."[3]

This Prophetic tradition is highly significant and it has given rise, through the ages, to numerous commentaries as to its meaning and impact. What is unanimously established in the Islamic creed *(al-'aqidah)* is that the Prophet of Islam is the last of God's Messengers and represents the final stage in the cycle of Prophethood. What the hadith tells us is that the Muslim community will nevertheless be accompanied and guided through the centuries by scholars and/or thinkers who will help it, every hundred years or so, to "regenerate" or "renew" the religion of Islam. This renewal of religion *(tajdid ad-din)* does not, of course, entail a change in the sources, principles, and fundamentals of Islam, but only in the way the religion is understood, implemented and lived in different times or places. This is precisely the point: scriptural sources (the Qur'an and Sunna) remain the primary references, and the fundamentals of faith and practice are left as they are, but our reading and our understanding of the texts will be "renewed" by the contribution of scholars and thinkers who will point to new perspectives by reviving timeless faith in our hearts while stimulating our minds so as to enable us to face the challenges of our respective times.

*Tajdid,* as it was understood by the classical tradition of scholars and schools of law, is thus a renewal of the reading, understanding, and, consequently, implementation of texts in light of the various historical and cultural contexts in which Muslim communities or societies stand. Muslims must, at a particular time in history, be able to rediscover the essence, ethical substance, and superior aims of Islam's message in order to implement them faithfully and adequately in sociocultural contexts that are essentially changing, in constant mutation. It is a matter of recapturing the original essence and "form" of the message, through renewed understanding, in order to remain faithful to it while lucidly facing the evolution of human beings and societies. The meaning of *tajdid*, as expressed in this Prophetic tradition, is indeed to "re-form" constantly, to *reform* in the name of faithfulness. In short, there can be no faithfulness to Islamic principles through the ages without evolution, without reform, without a renewal of intelligence and understanding.

This is also the meaning of the concept of *islah*, which appears several times in the Qur'an and in some Prophetic traditions *(ahadith)* and conveys the idea of improving, purifying, reconciling, repairing, and reforming. This is the meaning the prophet Shu'ayb conveys to his people when he says in the Qur'an: "I do not desire, in opposition to you, to do that which I forbid you to do. I desire nothing but reform [*al-islah;* also betterment, purification] as far as I am able."[4] Thus, divine messages through the centuries came to reform human understanding. Messengers called *muṣliḥūn* bring good, reconcile human beings with the divine, and reform their societies for the better. The notion of *islah* implies bringing the object (whether a heart, an intellect or a society) back to its original state, when the said object was considered to be pure and good: it is indeed a matter of improving, of curing, through re-forming, through *reform*.

It can be understood, then, that the two notions of *tajdid* and *islah* convey the same idea of reform and are at the same time complementary, since the former primarily (but not exclusively) refers to the relationship to texts, while the latter mainly has to do with reforming the human, spiritual, social, or political context. This revival of faith and religion through a constantly reforming approach of the understanding of texts *(tajdidiyyah)* and of the understanding of contexts *(islahiyyah)* is essential to the Islamic tradition and has been so since its early days. The first scholars who categorized the various spheres and manifold tools of Islamic sciences, particularly in the areas of law and jurisprudence, integrated those dimensions, when, for example, they referred to *ijtihad* (the critical approach of texts) or to *maslahah* (common good and interest). These latter notions will be discussed in more detail later on; however, it is important to state at this point that the use of the word "reform" is not at all foreign to the classical Islamic tradition, but that it is essential, from the outset, to define the aim, contents, and limits of the said reform.

## THE QUESTION OF SCRIPTURAL SOURCES

In the contemporary debate over "reform" within Islam's universe of reference, the status of the Qur'an is repeatedly stressed. It is as if no reform could actually take place if the status of the Qur'an itself, as the very word of God revealed to men, was not discussed or questioned. This condition is more or less clearly stated and sometimes in radical terms by some of our Jewish and/or Christian interlocutors in numerous interreligious circles and by a number of Muslim thinkers. They argue that Islam and Muslims will not "evolve," or be able to "reform" their religion and practices, unless they question the Qur'an's status as the absolute word of God and undertake a historical-critical reading and exegesis, which alone will permit a real aggiornamento of Islam similar to the Protestant Reformation or Vatican II.

This argument is highly successful in the West, and the answer one gives about the status of the Qur'an seems to have become the feature setting "true" reformers apart from "neofundamentalist" simulators.

It is indeed important, when starting this general reflection about reform, to make a number of points clear and to discuss some ideas that are commonly accepted and yet highly disputable. At the heart of the Islamic creed *(al-'aqidah)*, among the six pillars of faith *(arkan al-iman)*, lies the recognition of revealed books and the faith and belief that the Qur'an, the last Revelation, is the word of God *(kalam Allah)* revealed to mankind as such in clear Arabic language *(lisanun 'arabiyyun mubin).*[5] To the believing conscience, this is one of the pillars of faith, and no reform questioning one of the fundamentals of the creed, of the *'aqidah*, could be accepted, heard, or promoted by the Muslim faithful. It might be attractive to the restricted circles of rationalists, but it will always be perceived by the majority of believers, irrespective of their level of practice, as at best out of place and at worst a clear betrayal of Islamic teachings. Indeed, this "excess of rationalism" on the part of some early or contemporary thinkers has often led to simply disqualifying the notion of "reform" altogether, since it was perceived as dangerous because it undermined the principles of the Muslim faith or was imported from the Christian universe of reference.

One must add that the very terms of this debate have generated postulates that need to be questioned. Thus, people tend to believe that dogmatic or literalist approaches arise from the nature of the Qur'anic text and that a historical, contextualized reading would result if a human origin were ascribed to it.[6] However, this statement takes two dangerous shortcuts. The first is the assumption that the status of the text alone determines its readers' mode of interpretation, while this is far from obvious or inevitable. The history of religions and ideologies is filled with examples of texts produced by guides or thinkers that have been, and still are, read dogmatically by their adepts or followers. The status of the text can indeed influence the modalities of reading, but in the end, it is the mind and psyche of the reader interpreting it that projects its categories and the modalities of its interpretation onto the book. Up to very recent times, Marx's works were sometimes read and interpreted in most dogmatic terms by most atheistic Marxists. A text's human source by no means warrants a historicizing reading of its contents, and numerous Christian trends, while recognizing the various historical strata of the Gospels' elaboration, still advocate a literal reading of the New Testament. What must be assessed and questioned is often the outlook, psychological setup, and frame of reference of interpreting scholars, and the debate over the status of the text falls far short of resolving the issue of historical and contextualized interpretation.

The other shortcut is methodologically more serious and its consequences are far more harmful. It consists in exporting the experience of Catholic theology into the Islamic tradition: since the historical-critical approach was only possible in the Christian tradition once the human source of the New Testament had been acknowledged, it is assumed to be the same—by natural induction—for the Islamic legal tradition. However, this exogenous, imported outlook fails to do justice to the great legal tradition of Islam that has never, since the beginning, linked the status of the Qur'an (as the "eternal word of God") to the impossibility of historical and contextualized interpretation. Indeed, quite the contrary has been the case: from the outset, the Prophet's companions *(as-sahaba)*, the following generation *(at-tabi'ūn)*, then the scholars, the leading figures of the various sciences and schools of law, kept referring to the context, causes *(asbab)*, and chronology of revealed verses. The sciences and commentaries of the Qur'an *('ulūm al-Qur'an* and *at-tafasir)*, the study of the Prophet's life *(as-sira)*, and the classification of prophetic traditions *('ulūm al-hadith)* are so many areas of study that were constituted while taking into account the historicality of the revealed Word as well as of the Prophet's speech and action. The eternal Word of God was revealed within a specific history, over twenty-three years, and if some texts or injunctions transcend the human history that receives them, some other verses cannot be understood without being inserted into a particular time sequence. Then human intelligence alone can determine the contents of the timeless principle drawn from the text, while necessarily taking into account its relation to the social and historical context of its enunciation. This critical approach has been known and acknowledged since the beginning by all schools of law, and what was debated later on was not the legitimacy of the approach itself but the norms and limits of such contextualizing.[7] The debate already involves the elaboration of an applied hermeneutics.

The postulate—increasingly frequent in some academic or interreligious circles in the West—that only by questioning the status of the Qur'an can far-reaching reform be carried out thus turns out to be highly disputable both in terms of its theoretical assumptions and of its logic itself, and it is unanimously rejected by Muslim masses. It must be added that the contemporary trend that seeks to disqualify *ahadith* (Prophetic traditions) altogether as fundamental scriptural sources (for elaborating Islamic law and ethics) is being similarly rejected by Muslims all over the world, and will most certainly continue to be. The Sunna is indeed considered as secondary to the Qur'an, but it nevertheless remains an essential source for determining Islamic norms and practices: for instance, it is impossible to know how ritual prayer—the second pillar of Islam—should be performed unless one refers to the Islamic traditions *(ahadith)* that detail and establish its form, and that are unanimously acknowledged by Islamic scholars and believers alike.

It must therefore be stressed here that the status of the Qur'an for Muslims—considering it as God's word—as well as the necessary mediation of the Prophetic tradition (Sunna), are by no means obstacles to a historical, contextualized, and critical reading. What remains essential in this debate is to determine categories and norms that must make it possible to remain both faithful to the creed as such and coherent as to the questions raised by intelligence when faced with the evolution of sciences and of societies. Only within this frame of reference can the concrete implementation of *tajdid* and *al-islah*—as presented above—be efficient and fruitful.

THE IMMUTABLE *(ATH-THABIT)* AND
THE CHANGING *(AL-MUTAGHAYYIR)*

Just as the terms of the debate with certain trends defining themselves as "strictly rationalistic" must be clarified, it is also essential to question the methodological assumptions and some reductions performed by contemporary literalist trends that often present themselves as the only true *salafi.*⁸ Those trends, at the other end of the spectrum of interpretations, tend to reduce and level all the areas of study and methodological categories established by scholars through the ages. Because the Qur'an is eternal and revealed, the differentiation between the nature of principles, the classification levels of verses or Prophetic traditions, and interpretative methodologies, is reduced to a minimum. Literalists do admit that some principles and practices are more essential than others, but historical and contextual data (and, consequently, their influence on the texts' interpretation) are neglected, if not totally absent from the elaboration and fixation of the norms of practice and behaviour.

The contemporary literalist approach thus carries three reductions, or confusions, that restrict interpretation and in effect make it impossible to give adequate answers to contemporary challenges. The first reduction is fundamental and appears, all things considered, as a cause of the other two: it is the failure to distinguish between what, in the Revelation, is immutable *(thabit)*, absolute, and transhistorical, and what is subject to change, linked to the evolution of time and environmental changes *(mutaghayyir)*. A number of principles or practices belong to fundamentals and are absolute, true and/or to be implemented whatever the time or place one lives in. This is the case for the tenets of the *'aqidah* (the six pillars of faith) and of religious practice (the five pillars of Islam): a practicing Muslim will strive to respect those principles and remain faithful to the rules and forms of practice, which have never changed since the early days of Islam. Similarly, moral obligations or prohibitions (ethics of behavior, food prohibitions, etc.) are immutable and must be respected whatever the life context. This context must, however, be taken into account to determine the—necessarily changing—contextual modalities and conditions of application of those transhistorical prescriptions. While this is never necessary for the creed *(al-'aqidah)*, whose principles refer to conscience and faith and rarely pertains to ritual practices, although a number of possible allowances and alleviations *(rukhas)* exist in various situations and contexts, taking the environment into account is a constant necessity for implementing moral obligations in the sphere of social affairs and for all that pertains to local cultures and customs.

Injunctions, prohibitions, and recommendations may indeed be absolute and immutable in themselves, but their concrete implementation necessarily takes different and changing forms according to the environment. The scholars who dealt with the fundamentals of Islamic law and jurisprudence *(usūliyyūn)*, after Muhammad ibn Idris ash-Shafi'i (ninth century C.E.), actually made this distinction between the immutable and the changing even in the implementation of the "prescriptions defining the duties and obligations of responsible beings" *(al-ahkam at-taklifiyyah)*:[9] thus, marriage is permitted and recommended *(mubah* and *mustahab)* in general, but it can become almost an obligation *(wajib)* according to the person's situation, or, depending on the persons involved, it can be considered as a reprehensible action *(makrūh)* or as altogether prohibited *(haram)*. The context can thus make a single action move through the five categories established to define duties and obligations and thereby give a specific moral judgment. On a less technical level, one can find the same distinction—in social and cultural affairs—between respecting an absolute principle and the form its implementation will take: the principle of modesty and its rules (for both men and women) is established in Islamic ethics, but its implementation in any given society has always had to take into account local cultures and habits (types of clothing, colors, etc.).

By failing to distinguish sufficiently between the immutable and the changing—and never doing so systematically—contemporary literalists give rise to a series of other confusions involving most serious consequences. For on the level of relationships within human societies, distinguishing between the immutable and the changing makes it possible to draw a fundamental difference between principles and models. Principles can be immutable, absolute and eternal, but their implementations in time or in history—historical models—are relative, changing and in constant mutation. Thus, the principles of justice, equality, rights and human brotherhood that guided the Prophet of Islam indeed remain the references beyond history, but the model of the city of Medina founded by Muhammad in the seventh century C.E. is a historical realization linked to the realities and requirements of his time. Muslims must, in the course of history, try to remain faithful to those principles and strive to implement them as best they can according to the requirements of their time, but they cannot merely imitate, reproduce, or duplicate a historical model that was adapted to a particular time but no longer corresponds to the requirements of their own. Confusing eternal principles and historical models is in effect simplistic and, above all, and particularly serious, idealizing a moment in history (in this instance, of the city of Medina) leads to the thoughtless and guilty denial of that history and reduces the universality of Islam's principles to the dream of an impossible return to the past, to an irresponsible "nostalgia of origins." The same temptation can be found in some contemporary *salafi* trends that advocate an almost exclusively political commitment: they reduce faithfulness to the message to imitating, returning to, a specific historical political structure, a particular type of "state," or the reference to the "caliphate," which they set against any other possible political organization (dismissively arguing that these alternatives arise from the era of ignorance or opposition to Islam, *al-jahiliyyah*). Through a binary approach that is both simplistic and, unfortunately, appealing because it is so simple, they set one order against another and find it difficult to look into the nature of the principles on which either order relies.

The greatness and exemplarity of the city of Medina do not lie so much in its form proper as in the adequacy—at that particular moment in history—between the eternal principles stated and the historical implementation elaborated by the Prophet and his community. Thus, the historical model becomes a reference because its authors were able to achieve coherence between ideals and practices. The distinction between principles and models appeals to Muslims' conscience and requires them to display intelligence and creativity in order to achieve, at each moment in history and whatever their environment, a societal model as faithful as possible to the ethical principles they adhere to. Whereas for literalists being faithful to the Prophet, his companions, and the *salaf* essentially consists in imitating their behavior and simply trying to reproduce their historically dated achievements, it seems to us that essential faithfulness consists in recapturing their spiritual strength and intellectual energy in order to achieve the most coherent social model for our own time (as they did for theirs). The point is not to imitate the historical result achieved but to reproduce the ethical demand and human efforts through which it was achieved. It is not to repeat its form but to grasp its substance, spirit, and objectives.

The same intellectual stance can be found in the most ordinary daily realities and produces equally excessive and dangerous legal judgments. Confusing principles and models, a rule and its form, leads to exceedingly rigid and particularly exclusive reductions. Thus, modesty is prescribed to Muslims, but in the eyes of literalists, there is only one way of being modest (and thereby obeying Islamic prescriptions): imitating the Prophet, his companions, and the *salaf* and dressing just as they did, in identical clothes, and this is the only possible reference. One can see here how the principle of modesty is reduced to its actualization within a specific historical context. One could understand and accept such reduction if its advocates only expressed it for themselves. However, they do not, and that exclusive approach has equipped itself with legal tools to disqualify all other interpretations: thus, dressing in any other way than the *salaf* did is seen as a *bid'a* (plur. *bida'*), one of those guilty innovations the Prophet himself condemned. And this is where the third reduction mentioned above occurs: it is the failure to distinguish between, on the one hand, the legal methodology linked to the *'aqidah* (the creed) and the *'ibadat* (worship), and, on the other hand, that which deals with *mu'amalat* (social affairs). This distinction is essential, from the beginning. In the two spheres of *'aqidah* and *'ibadat*, we are confronted with the immutable teachings and practices that are determined by the Revelation and by Prophetic traditions, and in which human reason can add or delete nothing. We are here on the level of what could, by analogy, be termed "dogmatics": nothing can be said or stipulated in those two fields without relying on a verse, a hadith, a *dalil* (evidence). In this sphere, only what is written is allowed, and any addition or change is considered as a blameworthy, dangerous, condemnable innovation *(bid'a)*.

In the sphere of *mu'amalat* (social affairs), scholars established from the outset that the rule is exactly the opposite of that concerning *'aqidah* and *'ibadat:* here, everything is allowed, except what is explicitly forbidden by scriptural sources or scholarly consensus on the matter. The basic principle, in social affairs, is permission *(al-asl fil-ashya' al-ibaha)*, thus opening to men the fields of rationality, creativity, and research. So long as they remain faithful to principles and respect prohibitions, their intellectual, scientific, artistic, and, more generally, social, economical, and political productions are not innovations, but welcome achievements for the welfare of mankind. The reduction performed by contemporary literalists consists in failing to distinguish between those spheres (*'aqidah* and *'ibadat,* on the one hand, and *mu'amalat,* on the other) and extending the methodology of rule elaboration applicable to the first two ("only what is written can be done") to the totality of human actions. All that does not correspond—in its form—to what the Prophet and his companions did or produced is thus seen as a *bid'a* that has to be denounced. The consequences of such reduction are clear, and even though literalist scholars differ widely from each other in their degree of intellectual and legal sophistication, it remains that the theoretical framework underlying their approach not only opposes the reform of models but also adopts legal instruments of judgment that enable it to disqualify Muslim scholars who engage in that endeavor. This is not just a matter of disagreement, but of how one relates to Islamic norms, with the emergence of a scholarly authority that determines what is Islamic and what is not: the inflation of "innovator" or "*bid'a* promoter" accusations[10] is revealing of those tensions that run across the Islamic world as to the establishment of a framework of Islamic authority. The debate is sharp and the stakes are crucial.

That threefold confusion and reduction (immutable/changing; principles/models; and *'aqidah, 'ibadat mu'amalat*) clearly has major consequences on contemporary Islamic thought and in effect tends to disqualify any reform of the reading, understanding, and implementation of texts in a new historical context. It reduces faithfulness to the message to fixed reading, status quo, imitation *(at-taqlid)*, and blind reproduction of what was done before. Most of all, it results in oversimplifying the message of Islam and implementing its teaching in a way that, although it claims to be faithful to its historical form, sometimes contradicts its eternal objectives.

## IJTIHAD

All the Muslim scholars who have stressed the need for *tajdid*, for reform, have referred to the central notion of *ijtihad*. In the field of the classical study of the fundamentals of law and jurisprudence *(usūl al-fiqh)*, *ijtihad* has always consisted in promoting a critical reading of texts when they were open to interpretation *(dhanni)*, when the texts were silent about a particular situation, or when the context imperatively needed to be taken into account in the implementation of texts (even when those were explicit, *qat'i*).[11] The debates over the possibility, meaning, and limits of *ijtihad* have been, and continue to be, numerous and heated, but the legitimacy and necessity of such critical reading are rarely questioned, except by the narrowest literalist trends.

The human, social, political, economic, and cultural environment has always been more or less taken into account by the scholars who codified and implemented the principles of the fundamentals of Islamic law and jurisprudence *(usūl al-fiqh)* as well as by those who specialized in drawing up practical answers to the new questions of their time *(fuqaha'* working in the restricted area of *fiqh)*. When the former speak of "consensus" *(ijma')*, of "analogical reasoning" *(qiyas)*, of all the secondary sources *(istislah, istihsan,* etc.) and more generally of common good and interest *(maslahah)*,[12] they directly or indirectly refer to the practice of *ijtihad* that involves reading some texts in the light of the context and requires reforming our understanding of texts as well as of their implementation. This is exactly what jurisprudence scholars *(fuqaha')* do when they seek to implement some Islamic rules concretely in a new environment and/or time and sometimes have to draw up specific legal judgments *(fatawa)*. This dialectical relationship between text and context is an appeal to human intelligence to find the way to be faithful through the merging of two levels of knowledge: that of the eternal principles of practice and ethics and that of the ever-changing realities of human societies. Necessary "renewal" and constant "reform" thus lie at the very heart of the requirement of faith and faithfulness that accompanies the believing conscience through life and through history.

It must be added here that from the outset, Muslim scholars set strict, and indeed legitimate, conditions for the practice of *ijtihad*. Thus the interpretation of individual texts can only be carried out in the light of knowledge of the general message, of its various enunciation levels, of the categories of the sciences *('ulūm)* and methodologies, and of the rules *(qawa'id)* applied to scriptural texts, grammar *(nahw)*, semantics *(ma'na)*, and morphology *(sarf)*. Ijtihad has never been considered as a free interpretation of texts, open to critical elaboration by individuals with no knowledge of Islamic sciences or of the conventions and norms that text specialists and their practices are bound to follow. This pertains to the fields of applied science and law that by nature require appropriate training in the knowledge and mastery of the texts and the interpretative rules that apply to them.[13] It must be stressed again that—contrary to the argument one often hears nowadays in some self-termed "progressive" circles, that the "reform of Islam" will only be possible when all Muslims (whatever their degree of knowledge in the matter) have the right to exercise their own *ijtihad*—the renewal and reform of contemporary Islamic thought can by no means imply that one fails to respect the requirements of knowledge and science about our relationship to the Revelation, Prophetic traditions, and the productions of scholars in the course of history. The laudable will to "democratize" Islamic thought here takes on the dangerous aspect of downward leveling that disqualifies the basic conditions associated with the legal understanding of a text and the elaboration of its possible interpretations. In the field of law, such an attitude would amount to hoping that judges and lawyers faithful to the spirit of legal texts could magically emerge without ever having received any training on the subject (or, better still, *because* they never did). It also amounts to stating—most dangerously—that such immediate, free and nonspecialized access to scriptural texts ensures the emergence of more "open," more "progressive," and necessarily more "modern" readings of the Qur'an and Sunna: the violent and extremist actions committed in recent years in the name of Islam, and in the name of superficial readings of some Qur'anic verses, ought to convince us that this is far from certain.

*Ijtihad,* the critical reading of texts, must therefore be associated with very precise conditions that scholars have stated many times over. The very story of Muʻadh ibn Jabal, who was sent as a judge to Yemen by the Prophet, carries many teachings and determines the framework we should adopt when discussing *ijtihad* and reform. When Muʻadh was about to set off for his mission, the Prophet asked him: "According to what will you judge?" He answered: "According to the Book of God." "And if you find nothing?" the Prophet asked. "According to the tradition [*Sunna*] of God's Prophet." "And if you find nothing?" "Then, I shall exert myself [*ajtahidu*] to my utmost to formulate my own judgement,"[14] Muʻadh answered. The Prophet then exclaimed: "Praise be to God who guided His Messenger's messenger to what pleases His Messenger."[15] The first two questions and their respective answers directly mention the reference texts and their interpretation: Muʻadh ibn Jabal, whom the Prophet acknowledged to be one of the most competent in his community in the field of Islamic ethics,[16] states that he will first of all look for solutions in the Qur'an and in the Prophet's own practice, which he must therefore know perfectly. The third question is of particular interest, for it stipulates that Muʻadh will necessarily be confronted, in the new environment of Yemen, with situations of which nothing is said either in the Qur'an or in the Sunna. This question alone reveals two major teachings: the first is, of course, that not all answers can be found in the Qur'an and in the Sunna. The Qur'an indeed contains verses stating that "We have sent down to you a Book explaining all things,"[17] and "We have omitted nothing from the Book,"[18] but that refers to general principles, to essential and immutable rules, the practical implementation of which has to be thought out—through the mediation of the intelligence—according to circumstances and situations. The second teaching is directly linked to these situations: Yemen—though only a few hundred kilometers away—*already* in the Prophet's own time constitutes a different geographical, cultural, and legal setting, requiring the scholar to produce a reflection, an effort at extrapolation, reasoned and reasonable *ijtihad* in order to remain faithful to Islamic prescriptions. Muʻadh's last answer is no less edifying in this respect, since it directly refers to his own critical intelligence, which will have to face both the texts' potential silence and the new context. In such a situation, merely repeating or blindly imitating the Prophet *(taqlid)* in the form of his answers or in the practical implementation of rules is impossible: while one must remain faithful to essential and immutable principles *(usūl)*, it is no less necessary to take into account the context, culture, and common and public interest *(maslaha)* of the society at hand. Mu'adh, in the seventh century and in the Prophet's presence, thus showed that faithfulness of the heart and mind required lucidity and creativity from a human intelligence nurtured and inspired by the deep meaning of texts, and constantly setting them against the changing complexity of contexts. And he was strongly commended by the Prophet: "Praise be to God who has guided His Messenger's messenger to what pleases His Messenger."

All those reflections about reform lead us to the conclusion that there is indeed, in the classical Islamic tradition, a central reference to the need for a renewal, revival, and, consequently, *reform* of our reading and understanding. Debates have often—quite legitimately—concentrated on clearly determining the abilities and limits necessary for the practice of *tajdid* and *ijtihad*. When studying the history of Islamic law and ethics, one realizes that the advocates of the different interpretations were sometimes involved in tense, and often highly specialized, contradictory debates. While some called for the practice of *ijtihad* as a condition to faithfulness, others wanted to close its doors for fear of excess or because of excessive admiration for the works of the first great scholars who founded the legal schools, and others even went so far as to deny its legitimacy in the name of a rigid, literalist reading. What nevertheless remains the majority opinion among the critical mass of both Muslim scholars (whether Sunni or Shi'i, and from all legal schools) and Muslim communities, is that the rereading effort *(tajdid)* and the tool of critical interpretation of texts *(ijtihad)* are indispensable means to face contemporary challenges. Whether or not one chooses to be affiliated with a legal school *(madhhab),* whatever trend of thought one follows, it seems clear that new challenges require new answers. Muslim scholars must imperatively resume possession of the intellectual and legal tools of that renewal, of the necessary reform that stands out as a requirement of faithfulness from the very origin of the message's revelation.

NOTES

1. A verb of the same form whose root is *ja-da-da* is sometimes used to convey the idea of "innovating," "modernizing."

2. The Arabic word *man* used in the original can mean either an individual or a group.

3. Hadith reported by Abū Dawūd.
4. Qur'an 11:88.
5. Qur'an 16:103 and 26:195.
6. The author would then be the Prophet Muhammad or, from a more global methodological viewpoint, the text should be dealt with as a human work taking into account its chronology, or even its evolution and/or possible contradictions.
7. It must be added here that the heated debate that opposed Mu'tazili rationalists and Ibn Hanbal, during the reign of Caliph al-Ma'mūn (d. 833 C.E.), over the created or uncreated nature of the Qur'an, was totally distinct, for the advocates of both camps, from the question of whether or not the Qur'an should be given contextualized interpretation. Discussions today take over in a most biased and superficial manner the terms of the debate that began in the ninth century and went on through the tenth and eleventh centuries C.E., between Hanbali, Ash'ari, and Maturidi over the status of the Qur'an. The point was then to determine the status of the Qur'an in relation to the principle of God's oneness *(at-tawhid)*, and not the legitimacy of interpreting revealed verses in the light of the Prophetic experience and history that endow them with meaning. Thus, Ahmad ibn Hanbal, a fierce proponent of the uncreated nature of the Qur'an, never questioned the need for a contextualized legal reading: what he essentially opposed was the elaboration of dogmatics and of a theological-philosophical theory *(kalam)* that tended to acknowledge human reason only as its ultimate reference. The classical Islamic tradition (whether Sunni or Shi'i) was quick to establish—beyond the disputes over the status of the essence of God's Word, qualities, and names—that if the Word (the Qur'an) comes from God, the Word is not God, and the Text's revelation within human history requires the mediation of human intelligence to grasp and understand it and to remain faithful to it through time. Once more, the central issue was to determine the nature and limits of interpretation confronting the revealed Text.
8. *Salafi* literalists refuse the mediation of the legal schools and their scholars of reference when approaching and reading texts. They call themselves *salafi* because they are keen to follow the *salaf*, which is the title given to the Prophet's companions and the pious Muslims of the first three generations of Islam. The Qur'an and Sunna should therefore be interpreted directly, bypassing the divisions of legal schools, according to them.
9. Those prescriptions have been classified into five distinct categories: at the two ends of the scale of prescriptions, one can find *al-wajib* (or *al-fard,* though some scholars, particularly of the Hanafi school, make a distinction in status and value between *al-wajib* and *al-fard)* and *al-haram*: the first term refers to an action considered as mandatory, while the last means what is absolutely forbidden. If, for instance, a Qur'anic injunction is stated in the imperative, such as "Perform prayer and give the purifying alms" (Qur'an 2:43), or in the negative imperative, such as "And do not come near to adultery" (Qur'an 17:32), those injunctions will be identified as respectively an obligation *(wajib)* or a prohibition *(haram)*. Between those two extremes, ulama have identified three other statuses for human actions: what is "recommended" or "preferable" *(al-mustahab,*

*al-mandūb)*, what is "reprehensible" *(al-makrūh)*, and what is permitted *(al-mubah)*.

10. Those are serious accusations that make a scholar or thinker thus qualified to be considered as an enemy from within, an apostate *(murtad)* or a traitor.

11. See the discussion and analysis in Tariq Ramadan, *Western Muslims and the Future of Islam* (New York: Oxford University Press, 2003), p. 43.

12. See ibid., p. 31.

13. *Ijtihad* is not limited to that dimension. In other words, while the necessary text expertise must be recognized and respected, it is also urgent to reassess the importance of expertise regarding knowledge of the environment, and of the exact, human, and social sciences.

14. The verb *ajtahidu* comes from the same root *(ja-ha-da, ij-ta-ha-da)* as *ijtihad*.

15. Hadith reported by Abū Dawud, Ahmad, at-Tirmidhi, and ad-Darami.

16. The Prophet once said: "The man in my community with the best knowledge of the licit and the illicit is Mu'adh ibn Jabal" (hadith reported by at-Tirmidhi, Ibn Majah, and Ahmad).

17. Qur'an 16:89.

18. Qur'an 6:38.

CHAPTER 3

# Deconstructing *Epistēmē*(s)

MOHAMMED ARKOUN

## THE RELIGIOUS SCIENCES VERSUS THE RATIONAL SCIENCES

Exploring the tensions between religious sciences and rational sciences has been a main concern of monotheist religions since the emergence of Christian teachings. We know that the four Gospels selected by the Church were collected and transmitted in Greek, although Jesus expressed his message in Aramaic. The Greek language had been used five centuries prior to Jesus Christ to express two forms and types of knowledge: one based on *logos*, the other on *muthos*. While Plato used mythical narratives to express his philosophy, Aristotle elaborated his impressive philosophical corpus based on *logos*. Facing this dialectical intellectual tension between *muthos* and *logos*, the Hebrew Torah (called the *Pentateukhos*, or Pentateuch, in Greek) inaugurated another binary tension between the Word of God and prophetic discourse expressed successively in three Semitic languages: Hebrew, Aramaic, and Arabic.

It is very unusual that this intellectual and linguistic process be considered and studied in this long-term perspective, which includes the same approach that the Greek-Latin cultural and intellectual expansion has carried on in Europe and the West (Occident) until today. The same Islamic intellectual process, as a constitutive part of the global history of thought, unfolded in the geohistorical Mediterranean area. It is of critical importance to understand the intellectual processes at work in the historical development of what is currently known as "Islam" by laypeople and scholars alike. I take "Islam" here to refer to the intellectual output—the so-called "Islamic thought"—dating from the inaugurating moment of Qur'anic discourse. Up to now, Western scholarship has been content to treat the history of Islamic thought as the cognitive frame of a linear history of ideas. In so doing, it has confined its attention for the most part to the major texts of the formative and classical periods. Accordingly, it has been apt to neglect the long period of scholastic reproduction, collection, and summarizations of classical works, a period stretching from 1400 to 1800 C.E. The latter tends to be dismissed, in perfunctory terms, as a period of decay. The subsequent period, from 1800 to 1940, labeled the *nahda* ("awakening") has elicited more attention from traditional scholarship than from the new scholarship represented by the social and political sciences born in nineteenth-century Europe. This picture is part of a growing gap, still unremedied, between the creative and conquering dynamic of European societies, on one hand, and the stagnation of Islamic societies, on the other, where Islamic beliefs and their associated ethical, juridical, and cultural codes continue to shape their worldview and dictate their collective history.

The colonial domination of so-called Muslim societies was no doubt responsible for the political resistance to what is still called Western "cultural aggression" *(ghazw fikri)*. In this connection, it is important to note the attempts made by a small number of thinkers or scholars to introduce scientific research and modern education in Muslim contexts during the period that Albert Hourani forty years ago described as the "Liberal Age."[1] From the standpoint of the systems imposed by postcolonial states on "Muslim" societies during the second half of the twentieth century, their apparent receptivity to modern thought during the Liberal Age may seem very impressive indeed. Structurally, however, it was doomed to tragic failure. To this day, social structures and conservative, patriarchal conceptions of "truth" and "value," and the juridical codes and political practices that go hand in hand with these, continue to exert an undiminished impact on daily life at all levels, especially on the overall cultural codes of these societies. The new breed of scholars, mostly political scientists, who now pass as experts on contemporary "Islam" remain wedded to categories such as "fundamentalist Islam," "terrorists and martyrs," "jihad," "al-Qaeda," and so on. They are also fond of reiterating the familiar rhetoric pervading Islah, Salafiya, Wahhabism, and various other political movements. There are those among these commentators who share the common ritualized celebration to be found among Muslims of the so-called Golden Age of Arabo-Islamic civilization. They perpetuate the apologetic tradition that keeps reminding Europeans of their debt to the Arabo-Islamic civilization for having passed on the torch of the science and philosophy of the ancient Greeks after this had been translated and extended through the resources of the Arabic language.

However, such an apologetic stance serves only to distract attention from the intellectual, literary, and cultural failures, shrinkage of intellectual endeavour, and deep regression of scientific research in the crucial domain of the human and social sciences characteristic of the postcolonial period (1950–2011) in Arabo-Islamic societies, which scarcely receive serious or responsible attention.

These are the main reasons that first led me, in the early 1970s, to launch the ambitious project of what I have called a Critique of Islamic Reason. Through the ensuing four decades I have been writing extensively on this subject in tandem with a discipline I call "Applied Islamology." I take pains to distinguish the latter from both classical Islamology (i.e., Islamic studies), and contemporary political science. Muslims, in general, have welcomed this response to the unresolved issues arising from the nature of postcolonial single-party states *(parti-états)*, and of the political opposition to these that currently takes the form of the well-known fundamentalist movements. I do not intend to repeat here, in this connection, what I have already elaborated in two recent books.[2]

In the present chapter, I shall dwell on the concept of historical epistemology applied to what I call the "closed official corpora" of the Islamic creed. The focus of this approach includes the discourse of the Qur'an, hadith, *sira* (biographies of the Prophet Muhammad), Shari'a, and *fiqh*, as well as historiography. Each of these discourses has its specific linguistic and semiotic status. Each needs to be considered in its historical, epistemic environment. It is essential here to heed the lesson of the methodology of linguistic and semiotic discourse analysis, which reminds us that every articulation of meaning is built on explicit or implicit postulates that in turn need to be verified for their truth or falsity.

Let us take, as examples, the professions of faith in Islam and Christianity, which define a rigid theological divide between these two monotheistic faiths based on their respective conceptions of God, His manifestation in the world, and the content of His commandments and prohibitions. For Muslims, "there is no divinity but Allah, and Muhammad is the messenger of Allah." Christians, for their part, subscribe to their creed in the "name of the Father, the Son and the Holy Spirit." Each of these formulas, which govern the confession of faith and the rituals of the community concerned, serves to entrench it in its characteristic theological space of perception, interpretation, knowledge, and everyday behavior. In each, the original historical context and the genesis of doctrine through time is effectively abolished. Muslims are no longer aware of the strenuous social and political battles that took place with the three sociocultural groups, namely (in the vocabulary of the Qur'an), the polytheists, or *mushrikun,* and the two peoples of the Book *(ahl al-kitab),* the Jews and the Christians. The nature of the divine was originally contested as an integral part of these battles. Similarly, the second proposition, which proclaims Muhammad as the Messenger and the Prophet of Allah, represents a theological challenge to the historical conception of prophetic function and discourse elaborated in biblical narratives. This challenge was amplified in Qur'anic discourse in an increasingly polemical style in the face of resistance from all sides, such as the refusal of the polytheists to abandon their pantheon. It is in this vein that the Qur'an accuses the Jews of maintaining that 'Uzyayr is the son of Allah, and rebukes the Christians by insisting that Jesus was but the son of Mary and that he was neither crucified nor resurrected. Similarly, the Judaic tradition continues to repudiate the whole theological construction serving to elevate Jesus, the Jewish preacher from Nazareth, to the rank of Jesus Christ.

I emphasize here the *cognitive* dimension of the theology centered on the logos of God, enunciated in the Word of God, which is also called "Revelation." The Qur'an, echoing the Bible, declares that God taught the names of all things to Adam. These names are taken to delineate the real being and the true meaning of every entity featuring in the Word of God. Theological discourse in the Jewish, Christian, and Islamic traditions employed the conceptual and logical framework derived from the Aristotelian corpus to provide a degree of rational coherence to systems of belief and nonbelief in each of the three faiths. Once Islam had emerged not only as a religion but as a vast political and cultural empire, each of the these communities held uncompromisingly to the claim that its own system of belief and disbelief was the most faithful and comprehensive replica of the teaching of the true God, who Himself established and endorsed it as the true religion (the *din al-haqq,* namely, Islam, earmarked by Allah as the chosen faith for all humanity).

In our own day, there is a trend in Catholic theology supporting the idea that religions are not equally "true." Several criteria should be used to establish a hierarchy of truth considering its form, its level, its domain, its historical genesis, its effectiveness in daily life, and its theoretical axiology. In this connection, Pope Benedict XVI has employed a more strictly logocentrist argument to acclaim what he sees as the intimate bond between faith and reason in the Hellenistic extension of the *logos* in the history of Christianity. This claim is repudiated by Jews, Muslims, and by several Protestant denominations. The debate provoked by Pope Benedict's position could have provided an occasion for proceeding beyond the exclusivities promoted by so-called orthodox faiths that regard themselves as the unique expression of the uniquely true religion. But this hope would seem, in present circumstances, to be in vain. When we consider the worldwide expansion of systemic political violence from 1945 on, it seems unlikely that religions that thrive on dogmatic enclosures inherited from the past would accept any intellectual and cultural strategies designed to subvert their cognitive frames, their cherished certitudes, and the stranglehold of the even more destructive modern political and economic ideologies imposed on all contemporary societies by the powerful states that, since the nineteenth century, have arrogated to themselves the "monopoly of legal violence."

After World War II, which had been waged within the mental framework of the so-called emancipatory Enlightenment in modern Europe, it became obvious that scientific progress had contributed to the dispossession of the non-European world rather than to the liberation of the human condition from ignorance, oppression, material deprivation, and, in the sphere of mind and culture, regressive beliefs and representations.

The postwar *Machtpolitik* that prevailed among European national states is now spreading across the world. Currently, we live in the phase of a "clean war" *(guerre propre)* between enabled and disabled societies. A single victim of war in the camp of powerful allies is judged to be one too many; whereas numberless instances of those who are maimed or killed on the other side remain anonymous and unofficial.

Following the attack on 9/11, the notion of a just war was brandished as a new weapon of legitimacy. What resulted was a competition for the status of a victim. The powerful United States saw itself as a victim, while al-Qaeda emerged as an incarnation of Absolute Evil. Scarcely anyone dared to point out that the terrorists who inflicted havoc upon the World Trade Center saw themselves as obeying the commandments of the true religion, systematically demoted and disparaged since the nineteenth century. It is relevant here to invoke the seminal concept of "false knowledge" formulated by the French philosopher

Gaston Bachelard, as well as what sociologists call the *imaginaire* production of societies.³ These notions of knowledge versus ignorance, truth versus falsehood, good versus evil, justice versus injustice, the dominant and the dominated, and so on, are not mere philosophical abstractions. I refer rather to their continuous and concrete elaboration in the human sciences. By contrast, wherever classical scholarship prevails in research and teaching, the resulting epistemological cleavages generate radical ideological conflict.

In today's so-called interreligious or intercultural dialogue, the archaeology of meaning tends to be conspicuously absent. Thus, systems of belief and disbelief are taken as safe, unquestionable instances of truth, legitimacy, and certain knowledge. The normative postulates in place in the vast domain of the religious sciences (which include theology, sacred law, and ethics) remain unchallenged by considerations from critical history and the perspectives of "anthropology as cultural criticism"—a discipline cultivated by the likes of James Clifford, Clifford Geertz, Jack Goody, and Claude Lévi-Strauss. To say this is not to ignore theology—much less to dismiss it as a point of principle—and the orthodox systems of belief and nonbelief subsumed within it. Discourse analysis makes a point of including every aspect of such systems in religious as well as secular manifestations of cognitive reason. Nevertheless, it is undeniable that Christian theology is nowadays more receptive to the methodologies and changing *epistēmē*(s) of the social and political sciences than its counterparts in contemporary Islamic contexts. The cognitive issues inherent in the mutually contending perspectives of the will to power and the quest for meaning deserve greater elaboration.

CULTURE OF BELIEF VERSUS CULTURE OF DISBELIEF:
BEYOND BINARY THOUGHT

A number of contemporary Muslim intellectuals advocate an authentic "modern" Islam. Tariq Ramadan, a fellow contributor to this volume, is one of the more notable members of this group of thinkers. There is a crucial distinction, however, between the culture of belief upheld by every religious tradition, on one side, and, on the other side, the culture of disbelief rooted in a pragmatic alliance between modern scientific knowledge, technology, and the democratic order prevalent in modern states. It appears that advocates of "modern" Islamic thought who proclaim the superiority of faith resort to a time-honored polemic to counteract the alleged pretensions of scientists in favor of a knowledge that is more objective and trustworthy than that of the systems of the class of people whom Max Weber once described as "managers of the sacred."

It is interesting that this polemical gambit echoes the stereotypical rejoinder by students in Europe and America in the summer of 1968 to every attempt at serious intellectual argument. Anyone who made such an attempt was confronted by an aggressive, dismissive stance challenging the speaker to identify the partisan standpoint that allegedly lay underneath his arguments. The assumption here was that every piece of discourse is inspired by an ideology.

It would appear that there is but a single exception to the innate limitation of human reason. This lies in starting from and abiding forever in the postulate that the *Qur'an* in all its declarations is ipsissima verba, the very Word of God. We are thus left with a rhetorical device, a sophistic formula, on burning issues, with religious reason on one side and classical philosophical reason, in the form of Greek metaphysics, on the other. My contention is that the social and political sciences are unfurling new cognitive possibilities that allow reason to go beyond this obsolete binary frame of thinking. For centuries, theological reason and classical philosophical reason have shared the binary opposition between true and false, right and wrong, good and evil, just and unjust, the essential and the contingent, the created and uncreated, and so on. This binary thinking shackles reason with the logic based on the excluded middle, with Euclidian geometry, with metaphysical and theological categories in general, as well as with a linear chronology of terrestrial historiography, and the notion of the eternal speech of God that supersedes contingent human discourses. Shackled in this way, reason can only proceed in the closed and limited mental space of abstract, essentialist, substantialist, and transcendentalist speculation.

For its part, the new reason embraced from the eighteenth century on, until 1945, as historians of the Enlightenment have shown, was captive to what Michel Foucault describes as the "historico-transcendental thematic."[4] Even the postmodernism touted by some philosophers during the 1970s left reason bound to an inherited Eurocentric, linear history of thought and civilization. The intellectual and cognitive leaps undertaken by three major subversive thinkers—Marx, Nietzsche, and Freud—ended up becoming petrified into scholastic and ideological schools, with competing claims to orthodoxy by adherents at odds with one another, who in this way served to reproduce the sectarian religious rivalries of former times.

Postmodernism had a short life. The sudden collapse of Marxist-Communist ideology left the road clear for a liberal, pragmatic, and empirical philosophy that endorsed the sovereignty of the free market, hailed the end of history, and predicted an impending clash of civilizations. Meanwhile, sectarian nationalist movements promoted political violence in the new historical agenda encompassing the former Soviet territories and ex–Third World societies. All so-called Muslim societies are implicated, more deeply than ever before, in the new geopolitical strategy of the United States and the European Union, poles of hegemonic power unified conceptually under the name of the West. This is especially noticeable in references to the ideological polarization between "Islam and the West." All this is obscured by the fact that the trajectory of the Reason of the Enlightenment tends to be studied separately from the *Machtpolitik* or *Realpolitik* employed by the West in the geopolitical mapping of the rest of the world from the time the Yalta Treaty was signed in 1945 by the four major powers of the time. The explosion in Manhattan on 9/11 can be seen, in this light, as the climax of a tragedy, simmering underground, which was planned by political decision-makers in the West as well as by the postcolonial regimes born after 1945.

It is with a view to overcoming this Manichean use of reason, and the false legitimacy claimed by both religious reason and its secularized, modern counterpart, that I apply the same reflexive critical history, at one and the same time, to all the protagonists in the theater of modern history: the civil wars, the so-called wars of liberation, and the "just wars" fought ostensibly to eradicate the terrorist threat, all of which continue to inflict systemic violence on a worldwide scale today. It is no longer acceptable to preach democracy and human rights to regressive political regimes and the societies under their yoke. The burning question for all people in the world today is how to identify common, shared, viable forms of reason, critical knowledge, political legitimacy, overarching justice, and humanist thought and practice. The challenge is to recognize and encourage these potentialities in each and every culture and civilization that at present craves the protection of its right to difference, which is acclaimed and celebrated without self-criticism. Each civilization asserts its specific values, historical heritage, religious law, ethics, political legitimacy, artistic achievements, ancient glory, and its contributions to the universal good of mankind and its environment.

The right to the protection of "difference" should at all times be linked to the concrete capacity in each citizen to submit this "difference" to commonly espoused rules of self-criticism. This is far from being the case at present. What is more common, rather, are institutionalized forms of ignorance that are assumed and defended as universal values and knowledge in both religious and modern secular contexts. This is what I call the "competing perspectives" to be found in sectarian divisions and oppositions, and the mutual exclusivities to be seen in regressive, underdeveloped oppressed societies. We observe the same sectarian divisions in political parties, the class struggles and individualist interests of advanced, democratic affluent societies.

To date, I have described and elaborated a concept of "emerging reason" in several of my works, lectures, and tutorials. The term stands for every innovative answer given to the challenges of new historical pressures today, such as those of demography, social exclusion, the widening gaps within and between civil societies, the transgressions of political regimes, cultural regression or subversion, the failure of artistic creativity, the absence of charismatic leaders, the recurrent economic and monetary crises, the ecological threats, and the impact of violence at every social and historical level, all of which are rampant today. In every context, emerging reason faces the daunting recurrence of traditional forms of rationality that are sociologically dominant even in contexts where scholarship, scientific discoveries, freedom of thought, subversive criticism, and highly sophisticated technology are changing daily life at every level of society.

The emerging reason has to cope, on one hand, with a reactivation of ancient, idealized figures in the collective imagination that accompanies revivalism, and, on the other hand, with the new materialist divinities hailed by late modern forms of "tele-techno-scientific reason." The modes of inquiry and expression in emerging reason are not confined to the logocentrism of the Aristotelian corpus developed over the course of centuries.[5] It deals simultaneously with the imagination, with individual and collective memories, and with the relentless pressure of emotions, affects, sensibilities, hopes, and desires. At the same time, it seeks to elaborate a grammar of emotions, addressing the irrational and often violent episodes that occur during social or political demonstrations and the conflagrations of civil war. It pays critical attention to the ongoing metamorphoses of ancient notions or practices, such as the sacred, sanctity, ritual, spirituality, mysticism, supernaturalism, as well as the narratives, legends, mythologies, and superstitions that have up to now been seen as peculiar to religion. The very concept of religion needs to be revisited in light of the rise of secular religions and of populist religiosity and superstitious beliefs among supposedly modern, emancipated elites.

Modern positivist reason aimed to replace faith-based knowledge with scientific, objectivist knowledge. Mythical representations of truth and reality were dismissed as legends, fables, and superstitious beliefs. Religion was interpreted as a superstitious and phantasmic construction of reality. The Marxist positivist slogan that declared religion to be the "opium of the people" became the motto of a new modern religion that called itself "atheism." Atheism was presented as a scientific theory designed to eliminate false beliefs. The human subject was thus split into a rational, logical, logocentrist expert, on one hand, and an emotional, passionate, imaginative believer, on the other. This split still endures in the prevalent division between positivist, pragmatic, empirical sciences and the so-called human and religious sciences. A rigid positivist frame of mind continues to inspire schools of rationalism, atheism, or "neutral," "objective" *laïcité* (secularism) promulgated in state schools in France since the days of the Third Republic.

The ideological, political dimension of modern reason is now fiercely contested by the even more menacing return of religion that serves as the political springboard of so-called fundamentalist movements. We can see, in this context, the ideological pressures and the intellectual needs that call for the emergence of another reason, with its specific functions and horizons of meaning. Those who continue to invoke a global, abstract, idealistic, and supra-historical Enlightenment appeal desperately to modern democratic values as a solution. Emerging reason thus has a responsibility to combat both these competing ideological perversions of critical reason.

The verdict of emerging reason is that the proponents of a mythologized and ideologized Enlightenment are prisoners of the same erroneous reasoning as those who enlist faith-based wisdom and spirituality to legitimize the so-called "just war." When we consider the anti-humanist political and economic consequences of the retaliation against the aggression of 9/11, we can only conclude that neither religious nor modern enlightened reason has succeeded—intellectually, legally, ethically, theologically, or philosophically—in eliminating clashes of institutionalized ignorance, erroneous legitimacy, and arbitrary will to power. Both religious authorities and modern secular intellectuals or scholars were quick to give their backing to militant retaliatory measures designed to exterminate the enemy. There were very few on either the Muslim or the Western side who raised their voices, not in the familiar apologetic celebration of the true religion or the supremacy of democratic values, but along the lines of a radical, subversive criticism of a reason emerging precisely from these historical challenges.

I was one of those who voiced this perspective in lectures at the Library of Congress after the events of September 11, 2001. I elaborated it further in a book published jointly with my colleague Joseph Maila in 2003, immediately in the wake of the "just war" against Iraq.[6] But a few modest voices have little chance of being heard in the cacophony of thousands of books on Islamic fundamentalism that keep flooding the market, and of numerous vociferous interventions from those who have daily access to powerful media, both written and oral. In my most recent book, as well as in many articles, I have deepened the concept of "subversive criticism" based on emerging reason. I have coined new concepts in the process, among them "mytho-history" and "mytho-ideology," as well as "reflexive history, sociology, and anthropology of thought."

I have employed these concepts while focusing on the instructive case of Islamic thought as it developed in the "geo-historical, Mediterranean area" from 661 to 1400 C.E. The two concepts of "mytho-history" and "mytho-ideology" draw attention to neglected domains of historical, sociopsychological, and ethnological exploration. These domains are of crucial importance for the history of ideas. The cultures of belief as well as disbelief are rooted in, and driven by, mytho-historical narratives and mytho-ideological constructions of social, political, and religious imaginaries. In our modern discourses and didactic writings, we continue to find mythical and ideological representations mingling with historical, sociological, and ethnological observation. The rhetoric of political discourse in election campaigns appeals chiefly to the collective imaginary rather than to critical reason. Similarly, the teaching of national history is more inclined to celebrate the glorious past of the nation-state than to explain lived history. The same type of mythologization may be seen at work in the apologetic, self-glorifying discourse of various communities. In theocratic regimes, to offer a historical critique of the orthodox foundations of what is taken to be true religion is to find oneself in jail, or even sentenced to death. I have explained, above, how the French term *imaginaire* encompasses more complex domains of human culture and history than the English term "imagination" and its cognates. An oral or written discourse drawing on the imaginary is liable to be deeply and immediately effective because it elicits the emotional adherence of the listener or reader. By contrast, a rational reception involves a greater time-lag, requiring as it does a training in critical methodology, capable of evaluating the validity of various discourses.

Even sophisticated scholarship is not immune to mytho-ideological constructions of an imagined past, together with religious or secular values associated with various regimes of truth. Social imaginaries and collective memories are the vehicles of these modes. For a recent example, we can hardly do better than to refer to a book by a French scholar and professor, Sylvain Gouguenheim.[7] The author resurrects an old, recurrent argument in the enduring polemic between Islam and Christianity. After the theological revisions introduced by Vatican II, the geopolitical "West" has replaced Christianity. The historical thesis that Europe received and learned from numerous texts translated from Arabic into Latin between the tenth and thirteenth centuries, seems hard for Gouguenheim to accept. Christianity and modern, secularized Europe alike appear reluctant to acknowledge the existence of science and philosophy in the Arabic language in the High Middle Ages, before the period of European hegemony. The thesis and the style of the book in question are deliberately polemical. The arguments are short, often ad hominem, and directed at selected authors. As we know, the media pay scant attention to erudite debates. However, in the present case, the most influential French daily, *Le Monde,* applauded the book as an innovative, revolutionary vision establishing the true, historical continuity of the "Greek Miracle" in Christian Europe. It invokes the highly sanctified, mythologized Mont Saint-Michel, which is still visited by millions of pilgrims and tourists, including (just prior to his election) French President Nicolas Sarkozy. For the first time, however, eminent scholars were quick—well before Muslims, especially Arabs—to take issue not only with the author and the reviewer of the book, but also the prestigious publisher Seuil, which included it in a reputable series, *L'Univers historique* (The Historical World).

It is relevant to add that the debate has so far been confined to academic circles. It is unlikely that we shall see demonstrations in the street, as was the case with the Danish cartoons, or Pope Benedict XVI's lecture at Regensberg in 2006. In fact, there is a strong link between the general theses reiterated by Gouguenheim and the pope's claim to an unbroken, profound intellectual link between the Greek *logos* and the Catholic faith. Both viewpoints reflect the same apologetic mentality subscribing to Christian exceptionalism. This is ultimately inseparable from secularized European exceptionalism. Both utilize the inaugural, grand narrative joining the "Greek Miracle" to the founding narrative of monotheist revelation, culminating in the figure of Jesus Christ. This narrative is reasserted as a historical response to the forces of Evil incarnate, once again, in "Islam": the arch-adversary that first came to life in the Qur'an, declaring itself the final Word of God revealed to mankind.

Europe and North America are unified in the geopolitically privileged and powerful entity called the West. This West is depicted as the home of universal values, sacred hope, indubitable knowledge, and the achievements of Reason, and seen by many as the true promise of Eternal Salvation. These are to be nourished and transferred, without dilution, to the rest of the world. This grand narrative is countered by a decisive "No" from the Islamic grand narrative. This refusal dates back to Qur'anic discourse, but the contemporary refusal is more crudely ideological, in that it is dominated by a collective anger, even a destructive rage. It has for long been a mytho-historical position, employing the very same rhetoric as that of the Judaeo-Christian tradition. "You went wrong," so the Muslims have long been saying to the West, right from the start—namely, with your holy scriptures, which you deliberately perverted, as God Himself declared in His last Revelation, through His last messenger, Muhammad. The "sword" of God remains mightier than all your sophisticated engines put together, and all your illusory values.

*What Went Wrong?* is the title of a best seller published by Bernard Lewis in 2003.[8] The title epitomizes centuries of polemic on the "true religion," the authentic revelation that assures its adherents that others are guilty of corrupting the very Word of God. When Bernard Lewis proposes a historical account of "The Roots of Muslim Rage" (the title of one of his widely read articles), he implicitly appeals to his scholarly credentials.[9] In fact, however, there are a lot of mytho-historical and mytho-ideological constructions in his thesis.

Neither of the grand narratives at issue here is expressed in these explicit terms. The heart of the current conflict is implicit, however, in the theological constructions of the orthodox systems of belief and nonbelief. With its positive engaging spiritual connotations, the concept of faith covers the detailed contents and behaviors perpetuated with the vocabulary, the linguistic articulation, and the practices of beliefs and nonbeliefs, not only religious, but also those accredited by positivist social sciences applied to the colonized countries since the nineteenth century. When theology is practiced as "the intelligence of faith subject to continuous probation through time" (Dominique Chenu), beliefs are constantly scrutinized, eventually revised or even abandoned. But this kind of theology is suspected by the supreme doctrinal Magisterium.

Here we discover, once more, the specific tasks awaiting emerging reason. Much more needs to be done, by way of subversion, on the side of contemporary Islam, than that of Western European Christianity. It is interesting that self-criticism among both Catholic and Protestant Christians leads some among them to the view that it is now time to rethink the fate of religion "after Christianity."[10] It is now redundant to want to reform or (in accordance with the vision of the present pope) re-Christianize Europe. The new thinking must not be confused with either theological modernism or a secularist ambition to separate religion from politics. Gianni Vattimo belongs rather to the school of Paul Ricœur, Emmanuel Levinas, Hans Gadamer, and those philosophers who draw from the up-to-date *epistēmē* of the human and social sciences and postmodern hermeneutics. The idea of a nonreligious Christianity represents a deepening of the philosophical and anthropological dimensions of the Christian outlook independently of the traditional liturgical structure, which was intended to stabilize and essentialize its faith-based or religious expression. Vattimo's view resembles the well-known thesis of René Girard, according to which Catholicism is the only way out of the violence generated by mimetic rivalry *(rivalité mimétique)*. The Catholic construction of the human subject is likewise expected to culminate in a "religionless Christianity." These heuristic hypotheses, proposed by these two authors, are meant to enable Christianity to arrive at a new historical stage in the long march toward an emancipatory goal of human history.

In a recent private exchange with Vattimo, I objected to the exclusive, privileged status accorded to Catholic religion and history in both these views. There is no doubt that such a claim has an apologetic flavor. Unless it is grounded in historical, anthropological, and philosophical imperatives, it is liable to reactivate the mimetic rivalry traditionally responsible for positions of violent, reciprocal rejection in the three religions of the Book, or rather Books.[11] Since the intellectual, scientific, technological, and political triumph of the reason of the Enlightenment, we have in fact been embroiled in tragic structural violence on a worldwide scale. As a historian of Islamic thought, I am wary of giving succor to the rival pretension of "a religionless Islam." I favor instead a different cognitive and epistemological option, free from any apologetic attitude, as outlined in the second edition of my book *The Unthought in Contemporary Islamic Thought,* which I chose to retitle as *Islam: To Reform or to Subvert?*

My methodological and epistemological contention is that we can no longer allow the interpreting communities the monopoly of shaping and controlling the orthodox tradition specific to the monotheistic religions. New scholarship now reveals the significant features relegated by those orthodox traditions to the domain of the unthinkable and the unthought. There is a long list of seminal works that have altered, even subverted, naïve transmission and reproduction of systems of belief and nonbelief.[12]

Practically every day, we find new, challenging titles of works in various languages in the field of religious studies. Not all of them offer new emancipatory approaches or novel documents affecting the beliefs based on orthodox teachings in each of these traditions. The received version of the history of monotheism gets decisively altered when we read a collection like *Ce que la Bible doit à l'Egypte* (What the Bible Owes to Egypt) or Jacqueline Chabbi's *Le Coran décrypté: Figures bibliques en Arabie* (The Qur'an Deciphered: Biblical Figures in Arabia) (both published in 2008). Historical evidence increasingly invites a radical revision of the concept of religion. No doubt, the impact of this is confined to a small group of scholars. It rarely affects the majority of believers.

Sociologically, beliefs in recent years tend to become obsolete for an ever-increasing number of believers. This is not due to subversive knowledge generated by the social and political sciences, but to other decisive factors, such as the economy, technology, or the impact of political institutions, juridical norms, and artistic innovations, all of which enhance the culture of disbelief. Consequently, religious culture comes to be eroded and religious practice neglected. The result is a continuous drift to other styles of life, which are even more subversive of reflexive thinking.

The idea of a Christianity without religion leads me to reflect critically on the possibilities of a heuristic program on analogous lines aiming at an Islam or Judaism "without religion." The point at issue is the old dispute about the concept of the true religion, which continues to shape and guide theological construction of faith in every community possessing its own collective memory. The Qur'an deployed the concept of true religion to distinguish and isolate Islam from the surrounding religions of the time. Hegel and other modern philosophers, not to mention theologians, defended this concept in their own terms. When Kant pondered on "religion within the limits of reason" (in his two major works, *The Critique of Pure Reason* and *The Critique of Practical Reason*), he introduced a new problematization of the concept, and the field it occupied. But our present *epistēmē* and scientific scholarship are much more encompassing, and intellectually much vaster, than those of the eighteenth century. At the same time, so many cultures and societies still remain insulated from the debates on the subject that have taken place in modern contexts in Europe and North America.

Given these historical facts, there are a number of possible outcomes of the ongoing confrontations summarized as "Islam versus the West."

First, Muslims might move away from an ideological, political exploitation of Islam, toward the positive, emancipatory knowledge available in the shared body of the human, social, and political sciences, applied impartially and equally to all contemporary societies. If this happens, the present polarization will become obsolete and an age of solidarity between peoples, states, and cultures, with shared values and shared models of historical action, will be inaugurated.

Second, Muslims might cling to a dogmatic, apologetic adherence to the notion of the true religion superseding all other models of historical action. In this case, the West will feel entitled to defend its values through a battle against obscurantist, repressive ideologies and in favor of a humanist, democratic regime of truth and politics.

Third, Muslims might stick to their Islamic principles, beliefs, and nonbeliefs, and to regressive regimes of absolutes and oppressive politics. Westerners on their part would persist in a hegemonic will to power, relying on *Macht-* and *Realpolitik*. They might continue, in accordance with a policy of double standards, to profess to safeguard human rights and liberal democracy, on one side, while seeking strategic control, on the other side, of arbitrarily demarcated geopolitical zones. If this happens, weakened and marginalized societies and cultures will be doomed to ever greater suffering, and unabating, systemic violence will dominate the future of mankind for long years to come.

There is a fourth possibility, in the form of ideological polarization originating elsewhere—in regions like China, India, Japan, sub-Saharan Africa, and Latin America. We can only wait, scanning the horizon for tentative signs of new paradigms for the future.

As outlined here, my approach examines religious phenomenon in its anthropological dimension, and I must therefore stress a final encompassing condition. Any of the four possibilities just mentioned are tied up with the search for relevant scientific, philosophical, theological, and political answers to the following nodal question: Is it desirable and feasible to engage in inquiries in order to legitimate faith and religion-based moral, juridical, political, or social norms aiming at the regulation of common action in present pluralist, secularized, or democratic societies?

In some European and American societies, mainly in the United States, there are practical answers—more or less tolerated and intellectually relevant—to that question. In France, we know how the principle of *laïcité* assumes the protection of all religious cults but refuses any kind of legitimacy and coexistence in the public sphere to any faith or religion-based norm. Here, the epistemological impediment prohibits raising the question even as a heuristic hypothesis. That is why the necessity of insisting on the question for its heuristic fecundity should be recognized by all scholars practicing human, social, juridical, and political sciences, as well, of course, as by all philosophers and theologians.

Many urgent problems are included in the question as I have articulated it, among them: (1) the current metamorphoses of meaning, leading to the expanding in all languages and cultures of what I call "the semantic disorder"; (2) the lack and loss of any interest in teaching comparative history of philosophy and theology, especially in the United States, where theology is taught in divinity schools and theological seminaries for the believers of each religion, which is a more regressive than emancipating practice; (3) the well-known historical fact that the political decision to reduce religion to a private concern of citizens was forcibly imposed in a time (during the eighteenth to nineteenth centuries) when knowledge of religions other than Judaism and Christianity in Europe was biased and very superficial. The political and cultural consequences of this forcible imposition can be clearly evaluated everywhere in the systemic violence that combines sacralized religious violence with the violence of MacWorld. What sociologists describe as the return of religion, or the "revenge of God," is just the manifestation of the persisting impact and resources of religions in societies dominated and marginalized since the nineteenth century. Successive forcible impositions after 1945 of the so-called Reason of the Enlightenment promoted to global sovereignty a new omnipotent God in the shape of tele-techno-scientific Reason.

NOTES

1. Albert Hourani, *Arabic Thought in the Liberal Age, 1798–1939* (Cambridge: Cambridge University Press, 1983).
2. See Mohammed Arkoun, *Islam: To Reform or Subvert?* (London: Saqi Books 2006), and id., *Humanisme et islam: Combats et propositions* (Paris: Vrin, 2006). The concept of the *imaginaire*, widely employed in the human, social, and political sciences in several European languages, remains virtually ignored, for all its fruitfulness, in the English logosphere, where the word "imaginary" implies a fanciful, i.e., inaccurate or irrelevant, representation of reality. This is perhaps one reason why the populist religiosity preached by televangelists in the United States is nowadays confused with religious faith informed by the discipline of critical theological reason. See Mohammed Arkoun, "The Cognitive Status and the Normative Functions of Revelation: The Example of the Qur'an," in id., *The Unthought in Contemporary Islamic Thought* (London: Saqi Books, 2003).
3. Equally relevant are the concepts of the "social construction of reality" (Peter Berger) and "the social institution of the human mind" (Jean de Munck).
4. Michel Foucault, *The Order of Things: An Archaeology of the Human Sciences* (New York: Vintage Books, 1994), p. 371.
5. The concept of logocentrism has an important role in elucidating the linguistic and semiotic features of the discursive structure of discourses based on Aristotelian *logos;* this structure is then differentiated from the one specific to mythical narratives of both religious discourse and platonic philosophical discourse. See Mohammed Arkoun, "Logocentrism and Religious Truth in Islamic Thought," in *Islam: To Reform or to Subvert?* (2nd ed., London: Saqi Books, 2006).
6. Mohammed Arkoun and Joseph Maïla, *De Manhattan à Bagdad : Au-delà du bien et du mal* (Paris: Desclée de Brouwer, 2003).
7. Sylvain Gouguenheim, *Aristote au Mont Saint-Michel : Les racines grecques de l'Europe chrétienne* (Paris: Seuil, 2008).
8. Bernard Lewis, *What Went Wrong? The Clash Between Islam and Modernity in the Middle East* (New York: Harper, 2003).
9. Bernard Lewis, "The Roots of Muslim Rage," *Policy* 17, 4 (Summer 2001–2002): 17–26; this article originally appeared in the *Atlantic Monthly*, September 1990, www.theatlantic.com/doc/199009/muslim-rage (accessed June 16, 2010).
10. See, e.g., Gianni Vattimo, *Dopo la cristianità: Per un cristianesimo non religioso* (Milan: Garzanti, 2002), trans. Frank La Brasca as *Après la chrétienté: Pour un christianisme non religieux* (Paris: Calmann-Lévy, 2004).
11. This is a concept I have specifically used to go beyond the Qur'anic concept of the "peoples of the Book" (i.e., the heavenly Book). See Arkoun, "Cognitive Status."
12. A sample list of only the most representative of this category of works includes Jonathan Brown, *The Canonisation of al-Bukhārī and Muslim: The Formation and Function of the Sunnī Ḥadīth Canon* (Leiden: Brill 2007; Jacqueline Chabbi, *Le seigneur des tribus : L'islam de Mahomet* (Paris: Broche

1996); id., *Le Coran décrypté : Figures bibliques en Arabie* (Paris: Fayard 2008); Jean-Louis Chrétien, *Sous le regard de la Bible* (Paris: Bayard 2008); Régis Debray, *Un Candide en Terre sainte* (Paris: Gallimard 2008); *Organizing Knowledge: Encyclopaedic Activities in the Pre-Eighteenth Century Islamic World*, ed. Gerhard Endress (Leiden: Brill 2006); Israël Finkelstein and Neil Asher Silberman, *The Bible Unearthed: Archaeology's New Vision of Ancient Israel and the Origin of Its Sacred Texts* (New York: Free Press, 2001); Jean Flori, *Pierre l'Ermite et la première croisade* (Paris: Fayard, 1999); Thomas Hoffmann, *The Poetic Qur'an: Studies on Qur'anic Poeticity* (Wiesbaden : Harrassowitz, 2007); Jonathan Israel, *Radical Enlightenment: Philosophy and the Making of Modernity, 1650–1750* (Oxford: Oxford University Press, 2001); G.H.A. Juynboll, *Encyclopaedia of Canonical Ḥadīth* (Leiden: Brill 2007); Didier Lett, *Un procès de canonisation au Moyen âge: Essai d'historie sociale: Nicolas de Tolentino, 1325* (Paris: Presses universitaires de France, 2008); John P. Meier, *A Marginal Jew: Rethinking the Historical Jesus*, vol. 1: *The Roots of the Problem and the Person*; vol. 2: *Mentor, Message, and Miracles*; vol. 3: *Companions and Competitors*; vol. 4: *Law and Love* (New York: Doubleday, 1991–2009); S. Caroline Purkhardt, *Transforming Social Representations: A Social Psychology of Common Sense and Science* (New York: Routledge, 1993); Thomas Römer, *Ce que la Bible doit à l'Égypte* (Paris: Bayard, 2008); Uri Rubin, *The Eye of the Beholder: The Life of Muhammad as Viewed by the Early Muslims* (Princeton, NJ: Darwin Press, 1995); R.B. Serjeant, *Customary and Shari'ah Law in Arabian Society* (London: Variorum, 1991); Tilman Nagel, *The History of Islamic Theology: From Muhammad to the Present*, trans. Thomas Thornton (Princeton, NJ: Markus Wiener, 2000); id., *Muhammad: Leben und Legende* (Munich: Oldenburg, 2008); id., *Allahs Liebling: Ursprung und Erscheinungsformen des Mohammedglaubens* (Munich: Oldenburg, 2008).

CHAPTER 4

# Iranian Shi'ism at the Gates of Historic Change

MEHRAN KAMRAVA

Some three decades after its political success in establishing a theocratic "Islamic Republic," Iranian Shi'ism is undergoing a profound, indeed revolutionary change in its philosophical underpinnings and its overall orientation. Ironically, this change is precipitated by the very establishment and evolution of the political system to which Shi'ism gave rise in the aftermath of Iran's 1978–79 revolution. Initially, in the lead-up to the revolution, Shi'ism emerged as a potent source of mass mobilization, exciting the masses and the elites alike about the possibilities of revolutionary liberation and the dawn of a new era, loosely characterized as Islamic and essentially democratic. But the realities of the post-revolutionary era—marked by a chaotic immediate aftermath, a bloody and devastating war of eight years with Iraq, charismatic rule, unfathomable repression, and austere revolutionism—turned the revolutionary Shi'ism of the 1970s into an apologist for authoritarianism and autocracy for much of the 1980s. In more ways than most Iranians dared to vocalize, the political system ceased to be revolutionary and instead more and more began to resemble run-of-the-mill dictatorships. The regime's ideological underpinnings, in the meanwhile, similarly assumed dictatorial garbs in order to justify an increasingly narrow elite's hold on power and its machinations for purposes of political longevity and legitimacy. Overseeing, and in many ways orchestrating, the entire process was the overwhelming presence and personality of Ayatollah Ruhollah Khomeini, the regime's founder.

Like all other revolutionary ideologies, the political and ideological unity of Shi'ism congealed under the banner of the Islamic revolution in the late 1970s turned out to be quite ephemeral. The grand revolutionary coalition that had brought the clergy to power began breaking up almost immediately after the monarchy was overthrown, and the circle of revolutionary leaders became increasingly narrower as competition for the newfound power intensified and as the stakes increased. Accordingly, to the victors went the ideological spoils of the revolution, which by the 1980s began sustaining and supporting what was by now the political establishment's orthodoxy. But orthodoxy, and with it forced conformity, are only as sustainable as the larger repressive milieu of which they are a part, and once the reigns of repression began loosening ever so slightly, in the late 1980s, the forced ideological conformity of postrevolutionary Shi'ism also began to show signs of fissure. The late 1980s were fateful times for Iran. The country's long war with Iraq finally ended in 1988; the regime felt compelled to position itself as a champion of economic reconstruction; far-reaching changes were initiated to a political system that now seemed unworkable and broken; and, perhaps most important, Ayatollah Khomeini died in June 1989.

Thus began a steady rethinking of what Iranian Shi'ism was all about. Is Shi'ism revolutionary and a framework for political liberation, or the underwriting blueprint for orthodoxy, conformity, and austerity? What role does it envision for innovation and, more specifically, for *ijtihad*, independent reasoning? How and with which tools does or should Shi'ism address such questions of contemporary relevance as democracy and civil rights, globalization and modernity? How is religious knowledge in general and Shi'a hermeneutics in particular acquired and accumulated? And, to what extent does mainstream Shi'ism endorse or jurisprudentially support the notion of the position of *Velayat-e Faqih*, supreme jurisconsult, which Ayatollah Khomeini elaborated, later occupied, and had enshrined in the 1979 Constitution? These and other similar questions formed the basis of a process whereby Iranian Shi'ism became the cause célèbre of a growing number of public intellectuals throughout the 1990s. As far as possible, these writers and journalists began raising questions concerning the jurisprudential and theological genealogies of many of the precepts on which the political orthodoxy had become reliant. Not surprisingly, all too often, the answers they provided to these questions differed markedly and radically from those officially endorsed and propagated by the political establishment. Individually and collectively, they pushed Iranian Shi'ism further along the path of sustained, systematic change, one with lasting historical consequences.

This chapter examines some of the most salient themes in Iranian Shi'a thought today as articulated by four of the country's most renowned religious intellectuals, namely, former president Mohammad Khatami, Mohammad Mojtahed Shabestari, 'Abdolkarim Soroush, and Mohsen Kadivar. Each of these individuals comes from a different background, approaches the topic differently, and concentrates on a different aspect of Shi'a jurisprudence. Nevertheless, they all share certain fundamental beliefs regarding the proper role of religion in society and politics and the need to rid Islam—and more specifically Shi'ism—of the barnacles it has accumulated throughout history. Religion in general and Shi'ism in particular, they maintain, needs to change if it is to remain relevant in today's world. More accurately, it is not religion per se but our conception of it, the way we arrive at its dictates and junctions, that is, *ijtihad,* and the processes whereby religious knowledge is acquired and is passed down from one generation to another, its hermeneutics. The outcome has been the articulation of a vibrant discourse within Iranian Shi'ism that is decidedly "reformist" in its orientation and is democratic in its essence and its agendas, one that seeks to fundamentally transform the way religion is understood, knowledge of it is produced, accumulated, and socially and politically utilized. Together, Iran's reformist religious intellectuals are articulating the broad contours of an Islamic democracy. And, in the process, wittingly or not, they are pushing Iranian Shi'ism further afield along the path of historic change.

ARTICULATING AN ISLAMIC DEMOCRACY

In outlining the principles of an Islamic democracy, a number of religious intellectuals begin by clarifying their conception of religion in general and Islam in particular. In simple terms, most argue, like Mostafa Katir'i, that "religion is made up of a series of rules and regulations, comprising a divine worldview that the Almighty has sent to humans through His prophets."[1] More specifically, according to Hojjatoleslam Hasan Yusofi Eshkevari, religion has three interrelated components: a worldview, ethical (or ideological) commands, and practical commands.[2] Each of these components is driven by the two internal logics of "guidance" and "justice"—guidance for man's spiritual growth and refinement, and justice as the driving principle in social relations, economy, ethics, legal rights, and freedom.³

The arguments of the religious intellectuals are guided by two important assumptions, one having to do with the larger nature and functions of religion, and another with religion's relationship with politics. First, all agree that religion does, and should continue to, play a pivotal role in the overall life of society. Hashem Aqajari, for example, maintains, that secularism features internal logical contradictions that it cannot easily solve.⁴ Most of these contradictions revolve around the spiritual needs of societies and individuals. One of the best-known religious intellectuals who has articulated the need to address this spiritual hunger is Mostafa Malekian. According to Malekian, religion, and more specifically Islam, provides answers and solutions to a whole host of question marks that, if unanswered, would bring misery and ruin to a person's life. "The mind and soul of the contemporary person has problems and difficulties that are existential in nature," he argues. "It is essential that we explore the Qur'an's perspective on these issues fully and thoroughly; problems and difficulties such as truth, good, compassion, beauty, justices, doubt, belief, calm, disquiet, anxiety, fear, happiness, depression, hopelessness, loneliness, death, meaning of life, self discovery, self-alienation, selfishness, self construction, pain and suffering, the changeable facets of life, the unchangeable facets of life, the differences between people and the secret of these differences."⁵

Apart from nourishing the soul, religion has important political functions. Yusofi Eshkevari's arguments in this regard are typical of many others. Without religion—and therefore without justice, religion's centerpiece—a balanced and spiritually fulfilling life is not possible, he argues.⁶ This is where the second assumption in the religious intellectuals' arguments about religion comes in. While religion is an integral and important part of society's overall operations, including its politics, an overwhelming majority of religious reformists maintain that Islam does not mandate a specific form of government. Yusofi Eshkevari's emphatic arguments in this regard are typical of those made by other religious intellectuals. "Never in Islam has the act of governing been mandated as a function of religion."⁷ Government, instead, is a purely human endeavor, cannot possibly have one form and type at all times, and is contextually dependent on the times and the conditions.⁸ These and other similar arguments, typical of the reformist religious discourse as they are, put it directly at odds with proponents of the conservative religious discourse.

Let us explore the theoretical propositions of the religious intellectuals regarding "religious government" in some depth. According to 'Ezzatollah Sahhabi, the Almighty has given man complete free will to choose and decide his own fate and destiny, including the type of political system under which he chooses to live.[9] While God is all-knowing and omnipotent, nowhere in the Holy Book or in the traditions has He mandated a specific form and type of government. In fact, 'Abdolali Bazargan, another religious intellectual, claims that the Qur'an explicitly mentions—meaning endorses—a diverse variety of political systems, including those headed by women.[10] The Qur'an, in other words, does not mandate a specific type of political system. Also, the ideal political system does not necessarily have to be ruled by a prophet or a learned religious cleric. "We have had prophets who have governed, and we have had prophets who have only fulfilled spiritual roles and who have delegated military and political matters to qualified leaders."[11] There is a significant conclusion to be drawn here: "In sum, the ideal type of political system differs according to the conditions of the times and the people's knowledge and understanding, and insisting on a uniform structure of government [for all times] and giving it divine sanction is contrary to the logic and the contents of the Qur'an."[12] The construction of a religious system is man's prerogative, and this is precisely why Shi'a *fiqh* features such a diversity of opinions about the ideal political system.[13]

This subject has been extensively studied by 'Abdolkarim Soroush. Soroush divides the phenomenon of political rule into two distinct aspects, one administrative and managerial, that is thoroughly *a*religious, and another ethical and normative, in which religion can play a determining role.[14] Ideally, governments must attend to the material needs of the people so that people themselves can attend to their more subtle, spiritual needs. "Religious government is one that addresses the worldly needs of the people and enables them to nurture and sustain their own spirits."[15] Soroush makes an important distinction between a "religious government" *(hokumat-e dini)* and a "jurisprudential government" *(hokumat-e fiqhi)*. A jurisprudential government is a theocracy that seeks to impose religious dictates on the population. Compliance is different from belief, and the pretence of being religious is fundamentally different from the internalization and voluntary, knowing acceptance of norms and values. "If the people of a society are not truly free to choose their beliefs, that society cannot be called truly 'religious' even if it is ruled over by a government that claims the mantle of religion.[16] From this we can surmise what religious government is and is not:

> A religious government is not one whose method of management is religious, since method can never be religious.
>
> A religious government is not one that spreads and executes jurisprudential commands, since compulsion is not a yardstick for religiosity.
>
> A religious government is not one that is based on the religious credentials and rights of the rulers, since government must also rely on the nonreligious rights of the people.
>
> A religious government is not one that imposes belief on the hearts of the people, since religion cannot be imposed.
>
> A religious government is one that is based on the nonreligious rights of the people and the nonpolitical responsibility of religious individuals toward management and critique of power. Its first responsibility is to provide for the needs of the people (based on rational methods and precedence) in order to rid them of material needs, so that they can attend to matters that are more delicate and spiritual. The people can thus freely choose their beliefs and also transform society into a stage for the open and free choice of religion.[17]

Insofar as the religious intellectuals' discussion of the relationship between religion—that is, Islam—and government is concerned, democracy figures very prominently. In fact, as mentioned earlier, for these architects of the reformist religious discourse, reformism is the means through which democracy as the end can be achieved. For them, Islam and democracy are intimately and fundamentally compatible. The argument is simple: Islam has not mandated any specific forms of government except those that attend to the material and spiritual needs of the people. The ideal form of government, therefore, is changeable according to the needs and circumstances of the times, which, in the contemporary era, happen to be democracies. Islam, in fact, contains several built-in features and mechanisms that are consistent with and are supportive of democracy. What Muslim societies need, therefore, are Islamic democracies.

Among the crop of religious intellectuals, Yusofi Eshkevari has been at the forefront of articulating the relationship between Islam and democracy. He argues that "the democratic method is the most religious and the most appropriate manner to administer Muslim societies."[18] If the essence of religion is the spread of peace and justice, and if the guiding logic of democracy is checks and limits on political power and the right of all to participate in the political process, "undoubtedly then, religious justice is not possible without resort to democratic methods. At the very least, democracy is the most appropriate method for ensuring justice."[19] In the Qur'an, Yusofi Eshkevari goes on to argue, man is created as a free and thinking being, and any form of compulsion and imposition is contrary to the spirit and essence of Islam. There is an important conclusion to be reached here: "In the fields of government and politics, not only are Islam and democracy not incompatible, in fact, to the contrary, no Muslim government can be undemocratic."[20] A truly Islamic government is a democratic one.

Elsewhere, Yusofi Eshkevari makes an important distinction between religious democracy as a political construct and religious pluralism as a theological notion. Yusofi Eshkevari rejects arguments by Friedrich Hayek and Soroush that all religions are equally just and righteous. Islam is, indeed, the only right and just religion, as enunciated in the Qur'an and demonstrated by the deeds of the Prophet.[21] If taken to mean the equal merits of all religions, therefore, religious pluralism is wrong and misguided. However, if it is conceptualized differently, in the sense of the right to choose religions through free choice and dialogue, then religious pluralism makes sense: "As a Muslim, I know that my religion is more just and more complete. But I do not have a monopoly over the truth and I do not seek to monopolize others. In this sense I am pluralist. I also believe in dialogue, discourse, and mutual understanding among religions, and reject religious violence and force and compulsion, and in this sense I am pluralist as well. But I also defend the righteousness of my religion."[22]

Other religious intellectuals have been equally emphatic in their defense of democracy as one of the key aspects of Islam. Hashem Aqajari, for example, maintains that far from being contradictory, religion and democracy are mutually necessary and complement one another.[23] The ideal form of government is a "religious democracy," one that is based on two key assumptions: an acceptance of religious pluralism and diversity of beliefs; and an acknowledgment of democracy as the best method to run society and to handle social and political issues.[24] Religious government is one in which individuals govern based on their understanding of religious norms and precepts. For a religious government to be democratic, it must be open to a plurality of religious understandings. There cannot be a single, dominant reading of religion. Religious government is not the government of God but the government of man, and man is not infallible. Only when a government is guided by the spirit of religion and the logic of democracy will the chances for mistakes and embarking on the wrong path be reduced.[25] "Democratism in power, pluralism in religion"—for Aqajari, these are the core principles of religious government.[26]

Hojjatoleslam Mohammad Mojtahed Shabestari, another prominent figure in the religious reformist discourse, advocates an unconditional adoption of democracy even if it means the risk of a popular vote to set religion aside. Democracy, he argues, is neither a philosophy of rights nor a philosophy of ethics. It is, instead, a method of government in which people participate in their own destiny and in the running of their own affairs.[27] Democracy is not just an attractive form of government; it is a necessity. "In today's societies," he maintains, "it is only through democracy that the full potential of individuals in the reconstruction of society can be realized. It is only through democracy that collective, creative solutions can be formulated to address complex problems."[28] As a method of government, democracy has no contradictions whatsoever with people's beliefs and values, and today millions of religious individuals around the world live and practice their beliefs peacefully under democratic governments. Muslims can do so as well, and, if they so choose, they can use God's commandments as guides for making laws in a democratic framework.[29] Nevertheless, Mojtahed Shabestari goes on to argue, it is also theoretically possible for Iranians to democratically legislate religion out of public life, although the likelihood of this happening is remote, and it cannot used as a basis for denying the desirability of democratic rule.[30]

To be certain, as indicated by the careful attention to Islam by literally religious reformists in their discussions of democracy, religion and democracy are often viewed as intimately linked. In certain instances, in fact, as Aqajari's discussion of "religious democracy" demonstrates, there are some important theoretical differences between the conception of democracy as articulated by most Iranian religious intellectuals and the notion of liberal democracy as conventionally understood in the West. The sociologist Alireza Shoja'izand (b. 1959), for example, makes a distinction between *freedom of thought* in Islam, which he claims is unconditional, versus *freedom of opinion,* on which Islam imposes certain limitations.[31] Shoja'izand sees Islam as open to different viewpoints, unlike Western liberalism, which he sees as intolerant of other opinions. But Islam does respect the rights of individuals to hold opinions that differ from its teachings and does not seek to impose itself on others by force.[32]

For the most part, nevertheless, the democracy articulated by the proponents of the religious reformist discourse is not significantly different from that commonly found in the West. For Mostafa Tajzadeh, for example, religious democracy has the same underlying foundations as liberal democracy in the West—political liberties, respect for human rights, self-determination, and so on—but it is more thorough and complete. In Islam, political participation is a religious obligation, not just a right, as it is in liberal democracies.[33] Similarly, according to the reformist political activist and one-time Intelligence Ministry official Mohsen Armin (b. 1954), Islam recognizes all basic freedoms, including freedom of thought and expression, the right to vote on political and social issues, the right to live freely, and the right to equality.[34] Islamic *fiqh* recognizes freedom of thought and religion, and it grants all individuals, regardless of their creed and religion, equal rights and protection before the law.[35] A proper reading of the Qur'an clearly demonstrates that "freedom can be a basis for religion."[36] Religion in general and Islam in particular have important roles to play in the lives of societies, but this role should be limited and is not absolute. Ultimately, Armin argues, this role should be played within a democratic framework.[37]

Democracies derive their legitimacy from the people, feature political participation and limitations on the powers of rulers, and are buttressed by civil society. In these important respects, Islamic democracies are no exception. As outlined in the Qur'an and in the *Nahjolbalagheh*, which comprises Imam Ali's sermons and letters, Muslim rulers have important obligations to the people, chief among which is respect for the popular will. Equally important, no one can claim the right to rule based solely on religious rank and qualification.[38] A successful religious government, according to Soroush, is one in which people have the right to supervise and if necessary remove their leaders from power.[39] Also key is political participation. Maximum power and state capacity can be achieved when greater numbers of people participate in the political process, and by doing so deepen the Islamic system's legitimacy.[40] According to Ayatollah 'Abbasali 'Ameed Zanjani, the Qur'an (13:11) gives a clear command to individuals to actively partake in the social and political management of their societies: "Verily God does not change the state of a people till they change themselves."[41] This participation needs to be organized and orderly, structured so as to have maximum effect in limiting the potential abuse of power by the state.[42]

There are, of course, a wide variety of forms of political participation, voting being the commonest. One of the cornerstones of the Prophet's rule was the *Bey'at,* a ceremony in which an oath of allegiance was taken and the Prophet's leadership was reaffirmed. In fact, the Prophet personally engaged in *Bey'at* on eight different occasions, and the practice is mentioned in the Qur'an three separate times.[43] Today, voting and elections perform the same functions that the *Bey'at* did during the Prophet's time, albeit in a more thorough and complete fashion, and, therefore, must be integral parts of any Muslim political system.[44] This centrality of elections to the running of Muslim societies, modeled after the centrality of the *Bey'at* to the running of the original *ummah,* is a recurrent and significant theme in much of the religious reformist literature in Iran today.[45] Applied to today's context, elections and voting are seen as one of the most essential aspects of politics in Islam.

With electoral politics and popular political participation comes legitimacy. It will be recalled that in the conservative religious discourse, political legitimacy is often attributed to divine sources that are beyond man's reach and control. At most, man may be able to play a role in the "acceptability" *(maqbuliyyat)* of a political system but not its legitimacy *(mashru'iyyat).* Proponents of the reformist religious discourse explicitly reject this subtle and important distinction between acceptability and legitimacy and its accompanying assumption of legitimacy's exclusivity to divinely ordained personages and institutions. Ayatollah Mohammad Musavi Bojnourdi, for example, addresses this question directly and reaches the conclusion that Islam's insistence on the right to vote makes people central to a regime's acquisition of popular legitimacy.[46] Islam, he maintains, pays careful attention to the wishes of the people and sees them as the central locus of power. Although those running the affairs of the *ummah* may have to meet certain prequalifications, the vote of the people is essential in giving them the right to rule.[47] Yusofi Eshkevari is equally emphatic on the worldly basis of political power. "[Both] the legitimacy and acceptance of the government and its leaders come from the results of popular elections, not from somewhere else. And the responsibility for elections rests on the shoulders of the people, not with God, or His prophet, or religion."[48]

Conversely, if for whatever reason people cease to engage in political participation, from the perspective of Islam, the system loses its legitimacy and will have to resort to force to stay in power.[49] Without legitimacy, a political system becomes dictatorial even if it may continue to have acceptability. Not surprisingly, Aqajari maintains, legitimacy crises have been recurrent features of Iranian political history as traditional political forces have sought to locate their legitimacy not in the people but in aristocracy, patrimonialism, or charisma.[50] Today, a false distinction has been created between "legitimacy" and "acceptability" in order to remedy the existing regime's legitimacy crisis. But this is only a temporary solution, an attempt to justify a twenty-first-century version of the theory of divinely ordained kingship.[51] Substituting or mixing legitimacy with righteousness *(haqqaniyyat)* is only a recipe for dictatorship.[52] This, of course, is a not-too-subtle reference to the Right's formulation of the concept of the supreme jurist, or *Velayat-e Faqih*. Saeed Hajjarian agrees. Those conservative religious thinkers who see *maqbuliyyat* as a sufficient substitute for legitimacy, he maintains, are simply trying to justify dictatorial rule.[53] "The misleading distinction between *maqbuliyyat* and *mashru'iyyat* is a desperate theoretical device concocted by the Right" in order to rescue itself from the political dead end it has reached.[54]

Equally important in solidifying the legitimacy of political systems is consultation *(shura)*, which was used extensively by the Prophet, even in instances when the prevailing opinion was against his.[55] According to Hojjatoleslam Ayazi, the command to consult has been spelled out in the Qur'an (3:159 and 42:38). Consultation must, therefore, become the standard practice through which today's Islamic leaders are elected and political decisions are made.[56] Applied to today's circumstances, the best consultative process is parliamentary, with the legislature acting as a forum in which expert advice and opinion is formulated and taken into account.

Limitations on the powers of rulers, the people's right to vote, and the centrality of consultation all become easier to attain when civil society is realized. Civil society is one of the key ingredients of modern polities as it allows for a more balanced relationship between the rulers and the ruled.[57] Religious intellectuals have spent considerable energy defining and emphasizing the need for civil society, and elaborating on its consistency with and support for religion.[58] Here it suffices to note the writings of only a few religious reformists on the topic, beginning with Saeed Hajjarian's. Hajjarian argues that civil society has a number of defining characteristics, including roots in society and independence from the state; a voluntary, autonomous, and self-directed nature, as in clubs and associations, syndicates, and independent media; a conciliatory spirit and civic-mindedness; and the aim of furthering the greater good and increasing societal limitations on the state's power.[59] For the modern individual, civil society is key to learning from the experience, scientific knowledge, and the cultural dispositions of others.

> It is through civil society that individuals, each with their own unique personalities, learn how to live together and defend their mutual interests.
>
> It is through civil society that sociability and the cultivation of future generations take place.
>
> It is through civil society that individual and collective talents are nurtured and creativity thrives.
>
> It is through civil society that division of labor and functional differentiation occur, therefore giving individuals sufficient time to pursue creative endeavors and the finer aspects of life.
>
> It is through civil society that communication spreads and collective wisdom is deepened.
>
> It is through civil society that mutually beneficial exchanges take place and rational decision-making grows.
>
> It is through civil society that political pursuits become possible and the foundations for government are laid.[60]

Civil society, Hajjarian goes on to conclude, in no way contradicts religion. In fact, he argues, the various institutions of civil society are necessary for the successful implementation of many of Islam's directives in society.[61]

This mutually reinforcing and beneficial connection between society and civil society is explored by a number of other religious intellectuals as well. 'Emadeddin Baqi, for example, maintains that religious institutions such as mosques, Friday prayer ceremonies, seminaries, *Marja'iyyat,* and religious taxes are in themselves organs of civil society.[62] Similarly, Hashem Aqajari argues that since civil society is "a methodology for organizing social relations," it has few or no differences with the *ummah*.[63] More specifically, he says, "If we accept a pluralist interpretation of religion and do not equate religion with only one, exclusivist reading of it, then we can have a religious society that is also a civil society."[64] This, of course, requires the construction of a new hermeneutics of religion that is consistent with the norms of civil society and democracy. "If our ideology and our conception of religion is predemocratic and precivic, serious obstacles will appear on the path of the civil society project."[65] Aqajari's prognosis for the future is not very positive. "Unfortunately," he argues, "we face worrying deficiencies in this regard," especially the angry reaction of traditionalists, or, alternatively, the trap of Western-style secularism.[66] In his opinion, neither of these two extreme options would serve Iran well.

A discussion of civil society's conceptualization by the religious reformists would be somewhat incomplete without mention of some of former president Khatami's thoughts on the subject. Khatami made the realization of civil society one of his main campaign slogans in the 1997 elections, and, once elected, he discussed and talked about the topic whenever he got the chance to do so. For Khatami, the connection between Islam and civil society is organic and deep-seated:

> In the civil society that we have in mind, the culture and norms of Islam form the primary orbit and standards of activity. But there is no room in it for personal despotism, group dictatorship, or even the dictatorship of the majority. In this society, because man is who he is, he is respected and honorable, and his rights are observed. In an Islamic civil society, citizens can determine their own destiny, supervise their own affairs, and choose their own leaders. These political leaders are servants of the people and not their masters. They are answerable to the people, whom the Almighty has put in charge of their own future.[67]

Khatami goes on to argue that Islamic civil society is an inclusive society in which all citizens enjoy equal rights and protection before the law regardless of their religious beliefs. Civil society ensures freedom and liberty within the framework of the law, and, over time, helps legal freedoms become routine and institutionalized.[68] As an integral part of Islamic government, "consultation [shura] is the most important basis of civil society, as are political development, popular participation, respect for the rights of the people, and reducing the role of the government."[69] Like Aqajari, Khatami offers a sobering assessment of the prospects for civil society's future. "The task ahead is indeed difficult," he concludes. "I appeal to all distinguished thinkers, all seminaries, all universities, and all university students to help us realize this important opportunity so that we can [place the realization of Islamic civil society] as one of our highest priorities."[70]

## A QUESTION OF HERMENEUTICS

Viewing civil society, popular legitimacy, the right to vote, and democracy in general as deeply and innately consistent with Islam is the product of a specific line of *ijtihad,* a conscious effort to articulate a dynamic *fiqh* in which *context*—what is best for the community in a specific time and place—plays a central role. What we are currently witnessing in Iran is the articulation of a discourse of religious dynamism, one in which Islam is taken to be inherently adaptable to modern times and conditions. Even more, Islam is seen by the proponents of the discourse as an agent of change and progress, an invaluable blueprint for such contemporary necessities as democracy, equality, justice, peace, civility, and advancement.

At the heart of such an endeavor is the construction of a hermeneutics of jurisprudence that would make it changeable and fluid, ushering in a dynamic *fiqh (fiqh-e pouya).* 'Abbas Kazemi maintains that the architects of the reformist religious discourse have set a number of important tasks before themselves.[71] First, for them the articulation of a new hermeneutics of Islam has assumed the form of a "research project," which they go about in a reasoned, methodical, and academic manner. In the process, they seek to reform and update the application of Islamic dictums and teachings, separate religion as it really is from religion as it is popularly understood, and to present a nuanced, historically and situationally contextualized understanding of Islam. Another goal of the religious reformists is to relocate the place of religion in society by reframing the central question in the popular imagination: people should not be asking themselves: "What does religion expect of us?" Instead, they should ask: "What do we expect of religion?" This would "lessen the burden on religion," Kazemi quotes Abdolkarim Soroush as having said, and challenges the notion that *fiqh* is sacrosanct and untouchable.[72] Instead, the religious reformists maintain, as it presently stands *fiqh* needs to be complemented by the modern sciences and by reason *('aql),* as well as by more contemporary inventions such as democracy and human rights.[73]

Of these self-ascribed tasks in relation to *fiqh,* two merit more detailed attention. First and foremost, the proponents of the reformist religious discourse maintain, the principles of *fiqh* are woefully outdated and need major revisions in order to regain their relevance to the lives of Muslims. Secondly, at present, *fiqh* preoccupies itself with mostly personal matters and often neglects larger social issues. According to the religious reformists, over time this misplaced focus has reinforced the archaic nature of *fiqh,* since solutions to personal issues tend to be less complicated than those demanded by the problems of complex, changing societies. *Fiqh,* therefore, needs both to be updated and to become social in scope.

Historically, as Mostafa Malekian points out, hermeneutics has not made much of an inroad in Islam.[74] Today, therefore, there is particular need for hermeneutic studies that offer new and relevant interpretations of Islam and Shi'ism. These interpretative endeavors are made possible through *ijtihad*. As the scholar 'Alireza Feiz (b. 1925) has put it, "Because of accumulated historical dust, coupled with the residual effects of the travails of times and eras long gone by, the marginalization and indictment of Shi'ism, and the resulting personalism of *fiqh* and its distance from prevailing social and political realities, have all combined to distort the real essence of *fiqh* and *ijtihad*, make them devoid of vitality and dynamism, and make them irrelevant with respect to political, social, and even economic issues."[75]

Ossified *fiqh*—or outdated methods of *ijtihad*, for that matter—cannot deal with the complex issues of contemporary society and, therefore, must be constantly revised and updated.[76] Baqi concurs. "The reality is that our *fiqh* and our religious sciences belong to the pre-industrial age," he writes. "They show no traces of the complexities of [contemporary] capital, labor, economics, civil and political liberties, and medical and biological discoveries, or the needs of the computer age and satellite technology."[77] As a body of legal rights, Baqi maintains, *fiqh* is manmade and is not sacred, and, as such, it must be adapted to changing times and circumstances.[78] Hajjarian has a similar take on *fiqh*. Neglecting this need for dynamism could have dire consequences, Feiz warns: "A changing society needs a changing *fiqh*, and since *fiqh* is the governing law of society at all times and places, it must necessarily be changeable and dynamic as well. If anyone or any forces stand in resistance to this dynamism, they ultimately endanger themselves and their society. Eventually, if they continue resisting the natural changes that are necessary in *fiqh*, they will disappear themselves."[79]

Aqajari goes so far as to maintain that some of Islam's most central injunctions, such as "doing good and prohibiting evil," must be fundamentally rethought and reformulated if they are to retain any measure of relevance to today's circumstances.[80] Similarly, Soroush calls the articulation of a new hermeneutics of Islam to be a matter of "greatest necessity" as demanded by the times.[81] As Feiz puts it, "we must work on *fiqh* extensively so that it can once again regain the position of esteem and relevance to society that it once had."[82]

How does *fiqh* become dynamic? Reason *('aql)*, the architects of the reformist religious discourse overwhelmingly maintain, plays a central role; in fact, it plays *the* central role. "Research *within fiqh* is not enough" to make it consistent with the logic and tenor of the times, Soroush warns. "Changes within the basic sciences can result in fundamental changes to *fiqh* as well."[83] *Fiqh* becomes dynamic when reason becomes the guiding principle according to which it is constructed, namely, through *ijtihad*. When *ijtihad* is based on reason—when it conforms to and pioneers the logic of the times—then through it a contextualized, dynamic *fiqh* is formulated.[84] "If reason is allows to finds its way into *fiqh*," Feiz writes, "undoubtedly dynamism will become an integral part of *fiqh* and cannot be denied [or prevented] by any one individual."[85]

Concurrent with the rationalization of *fiqh*, a parallel effort is needed to expand the scope of its purview to the society at large and to put a stop to its preoccupation with personal matters only. According to Hajjarian, *fiqh* is nothing more than a collection of opinions issued by *mujtahids* in relation to various aspects of life. These opinions, derived mostly from interpretations *(tafsir)* of the Qur'an and the Sunna, may address specific problems and issues a person faces in life, but seldom do they take into account the complexities of modern economy, politics, and society.[86] Without much elaboration, Hajjarian calls for the codification of the *fiqh* as the basis of a social contract, one that, presumably, would be pivotal in leading society toward progress and "a better world."[87] This preoccupation with minutiae, says another religious reformist, is because most of today's jurists, even enlightened ones like Ayatollah Montazeri, are scientifically ill-equipped to conceptualize and tackle the complexities of the modern world. Instead, they spend their time addressing issues such as the undesirability of defecating under a fruit tree, whether or not a man should shave off his beard, how to pay the *khoms* tax, the age of maturity for girls, and whether or not a couple are permitted to have sexual intimacy while facing the direction of Mecca.[88] According to Feiz, having devoted much time to these and other similar personal matters, Shi'a *mujtahids* have developed something of a consensus over most of them. Such a consensus is lacking over larger social issues, however, precisely because of a lack of consistent attention to them by the ulama.[89]

The key to articulating a socially meaningful and dynamic *fiqh*, of course, lies in *ijtihad*, and, more specifically, in *ijtihad* that takes into account context, place, and time. According to Baqi, Imam Ali counseled his son Hasan on the necessity of *ijtihad* in accordance with the times: "In religious affairs, if you do not agree with the precedent set by your ancestors, do your own thinking and research, and seek help and advice from the Almighty, so that you do not sink into doubt and mistake."[90] More specifically, he claims, insofar as today's clergy are concerned, they need to stop pursuing a myopic "survival strategy," as they are currently doing, and instead embrace new sciences and teachings that would better equip them to solve today's complex problems.[91] Along similar lines, Yusofi Eshkevari criticizes the people who seek piety in modeling their own behavior after the supposed deeds and saying of the Prophet Mohammad. They forget, Yusofi Eshkevari claims, that what the Prophet did and what he commanded were specific to the Mecca and Medina of 1,400 years ago and may not apply to today's life.[92] Therefore, taking into account contemporary needs and circumstances should be the cornerstone of *ijtihad*. Ahmad Qabel, another religious reformist, for example, maintains that we cannot rely on existing, old interpretations of the Qur'an alone. Doing so would close the "gates of *ijtihad*" and would keep the resulting *fiqh* stale and disconnected from reality.[93] Over time, there are changes to science, logic, norms, and values, 'Alireza 'Alavi-Tabar maintains, and all of these innovations need to be taken into account when engaging in *ijtihad*.[94]

The religious reformist Hojjatoleslam Saeed 'Edalatnezhad has divided *ijtihad* into two basic kinds: reason-centered *('aql mehvar)* and oral tradition-centered *(naql mehvar)*.[95] In both the Sunni and the Shi'a traditions, he maintains, oral tradition-centered *ijtihad* has been historically dominant, therefore impeding the growth and spread of new and innovative jurisprudential interpretations. In this type of *ijtihad*,

> among both the Sunnis and the Shi'a, reason is seen as a tool to better understand the text *(matn)* and to resolve its initial contradictions. In their opinion, God has not given the *mujtahids* the key of reason so that they could unlock secrets. Instead, reason is the key to unlock the secrets of the "text" and to better understand it in order to solve the individual or social problems that Muslims encounter. Since God, through his Prophet (and for the Shi'a also through the Infallible Imams) has already revealed to mankind all that needs to be revealed, there is no longer any need for human thought and reason in this endeavor. The Shari'a needs to be learned, and in learning it, we must resort to the faculty of reason.[96]

Reason, in other words, is helpful only in better understanding revealed knowledge, not that which is so far unknown. In this respect, if it has any role in *ijtihad* at all, that role is only secondary.

> By contrast, reason-centered *ijtihad* places reason at the center of intellectual activity. Reason-centered *ijtihad* does not mean abandoning or ignoring [existing] religious texts. It means using reason as one of the sources

used [in interpretation] and, when there is a contradiction, giving primacy to reason over existing texts. Just as reason dictates that the interpreter not dwell on some Qur'anic precepts that contradict the laws of nature—such as the characteristics of God—reason also dictates that is there is a contradiction between existing texts and collective knowledge, primacy be given to the latter. [97]

Given its far-reaching nature, 'Edalatnezhad argues that this *jtihad* may also be called *"ijtihad* in fundamentals," some of the primary characteristics of which include careful and detailed attention to the influence of time and place; concern with justice; drawing connections between individual thought and reasoning to collective knowledge and wisdom; and situating the rich products of Islamic heritage in their proper historical and geographic contexts.[98]

For 'Edalatnezhad and other like-minded religious reformists, conservative religious forces have kept the "gates of *ijtihad"* historically shut. In fact, Tdalatnezhad claims, all too often, the reaction against new *ijtihad* has been quite severe: "Not only have the gates of *ijtihad* been closed for some time, if there is a new *ijtihad,* the prevalent interpretation that rules over the *howzeh* considers it deviant. This governing interpretation has turned the *howzeh* into a factory in which every *ijtihad* produced has to look like the last one and must have the same size, color, and functionality as the one before."[99]

Needless to say, the proponents of the conservative religious discourse deny this accusation. Ayatollah Montazeri, for example, directly addresses this issue, maintaining that the continued openness of the gates of *ijtihad* is one Shi'ism's strengths, and that not every interpretation ought to be discarded simply because it is old.[100] Nevertheless, he claims, reason cannot always be trusted, and nor is it always deep and evolved enough to guide the individual in understanding God's commands and His design. Reason must, therefore, necessarily be complemented by the Shari'a.[101] And doing so requires trust in and *taqlid* (imitation) from learned *mujtahids*. Just as individuals must seek advice from specialists and physicians on medical matters, they also need to seek the advice of religious specialists in regards to the Shari'a and religion in general.[102]

This point goes to the heart of another argument by the religious reformists: if reason is to be trusted and employed in *ijtihad,* then why have a clerical class at all? This is the logical extension of the argument by the religious reformists that reason—individual reason—can be a proper, and supposedly sufficient, guide to *ijtihad*. Every individual, therefore, is a *mujtahid* and can engage in his or her own *ijtihad*. Surprisingly, this argument has not received as much attention as one would suspect, largely, I believe, because of the political costs associated with advocating the clergy's irrelevance. Nevertheless, a few religious reformists have alluded to this point in some of their arguments. Yusofi Eshkevari, for example, mentions in one of his interviews that initially Islam did not have a clerical class. Today, he further asserts, no one group, not even the clergy, can have a sole monopoly over the specialization of any one field.[103] Ahmad Qabel similarly rejects what he labels a feudal mind-set based on the presupposition that people need keepers.[104] Mojtahed Shabestari is far more explicit. "Understanding the Qur'an and the Islamic tradition is not the sole preserve of any particular group or class," he argues, "and whoever possesses the scientific and methodological tools necessary for interpreting them can do so, and may not be criticized by others."[105]

## CONCLUSION

The efforts of Mojtahed Shabestari, Khatami, Soroush, and Kadivar, along with those of the many other religious reformists mentioned here, have collectively given rise to a vibrant, intellectually sophisticated, and expansive discourse of Islamic reformism. Although similar discourses in the past have been a part of the mainstream of Islamic thought in Iran for some time, this latest incarnation stands out for several reasons. To begin with, the current discourse is being articulated in a radically new context that, unlike any other time in Iranian history, features a heritage of Islamic revolutionism, a theocratic political system, a politically backed discourse of religious conservatism, and unprecedented levels of and speeds in the flow of information and knowledge. Equally significant is the relatively new focus of the current discourse as compared to its previous incarnations, with themes relevant to, and often a product of, Iran of the late twentieth and the early twenty-first centuries—civil society, democracy, civil liberties, hermeneutics, and the like. Today's architects of the discourse of Islamic reformism are indeed the heirs of a rich and historically resonant strand of Muslim thought. But the larger context within which they find themselves, and the themes and topics they tackle, bear little or no resemblance to previous epochs of Iranian history. In tremendously important ways, therefore, they are blazing new trails.

Up until recent years, there have been three primary obstacles to the appearance of a sustained reformation in Shi'a jurisprudence *(fiqh)* in contemporary Iran. The first has had to do with the role of the state, which initially suppressed and sought to marginalize Shi'a doctrine and then, after the 1978–79 revolution, used it as its own basis of legitimacy and institutional framework. This, in turn, led to a second impediment to the reformation of Shi'a jurisprudence, namely, the emergence of a clerical class many of whose members positioned themselves as the primary protectors of Iranian culture and society against an oppressive and intrusive state. Largely as a result of this, Shi'a jurisprudence became increasingly politicized and revolutionized throughout the twentieth century, its revolutionary posture undermining its attention to inner reform. A third impediment, and directly related to the latter two, has been the traditional role of Shi'a clerics as social mediators and as protectors of culturally salient rituals. This pervasive social influence marginalized the voices of those calling for reforming the *fiqh*. Partly as a result their own actual or threatened marginalization and partly due to their conviction, those calling for the doctrinal reform of Shi'ism never quite went so far as to call for its jurisprudential "reformation," often tempering their call for reforms and balancing it with resort to some of Shi'ism's more orthodox, and at time archaic, notions and value systems.

Today, more than a quarter century after the success of the Islamic revolution, only the first impediment to the reformation of the Shi'a doctrine remains—namely, the nature and role of the state in relation to Shi'ism—while the other two impediments are undergoing fundamental changes. Whether these changes are by themselves sufficient to foster a process of religious reformation, or will also propel changes to the remaining impediment as well, remains to be seen. I would not go so far as to argue that the reformist religious discourse has sparked a religious "reformation" in Iran. But it has indeed started a process that, *if given the right type of institutional support,* could result in a fundamental reformation of Iranian Shi'ism. At a minimum, the discourse of religious reformism has raised important questions whose answers, while not necessarily within easy reach, cannot be ignored indefinitely. The relationship between Islam and civil society, pluralism, dynamic *ijtihad*, and dialogue among civilizations—these are important questions whose answers may be politically unpalatable to the stewards of the Islamic Republic. But now that the taboo of asking them has been broken, they cannot be unasked. The curiosity and the intellectual impetus for searching for answers is there; now all that is needed is the right set of institutional support mechanisms that would facilitate the articulation and institutionalization of answers to these and other similar questions. What is certain, however, is that today Iranian Shi'ism stands at the gates of historic doctrinal changes.

NOTES

1. Mostafa Katir'i, "Hokumat az Didgah-e Din" (Government from the Perspective of Religion), in Ali Mohammad Izadi et al., *Din va Hokumat* (Religion and Government) (Tehran: Rasa, 1377 A.H./1998 C.E.), p. 25.
2. Hasan Yusofi Eshkevari, "Hokumat-e Demokratik-e Eslami" (Democratic Islamic Government), in Izadi et al., *Din va Hokumat,* p. 291.
3. Ibid., pp. 291–292.
4. Hashem Aqajari, *Hokumat-e Dini va Hokumat-e Demokratik* (Religious Government and Democratic Government) (Tehran: Zekr, 1381 A.H./2002 C.E.), p. 243.
5. Mostafa Malekian, *Rahi be Raha-ee* (A Path to Liberation) (Tehran: Negah-e Mo'aser, 1381 A.H./2002 C.E.), p. 493.
6. Eshkevari, "Hokumat-e Demokratik-e Eslami," p. 306.
7. Ibid., p. 299.
8. Ibid., p. 300.
9. 'Ezzatollah Sahhabi. "Emkan-e Hokumat-e Dini" (The Possibility of Religious Government), in Izadi et al., *Din va Hokumat,* p. 207.
10. 'Abdolali Bazargan, "Marz-haye Miyan-e Din va Hokumat" (Boundaries Between Religion and Government), in Izadi et al., *Din va Hokumat,* p. 114.
11. Ibid., p. 114.
12. Ibid.
13. Sadeq Haqiqat, *Touzi'-e Qodrat dar Andisheh-ye Siyasi-e Shi'a* (Division of Power in Shi'a Political Thought) (Tehran: Hasti Nama, 1381 A.H./2002 C.E.), p. 254.
14. 'Abdolkarim Soroush. "Tahlil-e Mafhoum-e Hokumat-e Dini" (Analyzing the Meaning of Religious Government), in Izadi et al., *Din va Hokumat,* p. 173.
15. Ibid., p. 186.
16. Ibid., p. 165.
17. Ibid., p. 187.
18. Eshkevari, "Hokumat-e Demokratik-e Eslami," p. 296.
19. Ibid.
20. Ibid., p. 298.
21. Hasan Yusofi Eshkevari, *Ta'amollat-e Tanha-ee: Dibacheh-ee bar Hermeneutic-e Irani* (Thoughts in Loneliness: An Introduction to Iranian Hermeneutics) (Tehran: Saraee 1382 A.H./2003 C.E.), pp. 147–148.
22. Ibid., p. 149.
23. Aqajari, *Hokumat-e Dini va Hokumat-e Demokratik,* p. 146.

24. Ibid., p. 155.
25. Ibid., p. 171.
26. Ibid.
27. Mas'oud Razavi, *Motefakeran-e Mo'aser va Endisheh-ye Siyasi-e Eslam* (Contemporary Thinkers and Islamic Political Thought) (Tehran: Farzan-e Ruz, 1378 A.H./1999 C.E.), pp. 138–139.
28. Quoted in ibid., p. 140.
29. Quoted in ibid., p. 142.
30. Quoted in ibid., p. 143.
31. 'Alireza Shoja'izand, *Takapoo-haye Din-e Siyasi* (Efforts of Political Religion) (Tehran: Baz, 1383 A.H./2004 C.E.), p. 206.
32. Ibid., pp. 206–207.
33. Mostafa Tajzadeh, *Siyasat, Kakh va Zendan* (Politics, Palace, and Prison), (Tehran: Zekr, 1381 A.H./2002 C.E.), p. 106.
34. Mohsen Armin, *Eslam, Ejtema', Siyasat* (Islam, Society, Politics) (Tehran: Zekr, 1380 A.H./2001 C.E.), pp. 10, 26.
35. Ibid., p. 12.
36. Ibid., p. 20.
37. Ibid., p. 220.
38. Mohammad Ali Ayazi, "Din, Azadi, va Mas'ouliyyat," in Mohsen Armin et al., *Rabeteh-ye Din va Azadi* (The Relationship Between Religion and Freedom) (Tehran: Zekr, 1379 A.H./2000 C.E.), p. 66. This important point, which stands in direct opposition to the conservative religious discourse's formulation of *Velayat-e Faqih,* will be explored more fully below.
39. Soroush, "Tahlil-e Mafhoum-e Hokumat-e Dini," pp. 170–171.
40. 'Abdullah Nouri, *Shoukaran-e Eslah* (Hemlock for Advocate of Reform) (Tehran: Tarh-e No, 1379 A.H./2000 C.E.), p. 11.
41. 'Abbasali 'Ameed Zanjani, "Ab'ad-e Fiqhi-ye Mosharekat-e Siyasai" (The Jurisprudential Aspects of Political Participation), in *Mosharekat-e Siyasi* (Political Participation ), ed. 'Ali Akbar 'Alikhani (Tehran: Safir, 1377 A.H./1998 C.E.), p. 32.
42. Saeed Hajjarian, *Jomhuriyyat; Afsonzedai az Qodrat* (Republicanism; Demystification of Power) (Tehran: Tarh-e No, 1379 A.H./2000 C.E.), p. 361.
43. Abolfazl Musavian, *Mabani-e Mashro'iyyat-e Hokumat* (Basis of Government Legitimacy) (Tehran: Zekr, 1381 A.H./2002 C.E.), p. 26.
44. Ibid., pp. 46, 126.
45. See, e.g., 'Zanjani. "Ab'ad-e Fiqhi-ye Mosharekat-e Siyasi," pp. 40–41; Mohammad Qoochani, *Dowlat-e Dini va Din-e Dowlati* (Religious Government and Government's Religion) (Tehran: Saraee 1379 A.H./2000 C.E.), pp. 28–29; and Asadollah Bayat. "Payambaran, Nokhostin Tarrahan-e Jame'h Madani" (The Prophets, the First Architects of Civil Society), in Mohsen Armin et al., *Nesbat-e Din va Jame'h Madani* (The Relationship Between Religion and Society) (Tehran: Zekr, 1379 A.H./2000 C.E.), p. 153.
46. Mohammad Musavi Bojnourdi, "Naqsh-e Mosharekat-e Siyasi dar Mashru'iyyat-e Hokumat-e Eslami" (The Role of Political Participation in the Legitimacy of Islamic Government), in *Mosharekat-e Siyasi,* ed. 'Alikhani, pp. 24–25.

47. Quoted in Razavi, *Motefakeran-e Mo'aser va Endisheh-ye Siyasi-e Eslam*, p. 68.
48. Eshkevari, "Hokumat-e Demokratik-e Eslami," p. 301.
49. Bojnourdi, "Naqsh-e Mosharekat-e Siyasi dar Mashru'iyyat-e Hokumat-e Eslami," pp. 26–28.
50. Aqajari, *Hokumat-e Dini va Hokumat-e Demokratik*, p. 34.
51. Ibid., p. 42.
52. Ibid., p. 156.
53. Hajjarian, *Jomhuriyyat*, p. 475.
54. Ibid., p. 476.
55. Aqajari, *Hokumat-e Dini va Hokumat-e Demokratik*, p. 23.
56. Mohammad Ali Ayazi. "Jame'h Madani va Nesbat-e An ba Din" (Civil Society and Its Relationship with Religion), in Armin et al., *Nesbat-e Din va Jame'h Madani*, p. 104. Bazargan. "Marz-haye Miyan-e Din va Hokumat," p. 117.
57. Nouri, *Shoukaran-e Eslah*, p. 9.
58. See, e.g., Armin et al., *Nesbat-e Din va Jame'h Madani*.
59. Hajjarian, *Jomhuriyyat*, pp. 356–357.
60. Ibid., pp. 355–356.
61. Ibid., p. 360.
62. 'Emadeddin Baqi, *Jonbesh-e Eslahat-e Demokratik dar Iran* (The Democratic Reform Movement in Iran) (Tehran: Sarai, 1382 A.H./2003 C.E.), p. 135.
63. Hashem Aqajari, "Jame'h Madani va 'Avemel va Maven'eh-e Sheklgiri-ye An" (Civil Society and the Causes and Obstacles to Its Formation), in Armin et al., *Nesbat-e Din va Jame'h Madani*, pp. 31, 43.
64. Ibid., p. 50.
65. Ibid., p. 70.
66. Ibid., pp. 70–71.
67. Mohammad Khatami, "Jame'h Madani az Negah-e Eslam" (Civil Society from the Perspective of Islam), in Armin et al., *Nesbat-e Din va Jame'h Madani*, p. 181.
68. Ibid., p. 188.
69. Ibid., p. 189.
70. Ibid., p. 194.
71. 'Abbas Kazemi, *Jame'hshenasi-ye Roshanfedri-ye Dini dar Iran* (Sociology of the Religious Intellectual Movement in Iran) (Tehran: Tarh-e No, 1383 A.H./2004 C.E.), pp. 137–142.
72. Ibid., 140.
73. Ibid., 142.
74. Malekian, *Rahi be Raha-ee*, pp. 35–36.
75. 'Alireza Feiz, *Vizhegi-haye Ijtihad va Fiqhi-e Pouya* (The Characteristics of *Itjihad* and Dynamic Jurisprudence) (Tehran: Pazhoheshkadeh-e 'Olum-e Ensani va Motale'at-e Farhangi, 1381 A.H./2002 C.E.), p. 91.
76. Ibid., p. 245.
77. 'Emadeddin Baqi, *Gofteman-haye Dini-ye Mo'aser* (Contemporary Religious Discourses) (Tehran: Sarai, 1382 A.H./2003 C.E.), p. 138.

78. 'Emadeddin Baqi, *E'dam va Qasas* (Execution and *Qasas*) (Tehran: Sarai, 1381 A.H./2002 C.E.), p. 39.
79. Feiz, *Vizhegi-haye Ijtihad va Fiqhi-e Pouya*, p. 93.
80. Aqajari, *Hokumat-e Dini va Hokumat-e Demokratik*, pp. 110–111.
81. Abdolkarim Soroush, "Fiqh dar Tarazoo" (*Fiqh* in the Balance), in *Andarbab-e Ejtehad: Darbar-ye Kar-amadiye Fiqh-e Eslami dar Donya-ye Emrouz* (On *Ijtihad*: On the Effectiveness of Islamic Jurisprudence in Today's World), ed. Saeed 'Edalatnezhad (Tehran: Tarh-e No, 1382 A.H./2003 C.E.), p. 23.
82. Feiz, *Vizhegi-haye Ijtihad va Fiqhi-e Pouya*, p. 245.
83. Soroush, "Fiqh dar Tarazoo," p. 33. Emphasis added.
84. Feiz, *Vizhegi-haye Ijtihad va Fiqhi-e Pouya*, p. 136.
85. Ibid., p. 100.
86. Hajjarian, *Jomhuriyyat*, pp. 461–462.
87. Ibid., p. 462.
88. Saeed 'Edalatnezhad, "Bab-e Masdood-e Ijtihad" (The Closed Gates of *Ijtihad*), in *Andarbab-e Ejtehad*, ed. id., pp. 54, 58.
89. Feiz, *Vizhegi-haye Ijtihad va Fiqhi-e Pouya*, pp. 70, 76.
90. Baqi, *Gofteman-haye Dini-ye Mo'aser*, p. 298.
91. 'Emadeddin Baqi, *Rouhaniyyat va Qodrat: Jame'hshenasi-e Nahad-haye Dini* (The Clergy and Power: Sociology of Religious Institutions) (Tehran: Sarai, 1382 A.H./2003 C.E.), pp. 176–177.
92. Quoted in Qoochani, *Dowlat-e Dini va Din-e Dowlati*, p. 32.
93. Ahmad Qabel, *Naqd-e Farhang-e Khoshunat* (Critique of the Culture of Violence) (Tehran: Saraee, 1381 A.H./2002 C.E.), pp. 143–144.
94. 'Alireza 'Alavi-tabar, *Roshanfekri, Dindari, Mardomsalari* (Intellectualism, Religiosity, Democracy), (Tehran: Farhang-o Andisheh, 1379 A.H./2000 C.E.), pp. 70–71.
95. Saeed 'Edalatnezhad, "Kodam Ijtihad?" (Which *Ijtihad*?), in *Andarbab-e Ejtehad*, ed. id., p. 8.
96. Ibid., p. 10.
97. Ibid., p. 11.
98. Ibid., pp. 11–12.
99. Ibid., p. 48.
100. Hoseinali Montazeri, "Bab-e Maftooh-e Ijtihad" (The Open Gates of *Ijtihad*), in *Andarbab-e Ejtehad*, ed. 'Edalatnezhad, pp. 36–37.
101. Ibid., pp. 44–45.
102. Ibid., pp. 46–47.
103. Quoted in Qoochani, *Dowlat-e Dini va Din-e Dowlati*, p. 36.
104. Qabel, *Naqd-e Farhang-e Khoshunat*, p. 161.
105. Quoted in Razavi, *Motefakeran-e Mo'aser va Endisheh-ye Siyasi-e Eslam*, p. 145.

PART II

# The Arts and Letters

CHAPTER 5

# History from Below, Dictionary from Below

NELLY HANNA

DICTIONARIES AND SOCIAL HISTORY

Dictionaries have a special place in the Arabic literary heritage given the importance attached to the Arabic language. Major dictionaries written in the medieval period (Ibn Mandur, Firuzabadi), and in the early modern period (Murtada al-Zabidi) are still in use today and continue to be basic sources for linguistic studies. Over the centuries, there were certain formats that were used for such dictionaries, following an alphabetic order, providing references or precedents in the ways that words were used, and so on.

However, as a genre of writing, one can also use them as sources of social history. In other words, they can be regarded, not only as part of a traditional genre that has its rules and follows a particular form developed over the centuries, but also as a reflection of the cultural or social trends of their own times. In other words, one can study a dictionary as the expression of the particular context that produced it, or to use it as a source for historical studies rather than only as part of linguistic studies. Thus, historians could consult Murtada al-Zabidi's dictionary *Taj al-'Arus* for information in the same way that a chronicle like Jabarti's *'Aja'ib al-Athar* has been used as a source for eighteenth-century Mamluk history.

Such an approach to the dictionary as social history can be put in context with studies that have used dictionaries in other languages or cultures. For instance, scholars have made use of the work of Samuel

Johnson as a source for eighteenth-century English history. Rather than study this famous dictionary in the framework of lexicography or of its evolution, these studies focus instead on the dictionary as a representative of the period in which it was written and as a product of its own context, notably as an Enlightenment genre, a piece of writing reflecting its own time.[1]

I think we have much to gain from using Arabic dictionaries as sources for social and cultural history, rather than exclusively in the realm of language studies. This has a special importance inasmuch as the cultural history of the Ottoman period is still rather obscure and so far our sources for this subject are few.

The dictionary I am particularly interested in, Yusuf al-Maghribi's *Raf' al Isar 'an Kalam Ahl Misr,* was compiled in the early seventeenth century.[2] It is notable for being a dictionary of the colloquial speech of Cairo in the first decades of that century—which is to say, during the lexicographer's lifetime. Moreover, unlike other collections of colloquial Arabic that aimed at showing its deviations from the classical language, al-Maghribi's dictionary, on the contrary, aimed at showing that most colloquial words used by the inhabitants of Cairo had their source in the classical language and were consequently acceptable linguistically.[3]

In short, al-Maghribi was a defender of the colloquial—an innovative approach for a lexicographer. He was not, however, the first to compile a dictionary of colloquial Arabic. Earlier, as Arabic spread, especially in the centuries that followed Arab conquest of new territories, it had incorporated words from the languages of these territories. Earlier dictionaries of colloquial therefore aimed at identifying Arabic from the encroachments of foreign words. The incorporation of local vocabulary into Arabic was considered a negative development. Al-Maghribi used the old format of this kind of dictionary, but to a new end. Rather than adopting a negative attitude toward colloquial, he was on the contrary in favor of this vocabulary. His work was, as far as one can tell, the first Arabic dictionary of the spoken word that was not only favorable to the colloquial but also treated it as worthy of scientific study.

This important issue deserves, I believe, to be seen in the context of al-Maghribi's time. The social relevance that the use of colloquial Arabic may have had in different historical periods is also a matter to be elucidated. Scholars working on the end of the nineteenth century have discussed the use of colloquial at some length. During that time, the question of colloquial Arabic took on a political dimension. Linked to debates over emergent nationalism, it involved many prominent intellectuals in heated discussions. This was especially significant in view of the fact that the use of colloquial Arabic in some writings was an attempt to reach those segments of the population that had a limited education. Thus, when used under these conditions, colloquial Arabic could be considered as a challenge to the elite or to the authorities.[4] There were also strong arguments against its use in the light of the nationalist trends that emerged as the Ottoman Empire was slowly coming to an end and searches for different identities were evolving. In other words, the study of colloquial Arabic in the modern period is part of the larger picture that involves some of the many crucial changes taking place at that time. Its use—whether in newspapers, in poetry, or in other literary forms—could have important social and political implications.

This was not the case with the study of colloquial Arabic prior to the modern period, when an entirely different position, for the most part negative, was usually taken on the subject. Because of this, the possible connections between developments in 1600 and those in 1900 are not well known, and little has been written about the way these earlier developments could have influenced the later ones.

In fact, the study of colloquial Arabic prior to the modern period is usually associated with decline of the language resulting from a general decline in cultural production, or more specifically from neglect of the Arabic language by the authorities. Sometimes, the Ottoman authorities are held responsible for having allowed this linguistic decline to occur. The few studies that deal with this matter are the work of linguists, and as a result the discussions thus often go around the technical aspects of the language and the way it is used. Furthermore, there are few attempts to link it to the social context that gave rise to it or to find out why, at that particular moment in time, was there an increased interest and use of colloquial Arabic in writing. The political dimension is also missing from most studies. One needs therefore to formulate the issues that could be relevant to understand this trend. One of the few to have done so is the historical linguist Madiha Doss, whose work on popular Arabic chronicles of the eighteenth century has broken new ground by drawing attention to the emergence and popularization of coffeehouses as forums for their recitation, with the result that the written versions of colloquial chronicles were closely linked to their oral forms. This link could account for the use of the colloquial in written chronicles, whose language is consequently explainable by their context.[5]

Yusuf al-Maghribi's *Raf' al Isar 'an Kalam Ahl Misr* can be approached along similar lines. We need to ask what context can explain, not only in this particular seventeenth-century work, but about the emergence of a number of other works (including some dictionaries) during that century. In fact, the seventeenth century produced two types of related writings. On the one hand, there are dictionaries focusing on colloquial Arabic, and on the other hand, it was used in written texts. In the decades following the appearance of al-Maghrabi's dictionary, a number of other dictionaries of the colloquial, or which included many words in colloquial Arabic, made their appearance. One of these is Muhammad Ibn Abil Surur al-Bakri's *Al-Muqtadab fima Wafaqa Lugha Ahl Misr min Lughat al Arab* (written about 1657, that is about forty years after al-Maghribi's work), was a direct response to al-Maghribi's dictionary, since it seems that al-Maghribi had given a copy of the book to one of his shaykhs who belonged to the Bakri family, as a result of which Muhammad Ibn Abil Surur found it in the family library.[6] Another one is Muhibbi's *Qasd al-Sabil*.[7]

In fact, there is still a lot for historians to learn by the study of one of the great dictionaries of the Arabic language, Murtada al-Zabidi's *Taj al-Arus,* a work still currently used as one of the basic tools for language study, written by one of the most prominent scholars of the eighteenth century. *Taj al-'Arus* was not written in the tradition of colloquial Arabic dictionaries like al-Maghribi's. Nevertheless, the reader will note that there is a high level of awareness by Zabidi of the colloquial. Interspersed in his dictionary of classical Arabic words are numerous references to words that he indicates to be *amiyya* (colloquial). Can we see this as a process of incorporation of the *amiyya* into classical Arabic? And could we see *Raf' al-Isar 'an Kalam Ahl Misr* as a source or inspiration for the later great work? In short, the approach to the study of the dictionary as social history could have a wider application for works along similar lines.

Numerous works of the seventeenth and eighteenth centuries were written in colloquial or semi-colloquial Arabic. Some of them are known, but many more are not, and a special effort would be needed to locate and identify them in the various Arabic manuscript libraries of the world. The most famous of these works in the colloquial is Yusuf al-Shirbini's *Hazz al-Quhuf,* a parody on seventeenth-century peasants, one of the few published literary works of this period. It is therefore significant to try to find out not only why this was happening but also why it was happening at that particular point in time.

## LITERATURE AND DECLINE

This is especially relevant in view of the fact that Arabic culture in general and the literature in particular of the period 1600–1800 C.E. is still an unexplored field. Most Arabic literary works produced during this period have remained in manuscript form and have not been studied by scholars. The result is that many of them have remained unknown to both the specialist and the general reader. Certain basic assumptions have nevertheless dominated the field for a long time. The written production of the period has been perceived in a negative light, often equated with decline and stagnation, a view applied generally to literary works as well as to works on religion. The seventeenth and eighteenth century have often been called "traditional" in the sense that they were devoid of innovation; that scholars were satisfied with repeating and elaborating on earlier works. The range of studies in educational institutions was limited, and teachers tended to teach the same textbook generation after generation.[8] The period was termed the "age of *hawashi*," one in which writers were content to comment on earlier texts rather than to come forward with new ideas. These views were not based on a close study of texts; rather, they were an extension of the idea of general decline that preceded the modern period. Needless to say, as long as such views dominated the scholarly world, there were few efforts to study or to publish the written production of the period.

All the more reason, then, to delve more closely in those works available to us, of which, the dictionary of colloquial Arabic written by Yusuf al-Maghribi is one. In short, this work can be a way to reconsider many of the statements that were made about the written production of the Ottoman period in general. By proposing new approaches to the study of these sources, one can open the door to a more general reconsideration of the period. More important, one can see a source for some of the developments that occurred later. In this way, nineteenth-century developments are not entirely cut off from their historical sources.

Historical studies have taken that same path for some time now. For the most part, studies of the Ottoman world have stopped using the decline and modernization paradigms that consider the centuries before the modern period in negative terms. They are experimenting with new ways to approach the early modern period. In fact, some historians are trying to bridge the gap between modern and premodern in such a way as to see meaningful connections between the two. Using literary or linguistic sources for the study of history is both an attempt to find new ways of understanding culture and society in the seventeenth and eighteenth centuries and a way of bridging the various disciplines dealing with this period.

*The Context for the Expansion of Written Colloquial Arabic*

What, then, is innovative in the seventeenth century in general or in al-Maghribi's work in particular? One can suggest a number of answers. These can be proposed as hypotheses whose objective is to include this genre, in particular, and the study of language in general, within the domain of social history.

One answer would be to draw a parallel with historical works. In the "classical" period of Islamic history, the period up to the fall of the Abbasid empire (1258 C.E.), historical works tended to cover enormous geographical regions. With the fragmentation of the Abbasid empire into smaller political entities, more and more, historians tended to deal with specific regions or localities, often with the history of specific cities or towns. Historical chronicles were written about Mecca *(Tarikh Makka)*, about Jerusalem *(Tarikh al Quds)*, about Cairo or about Hums *(Tarikh Misr al Qahira, Tarikh Hums)* and so on. The historians tended to restrict their horizons geographically to a given locality, and few attempted to write about the Islamic *ummah* as a whole after the fall of the Abbasid empire and the creation of smaller political entities. The writing of history was, in other words, affected by the geopolitical conditions of the times.

Should one draw a parallel with dictionaries of the seventeenth century that are focused on dialect? Dialect is usually linked to a specific region or locality, and in the same way as chronicles became focused on specific localities. Possibly, these same general geopolitical transformations may have been one of the factors that gave rise to a series of writings in colloquial Arabic. There are nevertheless important differences between history writing and language. The *fusha* language was to remain the dominant form used in scholarly writings and in dictionaries, and this never stopped being the case, unlike the chronicles in which focus on the Islamic world was replaced by a more local focus. Even when colloquial Arabic dictionaries and literary works in colloquial Arabic gained some popularity, they never approached the *fusha* in terms of volume or importance. One imagines that the weight of the educational establishments on the cultural scene was a factor in the stability of the *fusha*. Nevertheless, the dictionary of Yusuf al-Maghribi would be in part explained by the emergence of a different conception of space and of different geopolitical horizons.

Another factor could have contributed to the more extensive use of colloquial Arabic in the seventeenth and eighteenth centuries, and to the dictionary of colloquial Arabic that Yusuf al-Maghribi compiled. We know that by 1600, when the lexicographer was active, international trade had picked up after some decades of its interruption following the Portuguese takeover of Goa in India. The coffee trade was picking up. One of the immediate consequences in the expansion of the Red Sea trade was the appearance of coffeehouses in Cairo and the expansion in their use. One can presume that the spread of coffeehouses all over the city gave an impetus to popular culture. In fact, popular poetry and oral poetry was in all probability encouraged by the emergence of these new locales where they were recited, notably the coffeehouses, which become an important part of the urban picture. All parts of the city had coffeehouses. There were about a thousand or so by the eighteenth century. Coffeehouses provided a space not only for oral poetry and storytelling but for many other kinds of entertainment. Given the location, the type of client, and the entertainment aspect of this poetry or storytelling, colloquial Arabic would almost certainly have been used.

One could conjecture that a more intense commercial life had some kind of bearing on a work like al-Maghribi's. The theme of the commercialization is yet to be explored fully in relation to its impact on culture. Numerous questions could be asked: Did the increased world trade currents of the period, the influx of money, or gold and silver from the Americas have an impact on culture? Did it affect, in any way, the class of religious scholars, the *ulama,* and the works that they wrote? Or were they impervious to change? Was there an impact on nonreligious culture, on belles-lettres, for instance? All these issues are waiting to be considered in relation to the period under study. One could also argue for, as Peter Gran did in relation to eighteenth-century chronicle writing, the expansion of a utilitarian dimension in academic culture, an element that was linked to the expansion of a commercial culture. Certain aspects of commercial culture were being developed in the early seventeenth century, and therefore one can also argue here that it could leave a certain impact on the way that language was used.[9]

Suffice it to say, for the present, that the dominant views of an unchanging, static, monolithic culture, that in the seventeenth century was roughly the same as it had been in the tenth or the eleventh centuries, are no longer convincing.

A second possible framework within which we can study the dictionary as a source for social history is in relation to classes. The use of colloquial Arabic can be regarded, as it has in studies of the nineteenth century, as a way to propose alternatives to the established language. It would nevertheless be erroneous to link classical Arabic to the academics or religious scholars and colloquial Arabic to the others. Many of the people who wrote in colloquial Arabic, including Yusuf al-Maghribi and Yusuf al-Shirbini, were educated and used classical Arabic in some of their writings. Yet there is some room for exploration around this issue.

Colloquial Arabic was, in some cases, a social statement. What, exactly, this statement means could vary between one writer and another. In the case of Yusuf al-Shirbini's *Hazz al Quhuf,* the author made fun of peasants and the many aspects of their conduct, their food, and their clothes, as well as their speech. At times, al-Shirbini's use of colloquial Arabic satirizes peasants. The level of their language showed their ignorance. Language was, in short, a tool that could be used to convey a variety of messages. The social content of the use of colloquial Arabic can be detected in the work. It is in the eighteenth century that we find a work using colloquial Arabic with the explicit purpose of challenging the establishment. The writings of Muhammad Hasan Abu Dhakir are an excellent example of the use of colloquial Arabic for the purpose of creating distance with the class of religious scholars. Abu Dhakir explicitly states that the type of language he chose to use was to show that he was different. Moreover, colloquial Arabic was a better way to express his thoughts without being restrained by correctness or by rigid forms that language could impose.[10]

### The "Dictionary from Below"

We can use different frameworks in order to understand *Raf' al Isar* as social history. One of them is to examine this dictionary in the framework of a "dictionary from below," in the same way as we refer to "history from below." The basis for this framework is the fact that the author is concerned with the practice of language, with the words as they were used, as he heard them, rather than with theory, with sources, or with correctness.

Another particular feature in al-Maghribi's work can justify placing his dictionary as history from below. This is his reliance upon what he hears rather than on the tradition of dictionary writing. It is the practice of language that he focuses on rather than the etymology, the practice of a certain sector of the population, rather than the theory. The result of approaching words as they are used, or as practice, is that al-Maghribi is led to undertake a number of social divisions that correspond to various social groups and categories. In other words, the social content of the vocabulary is strengthened by this approach. Among these are the distinctions between the vocabulary used by the different ethnic, linguistic, professional, and even age groups living in Cairo at the time. Thus, al-Maghribi's approach allows him to see differences and specificities. In addition to its importance as an empirical approach, it also reflects the cosmopolitan character of Cairo, with its various components, each of which had certain peculiarities that a careful listener like al-Maghribi could denote. The dictionary has examples of the peculiarities in the vocabulary as used by the three most important non-Cairene communities living in Cairo, namely, the North Africans, the Syrians, and the Turks. Thus, al-Maghribi points out that a word like *shaqafa* (meaning "a piece") is used by Syrians,[11] or that another word has a specific meaning in the Arabic used by Turks or Maghribis. As for the Maghariba (people of the Maghrib: Morocco, Tunisia, and Algeria), they used the word *makhala* instead of *bunduqiya* (both meaning "rifle").[12]

He also makes other social distinctions between other segments of the population, providing words from the vocabulary of the *khassa* and that of the *amma;* and from the vocabulary related to specific certain crafts, a subject he must have been familiar with given his own background as a craftsman.

Furthermore, we can call this work "dictionary from below" based on both al-Maghribi's choice of words to include and the information about himself and his views on various issues—a kind of diary or set of autobiographical notes—inserted here and there. In short, the lexicographer included matters he found interesting that do not always fall within the scope of the genre of dictionary-writing, which had its rules and was essentially academic.

With regard to his choice of words, one of the striking subjects is a certain focus on the family and household, on matters related to the domestic sphere. We do not have many sources for this period or even for the earlier medieval period that historians can use if they want to write about private or domestic life. Al-Maghribi's dictionary of colloquial Arabic contains a number of words related to the realm of the private, on food on the kitchen, and even in the domain of housekeeping, since he provides definitions of words around the subject of cleaning the house.

In this context, we find him writing his own life story, his North African origin, his upbringing in an artisan family of makers of sword sheaths, his growing up in the market, his uncles traveling to sell their merchandise. This short section reads like an autobiography. But even autobiographies can vary. Some autobiographies of the seventeenth and eighteenth centuries focus on the public aspects of the writer's life, his teachers, his students, and his books. This is not the case with al-Maghribi. His work gives the reader insights into his personal life. It has a personal dimension, since he talks of his inner desires, his conflicts with his uncles, his dislike of the craft he was supposed to carry out. He talks of the nights he spent reading books, because during the day he had to work at the family craft. This form of life history narrative is certainly not unique. Like many other such narratives, autobiography was not so much perceived as a genre in itself, but was often interspersed in other literary genres. Dwight Reynold's study of this subject has brought out many such autobiographical narratives.[13] Nevertheless, it does help to place the dictionary that al-Maghribi wrote within the realm of social history and of history from below.

A further feature that justifies the term "dictionary from below" is his interest in subordinate groups. In recent decades, historians have been interested in the study of subaltern or subordinate groups, of those groups who rarely appeared in historical works because they were marginal or because sources available about them were hard to get. Al-Maghribi's dictionary thus fills a gap as a source about some of these, notably children and women. Among the most interesting are the words relating to children, a social category not much written about in either history books or literary works of the period. The dictionary deals with children in more than one way. It provides definitions of words used by children (child language or infant language). In this context, al-Maghribi shows that language or the use of a word could vary according to age of a person. Thus we have words identified with infant language *(lughat al-atfal)* such as *tata,* which in infant or child language means to walk.[14] He also includes words that are used by slightly older children, or boys (the words he refers to as *qawl al sibyan*), such as *baba* for father.[15] This is the language used by children or used to address children. Al-Maghribi was also interested in the words that referred to certain acts that children did. Two words, *zahafa al-sabi* and *haba* referred to the period prior to learning how to walk, when the infant crept on all fours.[16] Likewise some of the vocabulary is oriented toward women, both what they say, that is, the language specific to females, and what they do, or the acts specific to them, such as various tasks related to cleaning the house.

One could argue, on the basis of the above, that al-Maghribi's focus on providing a definition for colloquial words and a justification for its origin was not the only objective of the work. It was also a description of the language of his time, with the many variations and subtleties that a given population could give it. The academic aspect of lexicography was subordinated to the practice of the language. Therefore, we are not simply referring to the type of word that the dictionary chose to study, but to a particular concept of language that seems to be implicit in this work. The dictionary was the framework that he used, but he made use of it in a somewhat different way and with a conception of the language (the spoken language, language in practice rather than in theory) that was original. It was an old format used to convey new thoughts. Within this format, al-Maghribi integrated the language of several social groups, including the ordinary person, the craftsmen, women, and children, that many other sources omit to mention.

## CONCLUSION

A dominant trend in much of the secondary literature on cultural history has been to use Napoleon's Egyptian expedition (1798–1799) as the source for Egypt's modern cultural development.[17] Studies on the nineteenth century often attribute either state policies (state schools, educational missions abroad) or European influences (the foundation of museums or of the Opera House, for instance) as the main sources of culture. This approach has emphasized 1800 as a dividing line, with a before and an after, between modern and traditional, and along with it, between a static and stagnant culture before 1800 as opposed to a dynamic one after that date. The persistence of the decline framework has been one of the impediments to the study of the culture of the period in general, and more specifically of its literature and its language.

By considering al-Maghribi's dictionary as a "dictionary from below" one can suggest an alternative approach to this paradigm. In doing so, *Raf' al Isar 'an Kalam Ahl Misr* can be understood not only as a list of the colloquial words, whether these are perceived as being distortions of classical vocabulary, or whether, as is often the case in this particular dictionary, they have a justification in the classical language. This work can be seen as an attempt to draw a map or picture of the language used in Cairo in the author's time; at the same time, it shows the class and social diversity of the city along linguistic lines.

This approach to al-Maghribi's dictionary has another advantage. It can help us to tie up the writers of the seventeenth and the eighteenth centuries with those of the nineteenth century. There are certain lines of continuity between periods that are usually studied apart. We can see these links in the focus on social groups that are not elites; we can also see them in the use of, or interest in, colloquial Arabic, not as the language of popular culture, associated with the illiterate or semi-educated who were only familiar with the spoken tongue, but as a serious scholarly endeavor. What we gain from a study of works like that of Yusuf al-Maghribi is to be able to identify some sources for modern culture in the culture of the seventeenth century or to find a historical depth to some of the developments of the nineteenth century. We can, in this way, identify a historical depth for the works of writers like Abdalla al-Nadim rather than to study him as an unexplained phenomenon. In summary, we can consider this work to be, at the same time, innovative for its period in its treatment of colloquial Arabic as worthy of scientific study; and as a work that looked to the future in relation to the later cultural developments in the language.

NOTES

1. Carey McIntosh, "Eighteenth-Century English Dictionaries and the Enlightenment," *Yearbook of English Studies* 28 (Leeds, UK: Maney, 1998), pp. 3–18.

2. Yusuf Al-Maghribi, *Raʿ al-Isar ʿan kalam ahl Misr,* ed. ʿAbdul-Salam Ahmad ʿAwwad (Moscow: Soviet Academy of Sciences, 1968).

3. Elisabeth Zack, "Colloquial Arabic in the 17th Century: Yusuf Al-Maghribi's Egyptian Arabic Wordlist," in *Approaches to Arabic Dialects: A Collection of Articles Presented to Manfred Woidich on the Occasion of His Sixtieth Birthday,* ed. Martine Haak, Rudolf de Jong, and Kees Versteegh (Leiden: Brill, 2004), pp. 382–383.

4. Marilyn Booth, "Colloquial Arabic Poetry, Politics and the Press in Modern Egypt," *International Journal of Middle East Studies* 24, no. 3 (August 1992): 423–425.

5. See Madiha Doss, "Military Chronicles of 17th century Egypt as an Aspect of Popular Culture" (paper presented to the Colloquium on Logos, Ethos and Mythos in the Middle East and North Africa, Budapest, September 18–22, 1995), pp. 67- 79; "Some Remarks on the Oral Factor in Arabic Linguistics," in

*Dialectica Arabica: A Collection of Articles in Honour of the Sixtieth Birthday of Professor Heikki Palva* (Helsinki: Finnish Oriental Society, 1995), pp. 49–61.

6. Muhammad Ibn Abil Surur al-Bakri, *Al-Muqtadab fima wafaqa Lugha Ahl Misr min Lughat al-Arab,* ed. Hisham Abdul Aziz and Adil al-Adawi (Cairo: Academy of Arts, 2006), pp. 51–52.

7. Muhammad Amin Al-Muhibbi, *Qasd al-Sabil fima fil-Lugha al-'Arabiyya min al-Dakhil,* ed. 'Uthman Mahmud al-Sini (2 vols.; Riad: Maktabat al-Tawba, 1994). See also Radi al Din Muhammad Ibrahim Yusuf Ibn al Hanbali (d. 971 C.E.), *Bahr al Awwam fima assab fihi al awam,* ed. Shaban Salih (Cairo: Dar al thaqafa al arabiya, 1990); Shihab al Din Ahmad Khafaji, *Kitab al-Shifa al-Ghalil fima fi kalam al-arab min al dakhil* (Cairo: Al-matbaa al-wahabiya, 1856).

8. Gamal El-Din El-Shayyal, "Some Aspects of Intellectual and Social Life in Eighteenth-Century Egypt," *Political and Social Change in Modern Egypt: Historical Studies from the Ottoman Conquest to the United Arab Republic,* ed. P. M. Holt (London: Oxford University Press, 1968), pp. 118–121.

9. Peter Gran, *Islamic Roots of Capitalism: Egypt 1760–1840* (1979; reprint, Cairo: American University in Cairo Press, 1999), pp. 72–73.

10. Nelly Hanna, *In Praise of Books: A Cultural History of Cairo's Middle Class* (Syracuse, NY: Syracuse University Press, 2003).

11. Al-Maghribi, *Raf' al-Isar 'an kalam ahl Misr,* p. 69.

12. Ibid., p. 198.

13. Dwight Reynolds, *Interpreting the Self: Autobiography in the Arabic Literary Tradition* (Berkeley: University of California Press, 2001).

14. Al-Maghribi, *Raf' al-Isar 'an kalam ahl Misr,* p. 25.

15. Ibid., p. 26.

16. Ibid., p. 31.

17. Paul Starkey, "Modern Egyptian Culture in the Arab World," in *The Cambridge History of Egypt,* ed. M. W. Daly (Cambridge: Cambridge University Press, 1998), p. 394.

CHAPTER 6

# The Translation of the Qur'an: An Impossible Task

*The Classical Linguistic-Theological Roots of the Debate*

NASR ABU-ZAYD

INTRODUCTION

This chapter analyzes the Qur'an's repeated assertions that it was revealed in Arabic in light of the fact that some Qur'anic vocabulary has been deemed originally not Arabic, presenting the classical, theological, and legal background of the issue of translation. It then goes on to discuss the legal issue of the validity of prayer performed with the translated Qur'an, which leads to deeper questions of theology concerning the nature of God's word. The final part of the chapter focuses on "content" and "form," both of which are strongly connected with the doctrine of the *i'jaz* (inimitability) of the Qur'an, itself one of the central issues in the contemporary debate about the status of any Qur'anic translation. Does a translation represent the word of God, or does it only convey the "meaning" of it, which in its turn is subjective, individualistic, and has no function in any religious activity?

The present investigation will confine itself to explorations of jurisprudence, theology, and literary criticism. Since these three disciplines are intimately interconnected, it is very difficult sometimes to find the boundaries.

ARABISM VERSUS FOREIGN VOCABULARY

From the outset, it is clearly stated in the Qur'an that it was sent down to the Prophet in plain Arabic speech, *bi lissanin 'arabiyyin mubin*, because God always considers the language of the people to whom a message was directed: "And we never sent a messenger but with the language of his people, that he might make it clear for them."[1] With the realization that some Qur'anic words, such as *jihannam, firdaws, taghut, mihrab,* and *sijjil,* have no Arabic roots, this Qur'anic statement raised questions concerning the existence of originally non-Arabic words in the Holy Book.

There were two answers to this question. One, emphasizing the literal meaning of the Qur'anic statement, denied the existence of any foreign vocabulary in the Qur'an. This was, for example, the position taken by al-Shafi'i (Muhammad b. Idris, 150 A.H./775 C.E.–204 A.H./850 C.E.), one of the most celebrated thinkers in the history of Islamic thought, who institutionalized the essential principles still observed in Islamic jurisprudence.

Al-Shafi'i's position was based on the opinion that there are no foreign words in the Qur'an. He related the opposite position to "ignorance" of the Arabic language in its totality. A comprehensive knowledge of Arabic is impossible because of its unique depth and beauty. Arabic is so similar to revelation, he maintained, that only a prophet is capable of totally knowing it. "No foreign words exist in the Qur'an," al-Shafi'i claimed.

> It is purely and completely an Arabic text. Whatever similarities exist between some vocabularies of the Qur'an and some foreign vocabularies are merely plain similarities. People who ignore these vocabularies mistakenly think that they are foreign words. As the Arabic language is beyond the scope of any individual's knowledge, only a prophet is entitled to inclusive knowledge of it. Some people might know some of it but ignore the rest, whereas others know what are ignored by those people but ignore what is known to them.[2]

This identification of Arabic language with revelation was expressed in different ways in theology and literary criticism as well. In linking Arabic—*al-Lisan al-'Arabi*—with revelation, al-Shafi'i cites the example of the Sunna, which according to him is a mode of divine revelation that, although knowable by the entire community of *ulama*, by definition cannot be fully comprehended by any given individual or group.

The philologist Abu-'Ubayd al-Qasim b. Sallam (d. 224 A.H./881 C.E.) gave a second answer, explaining that although originally foreign, the words in question had been borrowed and used by the Arabs long before the revelation of the Qur'an. Some of the Qur'an's vocabulary was thus indeed foreign, but had been Arabized before the revelation.[3]

Accordingly, the Qur'anic statement is true as long as the Arabization of those words is understood.

Not surprisingly, the emphasis on the absolute linguistic purity of the Qur'anic text has led to a firm stand on the part of many Muslims against the validity of any translation. Over time, throughout the history of Islamic thought, the discussion of this issue has taken a number of different directions, depending on the disciplinary prism through which it has been studied.

## VALIDITY/INVALIDITY OF THE TRANSLATED QUR'AN IN THE *SALAT*

Insofar as Islamic jurisprudence is concerned, the question was first asked in connection with whether or not new non-Arab converts to Islam may perform the prayer in their original language. Al-Shafi'i insists that it is not valid to pray reciting a Persian translation of the Qur'an. More than that, "an Arabic recitation is not valid if the precise verse sequence is not followed, even by mistake; it is not even valid if the mistake is corrected because the reciter should start the whole chapter (the first chapter of the Qur'an) all over again in its sequential order."[4]

Before al-Shafi'i, Abu Hanifa (d. 150 A.H./775 C.E.), from a Persian family himself, saw no religious objection to a Muslim who was unable to understand or recite Arabic performing the prayer in translation. He even decreed that those who knew some Arabic but had difficulties reciting Qur'an in that language might do so in another.[5]

## LITERARY CRITICISM: THE PROBLEM OF TRANSLATION

In his well-known book *al-Hayawan* (Animals), al-Jahiz, Abu 'Uthman 'Amr b. Bahr (d. 255 A.H./870 C.E.), a theologian and a literary critic, insists on the impossibility of poetry translation, because "once translated," he argues, a poem's "rhyming system is broken, its beauty is gone, and, unlike prose, it is no longer enjoyable." Al-Jahiz here expressly means Arabic poetry, which was without equal in the widely accepted view of many Arab literary critics at that time, reflecting anti-Persian ethnic prejudice and chauvinism during the second A.H./eighth C.E. and third A.H./ninth C.E. centuries.

According to the Muslim theologian Ibn Qutayba (d. 276 A.H./889 C.E.), who wrote about poetry and poets, *al-Shi'r wa Shu'ra'*, the Arabs excelled in poetic eloquence before Islam; their language had reached its full richness in a variety of modes of expressions and multiplicity of styles. No other human language could compare with Arabic, the language in which God had decided to send down his last message to mankind. It is not very clear in the theologian's argument whether God chose Arabic for his last message because of its intrinsic superiority or bestowed that superiority on it because it had been determined from eternity to be the language of His last message. The concept of the Qur'an developed in Islamic theology, dealt with in the next section, gives some grounds for both possibilities.

## QUR'ANIC SUPREMACY

The notion of the inimitability, *i'jaz,* of the Qur'an is an essential concept in Islamic theology and literary criticism. It is very true that, by its unique linguistic features, the Qur'an had from the moment of its revelation captured the Arab imagination. The Arabs tried their best to explain its effect on them in terms of the types of text they already knew, and these explanations are mentioned and refuted by the Qur'an itself. When the Arabs explain the Qur'an as "poetry" and accuse the Prophet of composing it, the answer is: "We have not taught him poetry; it is not seemly for him."[6] When they say that Muhammad is nothing but a soothsayer, the Qur'an replies: "By thy Lord's blessing thou art not a soothsayer, neither possessed."[7] Since they regarded the Qur'an as nothing but some stories forged by Muhammad and falsely claimed to have been revealed to him by God, nonbelieving Arabs thought it would be easy for them to make a text like it. The Qur'an in turn challenged the doubters by asking them to bring forth "ten forged chapters like it."[8] When the nonbelievers failed to respond to this challenge, the Qur'an, pretending to make it easier for them, decreased the number of chapters from ten to only one.[9] The last step was to indicate the absolute failure of the Arabs to challenge the authenticity of the Qur'an: "And if you [nonbelievers] are in doubt concerning that We have sent down on Our servant (Muhammad) then bring a chapter like it, and call your witnesses, apart from God, if you are truthful. And if you do not—and you will not—then fear the Fire, whose fuel is men and idols, prepared to unbelievers."[10]

The fact that the Arabs failed to respond to this challenge affirmed the Muslim belief about the nature of the Qur'an, including its supremacy as a text. It is by no means comparable with any human text, whether written in the past, present, or future. Many stories are preserved in Islamic literature according to which even the unbelievers were fascinated by the overwhelming poetic effect of the language of the Qur'an, an effect incomparable with that of poetry itself. The notion of the supremacy of the Qur'an, or rather of its inimitability, was developed later and explained in terms of its rhetorical characteristics. In spite of their occasional eloquence, the Arabs failed to bring forth the like of even the smallest chapter of the Qur'an. They produced poetry and prose, but they could not produce anything remotely resembling the Qur'an.

THEOLOGICAL EXPLANATION

Many theories were introduced in Islamic theology to explain the inimitability of the text. At least two major issues were to be elucidated: First, what was meant in the challenge when the Qur'an asks for something "like it"? Second, why did the Arabs fail to produce something like the Qur'an without simply imitating its style? Ibrahim bin Sayyar al-Nazzam (d. 230 A.H./877 C.E.), who was a rationalist, Mu'tazili theologian, introduced the theory of *sarfah*. According to al-Nazzam, God had deliberately interfered to prevent the Arabs, who could easily meet the challenge, from bringing into being a text like the Qur'an. This intervention of God was a miracle in itself. As for the text, there is nothing peculiar about it. Nevertheless, its supremacy is due to the information contained in it whether about the past, unknown to Muhammad, or about future incidents.[11] Therefore, as an Arabic text, the Qur'an is not inimitable, but as a divine revelation containing divine knowledge, it is. It is the content, not the style, that is God's sign that Muhammad spoke the truth.

This theory that relates the Arabs' failure to God's intervention is not in accordance with the rational theological system of the Mu'tazilites, that is, God would not inflict a challenge on the Arabs while intervening to strip them of their power. This would be an unjust act that is not likely to be divine; God is just. Therefore, this opinion was refuted, not only by the opponents of the Mu'tazilites, but also by the later Mu'tazilites as well.

Abu-Hashim al-Jubba'i (d. 321 A.H./973 C.E.) another Mu'tazili theologian, further developed al-Nazzam's arguments. In order to include the syntactical structure of the Qur'an as another dimension of its supremacy beside its content, al-Jubba'i had to make a clear distinction between the "content" and the "form" of any discourse. Ideas alone, no matter how wonderful or magnificent they may be, do not explain the supremacy of the Qur'an, or that of any other text. Style and eloquence are just as important, although without ideas they are merely decorative. A combination, or rather synthesis, of ideas and style should be considered. The Qur'an is, therefore, supreme and inimitable because of its syntactically distinguished structure.[12] Because the "uniqueness" of the Qur'an lies in its syntactical structure—that is, in both its content and its style—the Arabs failed to meet the challenge it posed them despite being masters of poetic eloquence.

The notion that the "content" of the Qur'an was part of the challenge raised a theological difficulty. God's knowledge is absolute, whereas human knowledge is limited. Therefore, a challenge that contains knowledge is unjust to human capacity; it is like throwing a bound person into the sea and asking him to swim. So long as Divine Justice is concerned, the challenge should be directed toward what is in human capacity. Evidences to sustain this line of argumentation were taken from the nature of miracles performed by Moses and Jesus in support of their claims. The miracles of Moses were in the same field of activities in which the Egyptians were well versed. So were the miracles of Jesus. As the Arabs were the masters of poetic eloquence, the miracle of Muhammad, the Qur'an, is a textual one and is superior in this respect. In terms of poetic eloquence, rhetoric or *balaghah,* the Qur'anic style is certainly of the highest level. Al-Rummani, Abu al-Hasan Ali b. 'Isa (d. 386 A.H./1041 C.E.), a Mu'tazili philologist, counted ten categories of poetics employed in the style of the Qur'an.[13]

Abu-Bakre al-Baqillani (d. 403 A.H./1056 C.E.), an anti-Mu'tazilite theologian and jurist, devoted a book to explaining what distinguished the Qur'an from all other texts, including previous holy books. He began by refuting al-Nazzam's theory on the grounds that like the Qur'an, previous holy scriptures contained some prophecies. However, unlike Islam's Holy Book, they are not considered inimitable. It is, therefore, the linguistic characteristics of the Qur'an that should be considered.[14] The unique style of the Qur'an, according to al-Baqillani, is that it is neither poetry nor prose; it is a literary genre in itself. No human literary measures can be used or applied to evaluate it. All human texts, including the seven great poems of pre-Islamic era, are nonsense if compared to the Qur'an.[15] It is, therefore, the very nature of the speaker himself, God, that makes it impossible to compare the Qur'an to any other text.

As an Ash'ari theologian, al-Baqillani believed in the distinction between the "eternal" speech of God, *kalam Allah al-azaliyy al-qadim,* and its manifestation in the present recited Qur'an. Nevertheless, inimitability of the Qur'an, according to him, lies in the recited text of the Qur'an, not in the eternal divine speech of God. This unbridgeable gap between the Qur'an and other human texts exists despite the fact that both of them are formed from the same substance, namely, language.[16] The Qur'an is the miracle *mu'jizah* upon which the proof of Muhammad's prophetic mission is based. In his conclusion, al-Baqillani enumerates three aspects of the miracle of *i'jaz* in relation to the Qur'an, only the last one being its eloquence.[17]

One miracle is that the Qur'an contains information about the unseen, "and that is something beyond the powers of humans, for they have no way to attain it."[18] The second aspect is that it is well known that the Prophet was an unlettered man, *ummi,* who could not write, and who could not read very well. Likewise it was generally recognized that he had no knowledge whatever of the books of earlier peoples, nor of their records, their histories, their biographies. Yet he produced summaries of what had happened [in history], told about mighty matters [of past days], and gave the important life histories from the creation of Adam up to his own mission.[19] The third aspect is that [the Qur'an] is wonderfully arranged and marvelously composed, and so exalted in its literary elegance as to be beyond what any mere created being could attain. This is essentially the opinion expressed by learned theologians.

The famous literary critic 'Abdul-Qahir al-Jurjani (d. 474 A.H./1078 C.E.) was an Ash'ari as well, but he was "thoroughly familiar with the works of the Mu'tazili al-Qadi 'Abd al-Jabbar (d. 474 A.H./1081 C.E.), to the point of being able to manipulate his ideas creatively with his own theo-rhetorical system."[20] Al-Jurjani introduced the theory of *nazm,* syntax, in his well-known book *Dala'il I'jaz al-Qur'an* (Proofs of Inimitability of the Qur'an), in which he affirms the central importance of eloquence. His theory is based on the assumption that texts, whether divine or human, are constructed according to the same rules; they are built from the same material and constructed according to the same grammatical norms and laws. In order to explain the supremacy of the Qur'an, scholars should not confine themselves to general remarks of admiration marked by piety and faith; they should instead embark on rigorous study of excellent human texts, namely, poetry, in order to uncover the laws of *nazm,* without which no convincing explanation of the Qur'an's supremacy is possible.[21]

The great contribution of al-Jurjani is his successful effort to provide linguistic rhetorical explanations of the stylistic eloquence and supremacy of the Qur'an. Nevertheless, he could not avoid relating these features to the nature of the producer of the text, God. Did it really need all these efforts to explain a phenomenon that ends up being self-explanatory? God's knowledge is incomparable by any means with human knowledge.

THE THEOLOGICAL ROOTS

In the Ash'ari theology, it was always the nature of the speaker that accounted for the nature of the text. This notion of the nature of the speaker as the essential reason behind the supremacy of the text paved the way to establish another notion concerning the nature of language itself. According to this notion, language is not a human invention but a gift from God. It was not difficult to support such a notion by quoting the Qur'an itself, where it is mentioned that God taught Adam "all the names."[22] Explaining the teaching of names as teaching language made language a divine code of communication given to man as a blessing from God. Any comparison between God's speech and man's speech is definitely heresy. It has been recently very dangerous to open a new discussion or to start a new intellectual debate concerning this understanding of the doctrine of "inimitability," even in the way that al-Jurjani did. This emphasis on the infallibility of the Holy Book, in modern Islamic discourse, is nothing but the logical conclusion of the belief that the Qur'an is the exact verbal rendering of the utterance of the absolute divine reality. The literalist belief that the Qur'an is a form of "verbal inspiration" lends itself to extremist interpretations of Islam. Conversely, in Christianity, "theology worked on the basis of four Gospels."[23]

Around the end of the first A.H./seventh century C.E. and during the first quarter of the second A.H./eighth century C.E., a new trend of thought began to emerge in response to the Umayyad political theology that emphasized the creed of "predestination" to legitimize political power. Three thinkers were executed because they opposed the concept of "predestination" and emphasized human free will and, accordingly, human responsibility. They all agreed on "justice" as one of God's divine attributes, which was to be an essential creed of the Mu'tazilite system. These three thinkers are Ma'bad al-Jahni (80 A.H./723 C.E.), Ghaylan of Damascus (99 A.H./742 C.E.), and al-Ja'd b. Dirham (120 A.H./764 C.E.). Not much is mentioned about their thesis except for al-Ja'd, who is reported to have claimed that the Qur'an, God's speech, is not eternal but is created. It is also reported that the three thinkers were influenced by prevailing trends in Christian theology. As long as the line of the argumentation for their two theses—human free will and the createdness of the Qur'an—is missing, some speculation might be possible within the very limited factual information available. Concerning the nature of God's speech, al-Ja'd might have thought that the notion that the Qur'an is eternal stood in contradiction to the absolute unity of God. It would be suggestive of the Christian Trinity, which is rejected by the Qur'an. God's speech is created, al-Ja'd asserted. Like God's justice and human responsibility, the non-eternity of God's speech was to be an essential part of the Mu'tazilites' system.

In Islamic doctrine since the third A.H./ninth century C.E., however, the concept of eternity developed as an important component of mainstream Sunni dogma. The intellectual dispute concerning the nature of the Qur'an, which was particularly heated among Muslim theologians in the second A.H./eighth century C.E., was decided upon by political power. "Orthodoxy" and "heterodoxy" split according to the approach adopted toward the Qur'an. This issue has at least four theoretical aspects: two theories concerning the origin of language and the relation between language and reality, and two corresponding theories about the "createdness" versus the "uncreatedness" of the Qur'an.

The theories supported by the Mu'tazila tended to be more rationalistic. The analysis of the relationship between man, language, and the Holy Book concentrated on man as the addressee of the text, and on human society as the public to whom its teachings were directed. Language is a human invention because in relating sound to meaning, it reflects social convention. Language never refers directly to reality, but reality is conceived, conceptualized, and then symbolized by the sound system. This is exemplified by the fact that in Arabic, as in any other language, there are words lacking a referent in reality: a word like *anqa* (comparable to the English "phoenix") does not refer to any existing reality. The Mu'tazila, therefore, saw in the Qur'an a created action and not the eternal verbal utterance of God. Even in the Qur'anic language, the relationship between the signifier and the signified existed only by human convention. There is nothing divine in this relationship itself. According to the Mu'tazila, the divine word adjusted itself to human language in order to give prosperity and welfare to society. They insisted that language was the product of man mediated by a certain historical culture and that the divine word respected the rules and forms of human language. For the Muʻtazila, there was a bridge between human reason and the divine word.

The anti-Muʻtazilite school of thought had different views on language in general and God's speech in particular. Language, said the anti-Muʻtazilites, is not a human invention but a divine gift to man. If the referent does not exist in the real world it ought to exist in metaphysical reality. Here the anti-Muʻtazilites quote some Qur'anic verses that, taken literally, would support their assumptions about the divinity of language.[24] The Muʻtazilites, of course, favor a metaphorical interpretation of these verses.[25] Since the relationship between the signifier and the signified is, in view of the orthodoxy, created by God himself, it is divine. It was logically concluded that God's speech is not a created action but it is one of His eternal attributes.

The Qur'an is God's speech. About this view there has not been any disagreement among Muslims throughout the centuries. The disputed point, however, is whether the Qur'an is eternal or temporal and created. This has led to fierce disputes and even to persecution and physical annihilation of the adherents of one or the other of the two positions. The period of the great inquisition and the persecution *(mihna)* of those who opted for the eternity of the Qur'an was in the first half of the third century A.H. (218 A.H./833 C.E.–243 A.H./848 C.E.). Its hero was Ahmad b. Hanbal (died 240 A.H./870 C.E.), who firmly objected to the idea of the temporality of the Qur'an.

It is worth noting that the choice in favor of one of the two answers had important implications for other doctrines of theology. The belief that the Qur'an is eternal implies, for instance, that God preordained any event mentioned in the Holy Book and leads to idea of God's absolute predestination of human action. He who wants to deny predestination will believe the Qur'an to be created. And, to mention yet another example, those who advocate the doctrine of God's absolute unity and uniqueness *(tawhid),* and wish to take it in its strictest sense, deny the existence of an uncreated Qur'an together with God in all eternity. The notion of an eternal Qur'an leads to strict adherence to literal meaning of the text.[26] The Qur'an is believed to have preexisted in Heaven, recorded on a well-preserved tablet. Later belief embellished this notion even further: the preexisting book was written in magnificent Arabic letters, each of which had the size of the legendary mountain Qaf.

CONCLUSION

The view that God had from eternity chosen Arabic because of its eternal intrinsic features became the dominant one among Muslims. In this view, Arabic is a divine language invented by God himself. As far as the majority of Muslims are concerned, the Qur'an is God's word revealed exactly in its original Arabic language to Prophet Muhammad. Muslims venerate and glorify the holy words of God, whether or not fully understood by recitation. It is felt that the audible features of the Qur'anic language, which include its sound effect, bring the Muslim to God's presence and put him in direct contact with His actual speech. Since translation never does justice to a literary text, especially to poetry, and since Arabic, the language of the Qur'an, is a divine language by nature, translation of Arabic poetry is impossible. Last but not least, since the Qur'an is the supreme Arabic text, translation is not only impossible but forbidden. What is allowed is translation of the "meanings" for the sake of knowing and learning about Islam. For praying and performing religious duties, no translation is permitted.

NOTES

1. Qur'an 14:4, trans. A.J. Arberry, *The Koran Interpreted* (1955; New York: Simon & Schuster, 1996).
2. Al-Shafi'i, *Al-Risala* (The Treatise), ed. Muhammad Shakir (Beirut, n.d.), p. 42.
3. Al-Sayyid Ya'qub Bakr, *Nusus fi Fiqh al-lugha al-'Arabiyya* (Texts in Arabic Philology) (Beirut, 1971), 2 : 33.
4. Al-Shafi'i, *Al 'Umm* (The Compendium) (Cairo, n.d.), 1: 94.
5. Muhammad Abu-Zahra, *Abu Hanifa: Hayatuh wa atharuh wa ara'uh al-fiqhiyya* (Abu Hanifa: His Life, Writings, and Legal Opinions) (Cairo: Dār al-Fikr al-'Arabī, 1380 A.H./1960 C.E.), p. 241.
6. Qur'an 35:69.
7. Qur'an 52:29.
8. Qur'an 2:13.
9. Qur'an 10:38.
10. Qur'an 2:23–24.
11. Al-Shahristani, Abu al-Fath Muhammad b. Abu al-Qasim, *Al-Milal wa 'Nihal* (Sects and Doctrines), in the margin of Ibn Hazm's *Al-Fisal fi al-Milal wa al-'Ahwa' wa Nihal* (The Distinction of Sects, Prejudices, and Doctrines) (Cairo, n.d.), 1: 64. And see also Abū al Ḥusayn b. 'Othmān al Khayyāṭ, *Kitāb al Intiṣār: Le livre du triomphe et de la réfutation d'Ibn al Rawandi l'hérétique*, trans. Albert Naṡrī Nādir (Beirut: Lettres orientales, 1957), pp. 28–29.

12. 'Abd al-Jabbar Al Asdabadi, *Al-Mughni fi Abwab al-Tawhid wa al-'Adl* (The Sufficient in the Themes of Divine Unicity and Divine Justice), vol. 12 of *I'jaz al-Qur'an* (The Inimitability of the Qur'an), ed. Amin al-Khuli (Cairo, 1380 A.H./1960 C.E.), pp. 199–200.

13. *Al-Nukkat fi I'jaz al-Qur'an* (Insights into the Inimitability of the Qur'an), in *Thalath Rasa'il fi i'jaz al-Qur'an* (Three Treatises on the Inimitability of the Qur'an), ed. Muhammad Khalafallah Ahmad and Muhammad Zaghlul Sallam (2nd ed., Cairo, 1968).

14. *I'jaz al-Qur'an* (The Inimitability of the Qur'an), in the margin of al-Suyuti's *Al-Itqan fi 'Ulum al-Qur'an* (The Precision in the Sciences of the Qur'an) (3rd ed., Cairo, 1370 A.H./1952 C.E.), 1: 43–44.

15. Ibid., pp. 150–154.

16. Ibid., 2: 169.

17. *Islam: Muhammad and His Religion,* ed. Arthur Jeffery (New York: Liberal Arts Press, 1958), pp. 55–57.

18. One example, explained at length by al-Baqillani,

> is the promise Allah, Most High, made to His Prophet—upon whom be peace—that his religion would triumph over the [other] religions. Thus He—mighty and exalted is He—said [Qur'an 9: 33]: "He it is who has sent His messenger with guidance and the religion of truth, that he might make it victorious over all religion, even though the polytheists dislike it," and this he did. Abu Bakr, the first caliph, the trusty one, with whom may Allah be pleased, when he sent out his troops raiding, used to remind them of Allah's promise to make His religion victorious, so that they should be hopeful of victory and feel certain of success. 'Umar b. al-Khattab, the second caliph, with whom may Allah be pleased, also used to do likewise in his day, so that his army commanders were aware of it. So Sa'd b. Abi Waqqas [one of the prophet's companions]—on whom may Allah be pleased—and other army leaders like him, used to remind their companions of that, urging them on by it and making them hopeful. And they used to meet with success in their ventures, such that in latter days of 'Umar—with whom may Allah be pleased—they had captured all [the lands] as far as Balk and the land of India.

19. The second aspect has to do with what Muslims consider as fact, namely, that although Muhammad was illiterate and had no access to knowledge, biblical stories are cited in the Qur'an:

> He [Muhammad] makes mention in the Book, which he brought as his miracle, of the story of Adam—upon him be peace—how he was created, what brought about his being turned out of the garden, then somewhat about his progeny and his condition, and his repentance. He also makes mention of the story of Noah—on whom be peace—what happened between him and his people, and how his affair turned out in the end. Likewise [he told] about Abraham—upon whom be peace—and about all the other prophets mentioned in the Qur'an, and the kings and pharaohs who lived in the days of the prophets—on whom be Allah's blessings. Now we know for sure that he had no way to [obtain knowledge of all] this save that of being taught, and since it is known that he had no intimacy with antiquarians or those who stored up information [about such matters], and did not go frequently to get from them, and that he was not one who could read, so that he might have taken this from some book that could possibly have come to him, then the conclusion is that he did not obtain this knowledge save by aid from revelation. This is what Allah—mighty and majestic is he—has said

[Qur'an 29:48]: 'Thou wast not reciting any book before it, nor writing it with thy right hand, otherwise those who it worthless would have been suspicious.' He also said [4:105]: 'And thus do We change about the signs, and [We do so] that they may say: Thou hast been studying.' We have already made clear that one who was accustomed to go repeatedly to receive instruction and busy himself at becoming intimate with those who had skill [in these matters] would not have been able hide this from the people, nor would there have been any disagreement among them as to the way he was acting. It was well known among those who had knowledge of these matters, even though such persons were seldom to be met, and who were in the habit of going to such for instruction. It was no secret who were most learned in each of these matters and who were being instructed [by them] in them, so if [Muhammad] had been among the latter, this would have been no secret.

20. Margaret Larkin, *The Theology of Meaning: 'Abd al-Qāhir al-Jurjānī's Theory of Discourse,* American Oriental Series, vol. 79 (New Haven, CT: American Oriental Society, 1995), p. 12.

21. Al-Jurjani, *Dala'il I'jaz al-Qur'an* (The Proofs of the Inimitability of the Qur'an), ed. Mamhmud Muhammad Shakir (2nd ed., Cairo, 1989), pp. 8–9.

22. Qur'an 2:31.

23. J. Van Ess, "Verbal Inspiration? Language and Revelation in Classical Islamic Theology," in *The Qur'an as Text,* ed. S. Wild (Leiden: Brill, 1996), p. 192.

24. Qur'an 2:31.

25. Nasr Abu-Zayd, *Al-Ittijah al-'Aqli fi Tafsir* (The Rational Trend in Exegesis (Beirut, 1996), pp. 70–82.

26. J. R. T. M. Peters, *God's Created Speech: A Study in the Speculative Theology of the Mu'tazilī Qādī l-gudât Abūl-Hasan 'Abd al-Jabbâr bn Ahmad al-Hamadānī* (Leiden: Brill, 1976), p. 3.

CHAPTER 7

# Toward a New Understanding of Renewal in Islam

ADONIS

I

Let me start with a question about the concepts of truth in poetry, and truth in religious revelations (the *wahi*), for in these two concepts lies the key to understanding renewal in Islam.

Who is the poet in Arab consciousness, especially prior to Islam? In my opinion, the answer is not just he who feels what others do not, as they used to say, but goes well beyond that, to he who transcends what is seen and unseen, and claims to see what others do not. His awareness of the unseen does not draw from his natural being, but from his association with persons or forces beyond nature, that is, the jinn. Poetry was, therefore, never just a form of descriptive linguistic art—it had perceptive knowledge drawn directly from the supernatural and the unknown, through the intermediary of extraordinary creatures. This relationship between the poet's and the jinn's world is a special relationship that concerns no one but the poet. The fact that each poet had his own jinn to call his "companion" reminds us of the meaning of the word "companion," a designation that God bestowed on Abraham. We say Abraham is God's close companion, and Moses His interlocutor.

They used to say, even after the rise of Islam, that poetry was revealed to the poet, just as religious revelations were to the prophet. Hassan bin Thabit said in this context:

Translated from the original Arabic by Ellen Khouri.

> A rhyme strong with teeming night
> came down to me from the sky

We can thus understand why the Arabs could find no better words to describe the Prophet of Islam than to say that He is the "poet" and the "jinn" were His source of inspiration, or premonition. They said, "And they appointed a relationship between Him and the jinn" (As-Saffat, 158); they also said, "Are we to forsake our gods for a mad poet?" (As-Saffat, 36). Linguistically, a madman is he who is possessed by jinn, or inhabited by a genie. Moreover, there are similarities between the revelations having come down, and poetry coming down, despite the Qur'an's insistence that the Prophet was not a poet, in other words, not inhabited by jinn, or in any way possessed by them, as the poet was.

To underline the similarities between the coming down of revelations and poetic inspiration, texts in the Qur'an insist that Islam is instinctive, just as poetry was instinctive for the Arabs.

Islam is instinctive and came bearing the truth. In this sense, it suspends all that has preceded it. The fact that revelations alone, not poetry, have the power to uncover, at the same time, the meaning of both existence and the supernatural, is ample proof of that.

Because prior to Islam the Arabs saw the supernatural as one and the same as the jinn world, Islam said, God created the supernatural, which means He also created the jinn. However, since God is the one who sent the revelations to the Prophet, his prophet is neither mad nor possessed by the jinn, as the poet is. It follows then that his inspiration is from God, not from the jinn.

Thus, "the truth" became exclusive to religious revelations, as did the exclusivity of the Prophet's choice as their intended recipient. It is at this point that poet and poetry started to been seen in a different light. The poet became a "deviant" and poetry a "deviation." It went even further when the poet became a sinner because his poetry was from the devil: "Shall I inform you (O people!) on whom it is that the evil ones descend? They descend on every lying, wicked person." (Ash-Shu'ara', 221–222).

Islam did not do away with poetry, but changed its significance and role by bending it to its imperatives. Poetry was no longer the "truth," nor did it any longer speak the "truth"; one way or another, its role became confined to serving religion. In other words, it was no longer a principle of learning and aesthetics.

Religious revelations thus revoke poetic inspiration using the very language of poetry, the Arabic language, a language that existed before the revelations came down. The revelations teach that the message of Islam is God's final message to Man, delivered through his last prophet, "the ultimate one." As such, it is the final divine message comprising the entire and ultimate truth on all matters: there is no room for alternatives, no room for retreat.

Nevertheless, poetry soon regained its status after a period of concealment, while the faith was propagated further afield. Starting in the Umayyad period, it prospered outside the religious domain regardless of the limitations imposed by religion, and continued to exist as a parallel movement, free of religious control, unfettered and unmolested save for a few exceptional cases.

There exist a number of issues without which any talk of renewal in Islam is moot. Among these is the fact that the Arabic language was once a vehicle for transmitting divine revelations from other prophecies, prior to Islam. As such, it is a "second" language that carried forward earlier divine revelations, revelations that came down in a different language.

Therefore, based on the above, Arab Islam's origins are "foreign" or "non-Arab," embodied in the descendents of Abraham, father of the Jewish people. His message and that of his descendents was in a language other than Arabic, in Hebrew to be precise, and was contained in a non-Arabic book, the Torah. Thus, Islam finds its origins in Torah-inspired monotheism, in its prophets and its poetry. It also finds it in Abraham's paternity of the Arabs, a non-Arab father.

Perhaps it is necessary to add here that the word "origin," in this context, means the "first," or the "father," to use Freudian language. The son here does not just inherit his father's natural attributes, but also his thoughts and his way of thinking. What complicates matters further in Arab Islam is that the father is a composite of three fathers:

1. The Abrahamic father: Judaism and Christianity
2. The Arab father (pre-Islamic) language and the tribe
3. The Muslim father: the last prophet, last prophecies, final divine words and the ultimate truth

The notion of parricide thus appears to be alien to Islam. In other words, it is as if there is no room in it—as text—for the concept of renewal.

The doors close firmly in this concept's face when we remember that the meanings of "final message," "final divine words" and "ultimate truth" involve the belief that God Himself, the inspiration behind the three monotheistic religions, performed most completely and comprehensively in his revelations to the Muslim prophet, his last messenger.

The truth, as Islam sees it, therefore, lies in the revelations, that is, the text of the Qur'an; it is thus final and permanent. Whatever Muslim revelations have said, has been said once, and forever. Based on that premise, this truth is general and common to all, by necessity, and the virtue of being a faith and a dogma. There can be no rupture of any kind here: it is today as it will be tomorrow, and as it will remain forever, exactly as it was at the beginning.

Therefore, religious truth in Islam is associated with the concept of the "nation." The "nation," as traditional fundamentalist Islam understands it today, is a unit, a single entity, a "solid edifice." In this entity, there is no room for diverse currents or for political and intellectual pluralism, which explains why any deviation from the national consensus meant secession, and why those who deviated were, one way or another, expelled from it. Thus, at the heart of this union, the divine and the religious, the sacred and political, all become one.

This view of the nation as a uniform and closed unit lies at the basis of the violence with which politics has been associated in Arab-Islamic society since its earliest beginnings. This violence allows us to say that the divine truth is itself founded on violence, a truth that is not the outcome of research, doubt, common sense, questioning and testing, but of duress. This is what makes it, in effect, a component of despotism, rather than of mercy, wisdom, thought, and choice. This is why in Muslim religious life, copying and imitation triumph over criticism and renewal.

When we realize that Muslim texts do not refer us back to the Pharaonic, Greek, early *Jahiliyya* in the Arabian Peninsula, Sumerian-Babylonian, or Phoenician-Canaanite periods, but to the Torah and its prophets, we should concede that their reader was compelled to read them in light of their relationship with the Torah's prophecies, and the monotheism they preached.

In light of the above, the researcher cannot help but note that monotheism has destroyed the notion of multiple gods (the pantheon), and that this fostered a new conflict between the monotheistic religions, and within each of these religions.

II

We now ask what renewal means according to the religious truth, on the one hand, and to the poetic truth, on the other. I shall start with the latter and say that, based on historical experience, renewal for the poet means ushering in something new, something not known before. In poetic terms, it means presenting new relationships between words and things, between one word and another and between the human being and the world. This is what great poets have done in Arabic, and this is exactly what Abu Nawwas, Abu Tammam, al-Mutanabi, and al-Ma'arri, among others, have done. Each of these men presented us with something new, that is, offered a world of their own as vision and expression. In its essence, renewal therefore relies on the rejection of a priori standardization, rules that ought not to be written.

Renewal, according to the religious truth, is an entirely different matter. To begin with, there is a text, a standard to be adhered to, both as divine truth and based on its description as a faith. It is a standard that cannot be changed. It could at best be interpreted or construed only in a manner that does not allow it to be seen in light of the world or as part of the human experience, but allows the world to be seen in its light.

Renewal, as far as religion is concerned, has therefore an entirely different meaning than renewal in poetry. Renewal means reinterpretation that keeps both life and world within the confines of religion, and under its thumb. In fact, it is making life and the world more religious. If we couple this meaning with the notion that Islam is a "nation," it becomes clear that the interpretation of religious texts is linked to universal politics in a manner that makes them fit in with the text. Religious truth is therefore collective, the truth of the nation; this is why, as historical experience proves, renewal is impossible except through secession or violence. This analysis could help us also understand how Islam revolves basically around politics, instead of culture in its all-embracing creative and civilized sense.

It would be useful for us to go back to the linguistic origin of the words "renewal" and "modernization." In the Arabic *Lisan al-'Arab* dictionary, renewal means, "that which you are not acquainted with." On the other hand, what is modern is "the opposite of what is old," and a "happening" (which in Arabic has the same root as the word for modern) is "something that did not exist before." In general, renewal is collective, and the modern is personal, linked essentially to religion.

It is also said, according to *Lisan al-'Arab,* that novelties are "the bad things that deviants have created, and were hitherto unknown to our good forebears." The hadith cautions against innovations, referring to everything that is not included in a book or in the Sunna (the way the Prophet lived his life), or is not the object of Muslim consensus.

The hadith also says, in effect, that everything modern is a deviation, and every deviation leads to perdition. We could extrapolate from this that sinning is called "modernization": man "modernizes," creates something new, therefore he sins, woman "modernizes," creates something new, therefore she sins. This shows that modernization is not exclusive to the religious context, but involves society and its morals, culture, and politics, as well.

Renewal and modernization are, therefore, the exact opposites of religion. At the same time, poetry, if not renewal and modernization, is nothing at all.

III

At that level, poetry and poetic truth are the exact opposites of religion and religious truth. Truth in poetry is inconstant, endless and unclear; in this sense, it is outside the confines of the realm of religious truth. As such, it is something that is not necessarily collective or shared. Nothing stays as is in poetic reality; poetic creativity is a perpetual rupture or perpetual continuity in perpetual rupture. The era of poetry and the era of religion are, therefore, not one and the same: the former is one of change and motion, and the latter is one of eternity and immobility.

Religion is an answer, and poetry is a question; therefore, religion can never serve as a reference for poetry. Poetic language is, to the contrary, a dialogue between what is seen and unseen. In poetry, the unseen, the supernatural, is the object of questions and doubt, not of faith and submission. This is why we believe that, contrary to religious truth, poetic truth can be felt in the illogical and unknown.

Religious and poetic truths are two opposite ways of seeing the world, each with its own intent: religion is codification, teaching and affirmation, and poetry is a question, an overview of the future and doubt.

However, despite the revelations' denial of poetic truth, and turning poetry's identity from an instinct and a foresight that unveils the truth, and from an original and sovereign word, into a mere tool at the service of religion, or a means of spreading the Muslim truth, poetry continued to prosper as the original word, even prior to religion. How do we explain this prospering, and that of other forms of art, not to forget philosophy and science?

The answer is that creativity as a movement, in all its aspects and forms, was in fact a step aside, or a deviation, from religious texts. What we call Arab civilization or culture, was, at its height, mostly the outcome of the conflict with religious texts. The conflict started with the interpretation of texts, and ended by keeping its distance from it. I am talking about the cultural modernization revolution, or renewal, which coincided with the rise of the Umayyid state in 661 C.E. (41 A.H.), that is, around thirty years after the establishment of the first caliphate in 632 C.E. (11 A.H.), and ended with the fall of Baghdad, in 1258 C.E., meaning that it lasted for six centuries.

With Baghdad's fall, Arab society's political-cultural identity also collapsed, prompting the confused and perplexed Muslims to adopt the religious identity. The tendency toward seeking refuge in Islam exacerbated the cultural decline, social dismemberment, and foreign hegemony, a hegemony that started with the Ottomans, lasted around four hundred years, and ended with Western colonialism. To one degree or another, and in one form or another, this colonialism is still with us today. The process of collapse is, therefore, still ongoing, as is the trend toward seeking refuge in religion.

Let me, finally, pose the following question to highlight the contradiction, at its extreme, between the religious and poetic truths, and clarify why Muslim revelations and poetic inspiration are two opposites that shall never meet: Does the "other" have a place in the Muslim religious truth? There are two types of "other": one is within Islam and belongs to it, and the other is outside of it.

In the first case, there are Muslims who accuse other Muslims of apostasy in the name of Islam, meaning that certain Muslims have no place in it. In the second case, there is no place for the "other" in Islam except if he is a member of *ahlul dhimma* (Christians and Jews), that is, by defining him as someone who has less rights than the Muslim, or as a second-class individual. In both cases, Islam seems more of a closed and ritualistic political system, than one of learning and spirituality.

Let me put the question differently: does the "other" have a place in Arab poetry? The answer is yes. No matter who he is, the "other" is part of the Arab poetic self, since poetry is a constant migration, in and through language, toward the unknown, in other words, in the other direction. As far as poetry is concerned, the stranger is close by, and the other is the self. In essence, existence in poetry is to be with, to be in company with, and unity in poetry is in itself, unity in company.

I thus arrive at the conclusion that truth in poetry is discovered and lived either in total isolation from religious revelation or by staying out of its confines; and the same goes for other forms of art, and for philosophy and science. There is a schism between the religious and the poetic as far as method, approach, and means of expression are concerned. In fact, as mentioned above, poetry has historically lived alongside religion, in Arab Islamic life, like two parallel and contradictory lines, and still does.

It is important to say here that this cultural and daily life contradiction between religious revelations and poetry goes back to the very first changes in the lives of Muslims, starting with the Prophet's death and the establishment of the Rashidun ("rightly guided") caliphate. These changes were based on necessities in which revelations had no place except as interpretations and opinions, reflected in the views and actions of people seeking compatibility between the revelations and daily life. In this context, we could consider the first establishment of the caliphate as an attempt, in theory and in practice, to reconcile eternity, represented by the revelations, and temporality, which embodies the Muslims' activities. We could describe this attempt, in comparison with what preceded it, as a renewal or a form of modernization.

The Muslims' conclave to designate the caliph, and all that it involved, was modernity—both as aims and means. The same could be said about Wars of Apostasy (against defectors from Islam), the revolt against the caliph Uthman and his murder, and wars that took place under the fourth caliph, crowned with the establishment of the first Arab state under Mu'awiya. These were all acts of modernization. Likewise, Mu'awiya went on to establish *diwan*s (councils) and state institutions based on the Byzantine model, that is, an un-Islamic model.

In fact, it was the second caliph who paved the way for shifting Muslim politics from a practice exclusive to the prophet, as embodied by the Prophet Mohammad himself, into a human practice resting on the shoulders of his successor, the caliph. This created more opportunities for conflicts of opinion, unlike the norm during the Prophet's time.

This opportunity, by which I mean the space to shift from the Prophet's to the caliph's policies, has not been adequately studied. It is within this space that the deep theoretical revolution that would influence the history of Islam took place, by which I mean the beginning of what could be construed as a modern way of looking at religious texts—references, and understanding the relationship between them, and modernity and reality. It is at this point that eruptions in the relationships between religion and the world started in earnest, via its relationship with the state. We might find in those eruptions elements that help explain the often-bloody violence that characterized the conflicts among Muslims, immediately following the Prophet's death, conflicts that lasted the entire first half of the first century A.H., and saw the murder of three Rashidun caliphs. These conflicts reached their apogee when the Umayyad Caliphate was established, and religion became a mere tool in the service of the political caliphate, or a weapon to wield against the enemy. Religion started to disintegrate into dogmatic sects whose leaders' main concern was the annihilation of their enemies, rather than building the state.

The élan of modernization, renewal, and development continued unabated in various political, cultural and, especially, poetic, philosophical, and architectural domains, until the fall of Baghdad in 1258. From that point on, and especially under the Ottoman sultanate, values of renewal and modernization started to disappear.

From this perspective, the problem seems to lie in what we know as the "renaissance." It was in this particular period that the call for the return to traditional values and mores, in the name of authenticity, flourished. However, it flourished without the vision of practicality, freedom to emulate, adaptability or the changes and innovations that the Arabs had previously enjoyed. It turned this particular period into an age of internal decline, a continuation of the decline already brought about by foreign invasions.

However, during that particular period the Arabs could have taken advantage of the Western knowledge and technology revolution, and thus ensured continuity with the values of renewal and modernization in Arab history. A good example is the value of distinguishing religiously between the public and private domains, for Abu Nawwas has said in this context, "My religion is mine, and the people's religion is theirs"; in other words, he drew a distinction between matters that relate to city and society, and those that concern the individual. We can cite other values relevant to the sovereignty of natural-positive law, civic and social requirements, and human rights and freedoms.

The Arabs, however, did not take advantage of these values. Instead, they reverted to dogmatic sectarianism, that is, to various forms of violence and to imposing a zero-sum game among members of the same society.

This regression fostered a fundamentalist culture that puts time, in its entirety, in a past. What we call the future became a mere tool to actualize the past. In this culture, there is no room for the future as openness toward the unknown, and as potential for creating a better world. The most complete and the best, in all fields, has been achieved, once and for all, and is in the past. The present has no choice but be guided by it and dance to its tune. According to this culture, the world has a rotational structure and has neither a present nor a future, except as reflections of the past. The Muslim Arab seems like a clone in this culture.

Thus, today's Islamic fundamentalism puts people under a total cultural siege, and tells them:

Look, but only at that which you cannot see,
Speak, but only about what you cannot mention or change, and
Do, but only what God has willed you, or destined you to do.

## IV

Between a reading that makes a lie out of a text, and another that makes a new horizon out of it, the text, per se, no longer exists; it has become mere interpretation. This allows us to say that religion has become an ideology and that, as such, it ceased to be a future-looking intellectual force.

In fact, truth, as taught by the Qur'an, has been denuded, just as the Qur'an itself has been. In other words, it exists, but only in isolation of thought and practice, or is present, but only as ready-made formulas and molds rejected by renewal throughout Arab history, as politics, thought, literature, or art.

Manifestations of the competitive relationship with the text, and the freedom to deal with it, include the caliphate state, belief in the creation of the Qur'an, apostasy, denial of prophecies, and revelations, Sufism, and poetry at its zenith.

Fundamentalism itself has rejected this truism at another level; it held it hostage to political ideologization.

Despite the basic difference between these two kinds of rejection, we could deduce from them that it is not religion, but the human mind that makes renewal possible. When we say the mind, we are also saying questions and doubts, freedom and creativity, rejection and transgression. The mind is therefore incapable of renewal except to the extent of its irrevocable liberation from religion, in a society that also succeeded in liberating itself. It means that in this society, religion is neither an institution nor a law unto all, but a matter of individual faith that concerns the individual alone, and a form of practice that commits no one but the practitioner. In other words, there could be no renewal except to the extent that religion has ceased to be a cultural, social, and political system.

Therefore, there is no renewal except by severing all ties between religion and politics, and between religion and artistic and cultural creativity. The Arab historical experience confirms that Arab society has not progressed or renewed itself except in tandem with this severance.

The question that begs itself here is, why this insistence in Islam today on unity between what is religious and what is cultural, political, and social, particularly since this insistence reduces revelations, in practice, to a mere tool, and religion to a mere set of orders and legal interdictions?

It is an insistence that implicitly promotes the notion that Muslims are a "nation" in the traditional religious and legal sense of the term, brought together by a single factor, or a single final destination, by choice or necessity. It highlights the fact that the individual within society no longer exists, even if he is a Muslim, except as a member of the religious collective.

It is an insistence that renewal has no place in Islam, and that any truth that does not emanate from Islamic texts, or that religion does not approve, from the traditionalists perspective, has no value whatsoever.

Finally, it is an insistence that the "other" whom the nation sees as different from it, or from its final intent, has no place in Islam, whether he belongs to the faith or not.

In the spirit of fairness, we should point out that the history of Islam has known a form of practice that could be construed as being akin to democracy. It is the treatment of the "other," the non-Muslims living in Muslim lands, that is, the so-called people of the book, or *ahlul dhimma*, in particular Arabs and Jews. The practice we are talking about is tolerance. However, although at the time this tolerance was quite advanced in terms of forging an open relationship between members of the three monotheistic religions, in particular, and between the self and the other, in general, the Muslims were tolerant based on a firm conviction that they, alone, owned the truth. Their tolerance was therefore a form of condescension toward the "other," in other words, a different kind of restriction. In the final analysis, this tolerance conceals elements that contradict democracy, or disagree with its intent, the intent that calls for total equality between members of the community, regardless of their religious affiliation. In fact, it is another form of inequality.

We should also point out in this context that throughout history, Muslims failed to root the concept of tolerance among them, either on the theoretical or the practical level. Above all, this is due to the integral marriage, since the rise of the early Islamic state, between the religious and the political, and to the struggle over power in the name of religion, a struggle that gradually became an ideological means of gaining power. It is the position that Islamic political currents have adopted today. It is a struggle that started with violence and blood, in a manner reminiscent of Greek tragedies. Seen from this angle, Arab-Islamic history appears like a continuous war to erase all traces of diverse opinion within Islam, a war that still goes on, in one form or another. Moreover, it is not limited to the two major factions within Islam, but involves other smaller sects as well. This particular Arab-Islamic history is full of individual and collective massacres, starting with the Wars of Apostasy, early in the first Islamic state, to political rebellions and those that took place in philosophy, Sufism, and poetry, all labeled as atheistic and agnostic.

V

Despite the all-embracing humane and knowledge revolution achieved by humanity, especially in the fields of human rights and freedoms, Islam does not allow those born in the faith to leave it for another, or openly profess their lack of faith. Those who dare declare so openly could be slain legally.

It is important, in this context, to pave the way for a critical theory that opposes the political-doctrinal tradition, since the latter prevents thinking, and prevents the awareness that we do not think. It puts Islam itself in a large prison, transforming the "nation" and its "thinking" into an "essence," and a rigid one at that.

If we realize that Islam today is a theology imposed on society, even on those who do not believe in it, and that this is tantamount to violence and duress against humanity and human rights, we shall also realize that Muslims have two options: either they continue to stress the concept of the religious "nation" in matters of daily life and culture, or they abandon it in favor of another, more humane civic concept.

The first option holds mind and thought hostage to legal rigidity, and keeps society under the hegemony of violence and duress, in a continuous war between the "nation" and "society" within the same country, and among Muslims themselves. The second option liberates mind and thought, socially, culturally, and politically, from the doctrinal perspective and allows people to build a society, thus laying the ground for citizenship and for individual rights and freedoms, in total equality, regardless of religious or ethnic affiliations.

Nothing in the above means the abolition of religion, but rather how it is perceived, that is, viewing it in a manner that keeps it a personal matter for the individual to decide on, as he or she chooses, rather than for the "nation," "society" or the "state." The right to be or not to be religious is part, and parcel of individual rights and freedoms. This proves that the issue is not the abolition of religion, per se, but the building of an egalitarian society where people, whether in civil society, politics, culture, or institutions, are equal regardless whether the individual is a believer or an atheist.

Short of that, the mind will remain hostage to the enslaving religious narrative, which says that the truth emerges not from reality and experience, but from text and language. Therein lies the abolition of reality, and of language itself, by compelling it to withdraw inward, become self-absorbed and lose its vibrant relationship with people and matter.

In this context, the well-known slogan "Islam is the solution" seems nothing but a way to ascribe certain significances to religious texts from outside their domain, significances that are changeable by necessity given the advance in learning. This means that the slogan is far from being perfect and stable, is subject to the interpreter's knowledge and interpretation, and is therefore no more than an act of erasing, erasing of things and events, of truth and knowledge. What is the value of a notion that emanates from the belief, not only that everything has been said in the past, but that it was said in the most complete form possible? Why does such a notion exist to begin with? Any notion that sees the future as simply doomed to actualize and repeat the past is contrary not only to intellect and humanity but also to existence and life itself.

Needless to say, a society that truly believes in such a proposition and acts accordingly is incapable of accepting renewal or modernity; it would spell perdition, futility, and destruction for it. Therefore, the issue is not one of Islam's renewal as a religion, but renewal of the way we look at it, in other words, the renewal of Muslims themselves.

Let me say in conclusion, there is no renewal, modernity, or poetry in the revelations. Modernity and poetry are the work of those Muslims who allowed life and reality to triumph over text.

This allows me to conclude by asking three questions:

First: Can we discuss renewal or modernity in Islam in isolation from the issue of freedom? Freedom is not only the essence of humanity, but the essence of every renewal as well.

Second: What is it that religion can offer humanity, if not freedom, above all?

Third: If religion does not provide humanity with the opportunity to think freely about God, and about humankind and the world, why does it exist at all, and what is it good for?

CHAPTER 8

# Creation, Originality, and Innovation in Sufi Poetry

PATRICK LAUDE

If "innovation" is to be understood in its authentically spiritual, and eminently positive meaning in Islam, it cannot but be connected to the "science of the heart" that Sufism fosters and exemplifies. This is so because Sufi masters and poets relate any real "authenticity" *(asl)* in inspiration, creation, and innovation to the depth of inner perception and sincerity *(sidq)* from which it stems, that is, from the heart. *Tasawwuf* is most often introduced as being concerned with the heart. Although there may be as many definitions of Sufism as there are Sufi masters, if not more, given the variety of inspirations through which a given master may express himself or herself, it is not rare for these definitions to refer to a purification of the heart, an appeasement of the heart, or a change of heart, or an opening of the eye of the heart, and so on. In his *Minhaj at-tasawwuf,* Epistle on Sufism, for example, Sheikh Ahmad al-'Alawi emphasizes the need for a pure heart when writing that "the heart should show no bad character, neither jealousy, nor bewilderment, nor pessimism."[1] In parallel, *tasawwuf* has not uncommonly been designated as the "science of the heart," or the "heart of Islam." The term "heart," of course, has become highly polysemic, and not infrequently reduced to the seat of sentiments and to the physiological organ. Sufi writers understand the heart as a reality that encompasses a variety of levels, from the piece of flesh that pumps blood into the whole body up to the center of consciousness where the Divine touches the human. In a sense, all of the realities that are referred to by the term "heart" share in the same privilege of centrality, and lower manifestations of this principle of centrality are none but reflections of the higher ones, which means that the spiritual heart, which is both the goal and the principle of spiritual work, finds an analogical manifestation in the physical heart itself. This analogy is further reflected in the fact that the physical heart is the means through which blood is purified and pumped into the whole body. The symbolic analogy between the blood and the soul clearly indicates that the heart, as locus of contact with the Divine, is the organ of purification of the individual psychic substance that animates the whole being. A famous hadith refers to this principle: "Beware! Verily there is a piece of flesh in the body of man, which when good, the whole body is good; and when bad, the whole body is bad, and that is the heart."[2]

The Arabic term *qalb,* which is one of the most often used in Sufism, conveys etymologically a whole range of meanings that all have in common denotations of alternated motion, such as to turn, to reverse, to tip over, to upturn, to turn upside down, or inside out, and so forth. Although the heart is apprehended as central, intimate, profound and essential, it is not understood as static. The evident reason of these two seemingly contradictory aspects of the heart lies in its being the locus of encounter between the influx of the divine infiniteness and the limitations of the human individuality. The heart is a *barzakh,* an intermediary locus, at which the immensity of the ocean meets with the boundaries of the individual ego, thereby involving an ever-moving measure of alternation, change, and turbulence, as the waves on the shore. A Qur'anic source par excellence for such an understanding is to be found in *Surat al-Kahf,* the Chapter of the Cave, when the hearts of the young men of the cave are described as being both unmoving in their link to the Divine while being ever moved by the influxes of the latter:

> We gave strength to their hearts: Behold, they stood up and said: "Our Lord is the Lord of the heavens and of the earth: never shall we call upon any god other than Him." Qur'an 18:14

> Thou wouldst have deemed them awake, whilst they were asleep, and We turned them on their right and on their left sides. Qur'an 18:18

In this sura, the two divine motions of the heart are quite suggestive, if not instructive: There is first a strengthening (i.e., *rabatna*) akin to a binding or linking, which results in a standing and outer affirmation of faith. There is, secondly, an outer sleep that is in fact a state of spiritual wakefulness, in the sense that the sleepers are completely abandoned, forgetting their own will in sleep, while being awake in the spirit, obedient to the Divine motion that turns them left and right.

This fundamental disposition of Sufism, which some masters have equated to the situation of the corpse in the hands of the washer of the dead, bears a relationship with the notion of *waqt,* or instant, and appropriateness to this moment. Qushayri in his classic *al-risalat fi 'ilm at-tasawwuf* quotes al-Makki as stating that "Sufism is that the servant of God's behaviour in each moment be most appropriate for that particular moment."[3] The *waqt* expresses and manifests the will of God as it determines the *qalb* in its particular state. The discontinuity in the sequence of the *awqat,* which is metaphysically expressed in the Akbarian doctrine of *al-khalq al-jadid,* or renewal of creation at each instant,[4] is in fact none other than an expression of this unending series of alternations.

Any cursory review of Sufi poetry makes it plain that one of its main themes has to do precisely with this "changing heart." As the most fundamental manifestations of this changing heart, Martin Lings comments in his *What Is Sufism?* on the two basic spiritual expressions of proximity and distance, namely, expansion, *bast,* and contraction, *qabd,* as being the most fundamental manifestations of this changing heart.[5] These are analogous to the systole and diastole of the physical heart, which are themselves outer reflections of the metaphysical ambivalence of creation. This is the "magic" of the universe, which is neither "pure being" nor "pure nothing." Being is as it were on loan from the Divine, while nothingness is only a tendency that is never reached, as Frithjof Schuon puts it.[6] This is another way of saying that metaphysical continuity is from God, or more precisely from the Divine Essence, or subjectively from the heart, whereas metaphysical discontinuity proceeds, as a mere appearance, from the point of view of separativeness, a point of view that results from an inadequate perception of reality on our part. "We are closer *[aqrab]* to you than your jugular vein" states the Qur'an (50:16). While humans are the victims of their own *ghaflah* (heedlessness or inadvertence), the Qur'an refers frequently to those who forget that their metaphysical origin is in God as *ghafilun* ("the heedless ones"; e.g., Qur'an 30:7; 7:179 and 205).

Sufi poetry is an expression of, and a response to, this human sway between presence and absence. The thrust of this paper will deal with this fundamental aspect of the question in relation to the questions of creativity, originality, and innovation, but I would like, first of all, to introduce these reflections by a consideration of the concept of poetry in Islam, which is not without relevance to the substance of my argument.

Sufism is considered by many, today in Europe and in America, as the form, or the movement which, in Islam—when it is in fact deemed to be part of Islam—is the most conducive to creativity and the most independent from the dogmatic, formal, and conventional limitations with which this religion is frequently associated. The usual pairing of mysticism and poetry highlights this sense of freedom and unshackled authenticity that has become the hallmark of Sufism, at least as understood in the West. However, my contention is that such a reputation for originality and innovation cannot be adequately buttressed without a full consideration of the profound anchoring of Sufi poetry in scriptural sources and tradition.

The relationship of Islam with poetry is encapsulated in two passages of the Qur'an, which allow us to understand the ambiguity of the poetic word in Islam.

> And the Poets, it is those straying in Evil, who follow them:
> Seest thou not that they wander distracted in every valley?
> And that they say what they practice not?
> Except those who believe, work righteousness, engage much in the remembrance of Allah.
> Qur'an 26:224–227

The main reproach directed at the poets by the Qur'an—that they "say what they do not"—emphasizes the role of words as a distraction from being and a substitute for action. The "wandering" aspect of poets is both a historical reality that pertains, in pre-Islamic society, to the somewhat unstable and socially marginal existence of poets, such as Hassan ibn Thabit, and to the symbolic straying of their aesthetic "lies."[7] These are no different than the complacencies and the perils that Plato had in mind when he proposed to banish poets from the city.[8] Plato condemned the poets for allowing themselves to express images that are not in conformity with the Good, thereby indulging in the realm of moral weaknesses and ontological *phantasmata*, the illusory appearances that prevent us from gazing at archetypal realities. He was therefore focusing on the negative, potentially alienating aspect of poetry. In an Arab context, the perspective in which "poetic lies" are envisaged might be less metaphysical than moral and aesthetic, but it still bears witness to the reputation of poets as verbal magicians, soothsayers and experts in imaginary fallacies. Be that as it may, the Qur'anic "exception" *(istithna')*, "except those who believe and work righteousness," accounts for a kind of bifurcation into two poetic paths, one highly compatible with Islam, and the other not, a bifurcation analogous to Ali Lakhani's judicious distinction between T.S. Eliot's "poetry of accomplishment" and a mere "poetry of surfaces."[9] Such distinctions lead us to conclude that there are, fundamentally, two kinds of poets, whom we could respectively call "phantasmatic" poets and "iconic" or "ayatic" (from *ayat,* "signs") poets. The first are "magicians," inasmuch as they transform and deform reality, whereas the second are gifted with a power of perception—from *sha'ara* ("to perceive," "to feel")—that is normally unknown to other men.

It is in this context that the "innovative" reputation of poetry needs be approached. Let us begin by specifying that the term "innovation" *(bid'a)* is not in and of itself pejorative in Islam. In fact, much of its negative coloring results from the recent ideological influence of pro-Salafi modes of understanding Islam. Normatively, all that can be said is that there is an etymological and metaphysical connection between *bid'a,* innovation, and the creative power. God alone is, in a sense, entitled to *bid'a,* since he alone is *Mubdi'* as being the first Creator, Originator of all things, hence the suspicion, sometimes obsessive, concerning human innovation in religious matters in Islam.[10] Actually, the root BD' is to be found in the Qur'an to refer to God's ability as *Badi'u as-samawati wa'l ard* (Originator of the heavens and the Earth) (Qur'an 6: 101) to create, or more specifically to create for the first time, to originate. Human "innovation," and poetic "innovation" in particular, has been read, in that perspective, as a kind of usurpation of God's power, and a betrayal of the fresh and authentic originality of his creative Word. By contrast with the Qur'an, any human words would seem "inauthentic." God is the first and only Creator, which means that every other act of "creation" can only be regarded as a copy of the original, and a copy that can only be either a poor distortion or a dangerous substitute. Insofar as Islam is centered on the sense of pristine origin, or *fitrah,* it manifests a particularly acute sensitivity to the alterations and deformations to which this origin may be subjected.

However, poetry is, by definition, a kind of "creation" and "innovation,"[11] and this is in fact the essence of poetic perception. According to the eleventh-century rhetorician 'Ali Ibn Rashiq, "if the poet did not conceive a concept or invent one, or embellish an expression,[12] or give it an original twist, or expand the concepts others treated wrongly, or shorten the expressions others made excessively long, or use a concept in a different way than it had been used before, then the name of poet would be given to him in a figurative sense and not in a real one."[13]

Even though the innovative character of poetry is primarily envisaged by poets on a formal or verbal level, or as belonging to the domain of intuitive perception, the two being in fact subtly related, it must be acknowledged that a concern for "originality" is part and parcel of the practice of poetry. Notwithstanding such an acknowledgment, it must be granted that originality may be given quite distinct meanings. "[T]he word 'original' has become encrusted with meanings which do not touch the essence of originality but which are limited to one of its consequences, namely difference, the quality of being unusual or extraordinary," Martin Lings observes. "The original is that which springs directly from the origin or source."[14]

In point of fact, mystical poetry is particularly intent on reaching this origin that is the inimitable seal of true originality.[15] To the extent that it is profound, poetry is *dhikr,* a remembrance of the Origin; this remembrance being understood not only nor primarily in a temporal sense, but in a metaphysical, therefore ever concrete and immediate, sense. It bears stressing that *dhikr* is both mention and remembrance. When the Qur'an reminds its auditors of those whom "neither trade nor business distract from the *dhikr* of God," it must be suggested that there may be more, in this remark, than a mere reminder of the ever binding moral imperatives of the consciousness of God, or more than a reference to a purely intentional and general recognition of God: the term *dhikr* is actually more encompassing than this expedient interpretation would allow us to think, reaching to a point that conventional religion cannot envisage for lack of a sense of the self-transcendence involved in the spiritual path. The best evidence of the spiritual demands of the Qur'an lies precisely in the fact that *dhikr* is not only remembrance but also mention.

As mention, *dhikr* is presence by and through utterance of the Name of God, while as remembrance it bears witness to an absence that it fills, precisely, by remembering. *Dhikr* is both mantic and mantric: it pertains to *manteia* and to *mantra,* to prophecy and to invocation. As remembrance it is prophetic or mantic in the sense of speaking of what is absent, and for what is absent. It evokes, quasi-magically in fact, what is not available to the senses; and it does so by means of its mantric power as mention. Sufism in fact derives its strong faith in the "presential" *(huduri)* function of the Names of God from the fact that these Names flow from the same source of revelation as the Qur'an itself, being both parts of it and the main messages from it. The dialectic, or coincidence, between presence and absence in mystical poetry is evident in its inspiration. Thus mystical poetry involves both a "manic" inspiration and the language of "logic," what in Islam is called *mantiq*. With respect to the first of these characteristics, let us recall that Plato describes poetry as a *mania*, or madness;[16] in other words, there is a divinity that moves the poet, and that we refer to as "inspiration." It results from it that poetry is not "art," in the sense of a technique to be acquired, but "inspiration," in the sense of an inner state of "enthusiasm" that takes hold of the poet. In Sufism, an analogon of such a state is to found in the *shath*, which can be defined as a kind of divine commotion and unveiling.

This "manic" dimension is, as it were, the divine side of the poetical work, the grace without which the poem would be nothing more than an assemblage of words, be it relatively harmonious. Attar's *Mantiq al-tayr* (Language of the Birds) suggests, moreover, an interesting connection between such a "poetic" state, which we today conceive as "irrational," and the domain of rationality. In fact, the *Mantiq al-tayr* refers to a "logic," or a "conference," or a "discourse" of birds, thereby suggesting a bridge between the world of poetics and that of logic. The term *mantiq*, in Arabic, refers both to language and to logic, which suggests a connection between the realm of intelligence and that of poetry. As Seyyed Hossein Nasr observes, the disconnection between the realm of poetry and that of logic, which contemporary discourse tends to highlight, is in outright opposition to the traditional doctrine "according to which poetry and logic refer to a single Reality that binds and yet transcends them."[17] This traditional conception echoes the "language of birds," an intellective intimation of the divine, cosmic "numbers" of things that is a prerogative of the traditional poet. The fundamental bond between the two domains is moreover reflected in the fact that traditional poetry includes a logical dimension, while doctrinal expressions of a logical nature often incorporate a poetical aspect. Among Sufi texts of a purely doctrinal nature, the greatest, such as the *Gulshan-i raz* of Shabistari, are also poetical masterpieces.

What is the relevance of this twofold understanding of poetry as manic and *mantiq* to the question of presence and absence? Poetic *mania* refers to a human absence in the context of divine presence, in the sense that it presupposes a suspension of ordinary consciousness, which is superseded by divine inspiration, or by a divine mode of consciousness. This is illustrated by a number of poetic utterances that, in the context of Sufism, imply a kind of substitution of identity. The poetry of Hallaj is particularly characteristic of this kind of "theopathic" utterance:

"Ana man ahwa wa man ahwa ana . . ." ("He am I whom I love, He whom I love is I . . .").[18] By contrast, poetry as *mantiq* or logic points to a human presence that is as if delegated by the divine Absent. Poetic logic is like a gift, or a legacy from God to man, so that man may recover something of the Divine Presence in the Divine Absence. This is, as it were, the human side of the poetic equation, the human reflection of the Divine Intellect.

It results from the preceding lines that mystical poetry is both analogous to the Qur'an and dissimilar to it. It is akin to the Qur'an as *dhikr*, and also in the phenomenology of inspiration as a suspension of ordinary consciousness, as *mania*. However, poetry is also "logical," that is, it obeys a certain human, formal logic, of which the rules of prosody are so to speak the formal reflection. The Qur'an is freed from such human, formal constraints, and such is, in a sense, the secret of its incomparability. The Qur'an is not only inimitable in terms of its formal, logical, or conceptual content but, above all, because of that to which it leads by virtue of its belonging to a higher degree of reality. The Qur'an testifies to its divine nature not so much in terms of what it is itself, as a verbal system, as by what it alludes to by virtue of its divine inspiration. While poetry is like the language of *presence in absence,* springing forth, as a compensation, from a longing of the heart for the Divine Presence from within its very absence, the Qur'an, by contrast, is akin to a pointer to God's absence, or rather transcendence, within the very texture of His Word as presence. God is present in his Book, but this book is also a recurrent reference to what lies beyond, and cannot be accessed. We could almost say, in a most paradoxical fashion, that with the Qur'an there is a kind of mysterious *immanence of transcendence.*

With respect to poetry, it must be emphasized that it is, in large measure, a language intent on filling the void left by the divine parting from the soul. Let us quote Martin Lings on this aspect of presence in the midst of absence:

> [H]ere below Saints are no longer in the Paradise of Eden, and as things are and have been through historic times, the sense of separation from God and the return to the intrusive imperfections of this lower world can be overwhelming, despite the certitude of the Saint that the state of Union cannot be lost and that every apparent absence is within the framework of Presence. The soul spontaneously seeks a means of relief, and the chief means, needless to say, is prayer. Another means of relief, not altogether unconnected with prayer, is to give birth to a poem.[19]

Poetry, like prayer, stems from the gap that is left when the immediacy of union, or presence, has released its blissful hold on the soul. Opposing mystical experience and poetical expression—as has sometimes been done under the pretext that the former thrives on fullness and presence while the latter flows from emptiness and absence—is therefore inaccurate. It would be more adequate to write that poetry is like the resplendent shadow, if one be allowed this oxymoron, of the pure light of presence. Martin Lings's analogy between poetry and prayer is therefore highly suggestive of the ambivalent, half-human–half-divine, status of poetry. However, his statement also implies that prayer is a more central "means of relief" than poetry, its divine focus reabsorbing, as it were, its human locus. This is particularly true of jaculatory prayer *(dhikr Allah)* in which, as Frithjof Schuon has indicated, it is in fact God Himself who utters, in a mysterious but most real way, His Name in us.[20] In poetry, by contrast, the reciprocity between the Divine and the human, conveys a sense of reverse analogy in which the human absorbs the elixir of divine presence, and thereby transmutes the terrestrial language of man.

There is a sense, however, in which this contrast between poetry and the Qur'an must be qualified and as it were reversed. Let us note, in this respect, that the mystic generally aspires to become consumed into silence, and that poetry tends toward silence, which is pure presence. This cannot be better exemplified than by Khamush, the Silent One, which is Rumi's nickname. Fatemeh Keshavarz, commenting on Rumi, encapsulates a major dimension of Sufi poetry in general: "One may see the Divan as an intense expression of the desire to abandon the spoken word and embrace silence."[21] This longing for silence, far from being akin to an annihilation, can, in fact, be regarded as an ontological fullness. It is extinction, or *fana'*, from the point of view of analytic manifestation, while being permanence, *baqa'*, from the point of view of synthetic implicitness.[22] The higher reality always appears as a "nothing" from the standpoint of the lower one. Schuon's definition of the poem as "form in motion toward its essence" highlights the ontological primacy of the meaningful "silence" that constitutes the archetype or the entelechy of words. In that sense, the silence that inhabits and mysteriously informs mystical poetry as a longing testifies to a feeling that language is "not enough." It is the sign of language's impotence and limitations, but also, paradoxically, the index of an excess of language: the need for silence amounts to opening a space in the false "plenitude" of language in order to suggest the infinitude of the beyond, which words cannot capture. Language, especially in poetry, can in fact obstruct reality by making a potential idol of its verbal arrangements.

This twofold relationship between poetry and silence results from the Word being both a reflection of God and a separation from God, from its source, a mere echo. And this leads us to the recognition of two types of silence, both of which are at work in poetry. The first type of silence hints at the deepest layer of Reality as the unutterable essence of all words. This is the initial and final silence, which bears no connection to the words that follow and precede, while being the underlying substratum of all sounds, like the subjacent silence of a music. It is, as it were, an unarticulated fullness of language from which language derives and to which it returns.

The second type of silence is relational, and is therefore always relative to words. It proceeds by contrasts and alternations. This is silence as the "interstice" between the words. It can be a way to expand the effect of words, thereby suggesting both their power and their limitations. In such cases, the imperfection of language is hinted at by silence, but this same silence can also be a resounding space for the suggestive power of words. So the immanent charge of the poetic word is also informed by a call to transcendence.

Conversely, the transcendence highlighted by the Qur'an, as exemplified by its status of *i'jaz* (incomparability) and its leitmotiv of *tanzih* (abstraction) and ever furthering distance, tends to be turned inside out *(qalb),* as it were, by the Sufi unveiling of the dimension of immanence, in and by the quintessential synthesis of the Book, which many Sufis understand to be the *Shahadah* and the divine Name *(al-ism al-'azim).* In Sufi practice, the Divine Name becomes the epitome of Divine Presence. The *dhikr* is in fact understood, at its height, as an actualization of Divine Presence, a spiritual synthesis of the whole Qur'an.

Let us add that the alternation of presence and absence[23] that lies at the heart of mystical poetry is not only a subjective reality.[24] It finds its deepest foundation in the very structure of Reality as a veil upon the Divine Face. As the heart that moves back and forth from presence to absence, and alternates days and nights, the world of manifestation is itself both a veil that hides and one that reveals. In fact, the objective and subjective aspects of this metaphysical hide-and-seek are intimately intertwined. Thus is expressed the ambiguity, or even the mobility, of creation in a famous passage by Mahmud Shabistari:

> Were She to shake those fragrant tresses from her face,
> Not one impious soul would be left in the world.
> Were She to hold them still so as to hide her face,
> Not one true believer would be left to existence.[25]

The "fragrant tresses" are, in Shabistari, the multiplicity in which the Divine both hides itself and manifests itself. Behind this veil lies the unity of the Divine. When moving or shaking, these "tresses" reveal that which they hide, when set in their place, they hide the face of the Beloved. Creation is a play of hide-and-seek, as expressed by Ibn al-'Arabī: "The universe is neither pure being nor pure nothingness. It is entirely magic: it makes you believe that it is God and it is not God; it makes you believe it is creation and it is not creation, for it is neither this nor that in all respects."[26] The ambiguous status of creation accounts, metaphysically, for the interplay of silence and words, presence and absence, that is so characteristic of Sufi poetry.

"It makes you believe that it is God" points to the principle that the world leads us into thinking it is the real God inasmuch as it wants us to envisage it independently from God, while it is actually real only by and through God. So it can make you believe, in "its own terms," that it is in fact God, by making you oblivious of the fact that the unity is to be realized on the level of *wujud* (being) and not *mawjud* (relative beings), on the level of Divine Substance, not accidents. Conversely, the universe of manifestation "makes you believe" it is creation insofar as it is separated from God, and because it makes you envisage this separation as somehow "absolute" by virtue of it being "not nothing," by and through God. So the separation, albeit relative, is made apparently absolute in that it is not nothing, therefore a reflection of the absoluteness of the One. The universe is therefore a kind of perpetual alternation between an Absolute that is never fully realized in relativity, and a nothingness that is never reached.

This alternation appears, in a symbolic way, in the very manner in which poetry reveals itself as a spiritual medium to Ibn al-'Arabī:

> The reason which has led me to utter *(talaffuz)* poetry is that I saw in a dream an angel who was bringing me a piece of white light; as if it were a piece of the sun's light. "What is that?" I asked. "It is sura al-shu'arā" (the sura of the Poets) was the reply. I swallowed it, and felt a hair *(sha'ra)* stretching from my chest up to my throat, and then into my mouth. It was an animal with a head, a tongue, eyes, and lips. It stretched forth until its head reached the two horizons, that of the East and that of the West. After that, it shrank back and returned to my chest; at that moment I realized that my

words would reach the East and the West. When I came back to myself, I uttered verses that came forth from no reflection and no intellectual process whatsoever. Since that time, this inspiration has never ceased; and it is because of this sublime contemplation that I have collected all the poetry that I can remember. But there is much more that I have forgotten! Everything that this collection contains is thus, thanks be to God, nothing other than [the fruit of] divine projection, a holy and spiritual inspiration, a splendid, celestial heritage.[27]

There is here, besides the obvious sanction of, and justification for, spiritual poetry as a kind of prolongation of the Qur'an itself, quite a suggestive alternation between the smallest reality, symbolized by the hair, and the widest, expressed by the expanse of the horizon. The piece of light, the very element of vision, becomes, when ingested, a hair that is imperceptible to the eye but still perceptible inwardly, in the chest, presumably as an element of discomfort or unease that can only be released through the throat and the mouth. The spiritual reality of the sura "The Poets" is interiorized by Ibn al-'Arabī, and becomes itself the principle of the production of poetry. This means that the negative assertions of the sura toward poets can only be deemed to be extrinsic, and do not touch upon the essence of spiritual poetry. The ordinary *tafsir* (interpretation) of these verses asserts that the negative reference to the poets is a way to highlight that the Prophet was not himself a poet and a soothsayer. Poets are to be condemned because they create a verbal reality that does not correspond to what is, and they do so through excessive praises, lies, and soothsaying. They do so because they do not perceive reality as it is *(tawhid)* in the first place, and they are "associationists" inasmuch as their ego is involved in this poetic construction of reality on the sands of delusory words.

In sharp contrast to this illusory, phantasmatic reputation of poetry, it follows from the symbol of the hair, the smallest atom of visibility or perceptibility, that the production of poetry originates both from an assimilation of the Qur'an and from an inner, quasi-irresistible, urge, since a hair cannot remain in the throat without producing a discomfort that needs to be resolved in and by outer production. Moreover, commenting upon this passage in her biography of Ibn al-'Arabī, Claude Addas has mentioned that the imaginal transformation of the hair into an animal spreading over the horizon alludes to the universality of the message of Islam and Sufism, particularly as expressed in Ibn al-'Arabī's works.[28] Inwardness and universality are the two poles of the Muhammadan inspiration, as stemming from this passage. This twofold aspect is expressed by the alternation between the inner locus of perception, the chest, and the outer horizon, the two intermediary elements, or steps, being the mouth and the animal. The most imperceptible, the hair, comes to the mouth, where it becomes word, and then "animal" in the sense of a universal message perceptible by the senses, reaching finally the whole horizon. The near imperceptibility and subtlety of the hair, which is explicitly connected by Ibn al-ʿArabī to the Muhammadan Seal, may also be read as an allusion to the principle that the junction between the Divine and the human is of such a subtle nature as to be almost imperceptible outwardly until it manifests itself in and through outer creation, word or poetry. Poetry proceeds from an imperceptible reality that outpours into creation, with a final view to bring us back to the "original" heart.

As production, or creation, poetry connects the innermost and the outermost, it attempts at expressing the imperceptible in the language of the perceptible. The imperceptible is intuitive insight, mystical union, and the perceptible is couched in a language that speaks to the senses and sentiments. Hence the alternation of poetry between presence and absence, success and failure, fulfillment and lack. These alternations are thus expressed by Rumi:

> To capture love whatever words I say
> Makes me ashamed when love arrives my way,
> While explanation sometimes makes things clear
> True love through silence only one can hear:
> The pen would smoothly write the things it knew
> But when it came to love it split in two . . . [29]

In the language of Rumi, love is presence, and intellect absence, while poetry is as if oscillating between the two. If love is experience of spiritual fruition by presence, and intellect discursive distance, therefore exteriority vis-à-vis the mystical source, poetry cannot but be situated on the ambiguous and unstable locus of a kind of "necessary impossibility." It aims at distilling presence, but cannot do so without a measure of absence. This imbalance accounts for the fact that mystical poetry shifts back and forth between "theopathic utterance" and "theoretical explanation." This is a paradoxical position, since both ends take us away from poetry as such, the first end verging upon unitive experience, and therefore immediacy and silence, the second end leading into verbal insubstantiality, and even artifice.

What precedes leads us to conclude that the practice of spiritual poetry could be schematized in the form of a triangular structure, namely, an inverted triangle, the summit of which is the heart as seat of the divine presence. The upper, horizontal line of the triangle ranges from the mind as organ of mental crystallization and metaphorical representation of presence to the poem itself as linguistic production. The upper left angle, where the mind is situated, is in fact the very locus of ambivalence, since it can either faithfully transmit or appropriate and betray the immediacy of the heart's intuition springing forth from the inverted summit, hence the ambiguity of poetry that the Qur'an suggests: "They say what they do not." In that sense, the pretension and hypocrisy of poetry is akin to a more general flaw, which is referred to in Islam as *ri'a*. 'Alī ibn Muḥammad al-Jurjānī (1339?–1413 C.E.) defines *ri'a* as a "renunciation to *ikhlas* (sincerity, rectitude of intention) by paying attention to other than God in the accomplishment of outer or inner acts."[30] The term is akin to the root of *ra'a,* to perceive, to see, to notice, and also *ra'a,* to dissimulate. So *ri'a* is not only a dissimulation, but an excessive concern for self-perception and even ostentation, that is, "aesthetic ornamentation."

The closeness and association of the two roots to see *(ra'a)* and to dissimulate or to feign *(ra'a)* suggest that seeing is a form of dissimulation of the true Seer: a self-consciousness that obliterates the true *Shahid,* the Divine Witness who alone can say: "La ilaha illa Ana" (I am God) (Qur'an 20:14). It amounts to an inner *shirk,* a veiling or a covering *(kufr)* of the eye of God, as it were. If poetry is a compensation for the "flowing back" of divine presence, or a nostalgic remnant of that presence, it also runs the risk of substituting itself for the "absence" it sings, thereby closing the door to the grace of true inspiration. It is at this point that we reach the ultimate paradox of poetry as a genre. Poetry is a *shirk* to the extent that it favors, and savors, self-reflection over pure seeing. The poetic creation is indeed an inner perception that has been verbally crystallized, while simultaneously the object of an outer perception as product (poems, images, ideas, etc.). It may become complacency, self-reflection in the first sense, that is the hypocrisy and insubstantiality of the sura's poets, and outer *shirk* in the second, like Plato's poetic lies. Poetry can reveal, transmit, translate, but it can also cover, hide, and obstruct.[31] This has to do, undoubtedly, with the very modalities of poetic language, which is suggestive and allusive, connotative and imaginal, and therefore little adapted to the didactic and legal needs of the outer religious community. But there is another sense in which the allusiveness and subtlety of poetic language may be envisaged as ambiguous, and perhaps even perilous in the absence of a proper spiritual context and an adequate inner intention. In this sense, mystical poetry is perilous because it lies close to the source, and may very well spoil its purity. There is in poetry the seed of a kind of inconspicuous *shirk* that some Muslim traditions symbolize in the form of the track of an ant over a black stone on a dark night.

Because of the subtlety and profundity of its means and goals, it is not surprising that poetry occupies a paradoxical and highly ambivalent situation in the way to the Divine. Louis Massignon used to refer to this ambivalence by contrasting the naked witnessing of the *shath* (divinely inspired utterance) resulting from a mystical unveiling, *kashf*, such as he would see flow from the works of Hallaj and Shushtari, with what he conceived of as the aesthetic and philosophical constructions and complacencies of Ibn al-'Arabī and 'Umar Ibn al-Farid.[32] The latter's "preciosity" was, to his mind, a symptom of self-reflexive inflation. By contrast, Massignon perceived the seal of authenticity of mystical poetry in a certain elemental disorder, or even formal awkwardness, bearing witness to the absence of any formal *ri'a'*. One certainly does not need to agree with Massignon's particular idiosyncratic preferences and arguable biases[33] to acknowledge that spiritual poetry is genuine to the extent that it conveys a fresh sense of contact with reality, an immediacy that bears witness to its origin. Sufi poetry eschews *shirk* and *ri'a'* to the extent that it flows from the heart's intuition and abandonment with the selfless spontaneity of a sign of God, of a sign from God: a traditional "innovation" in metaphysical originality. I would like to suggest that this might also be a lesson for "innovation" in Islam at large. Beyond rationalistic, historical and ideological recipes for adaptation to circumstantial norms, innovation must be "original" in the sense of being concretely grounded on a consciousness of, and concern with, *tawhid*. When understood in such a specific—and arguably rather uncommon—way, the meaning of "innovation" is traditional in the deepest sense. "Innovation" disconnected from metaphysical and spiritual "originality" may confine itself to ideological patchwork or trendy bricolage. By contrast, tradition remains an inexhaustible source of authentic "innovation." As Henry Corbin put it, "a tradition transmits itself as something alive, because it is a ceaselessly renewed inspiration, and not a funeral cortège or a register of conformist opinion."[34] In keeping with such an understanding of tradition as a living source of inspiration, Sufi poetry is innovative by espousing and suggesting the renewed creation of the instant, finding therein, without seeking it, the pristine originality of the Real.

NOTES

1. Shaykh Ahmad al-'Alawi, *Minhaj at-tasawwuf* (Beirut: Albouraq, 2006), pp. 30–31: "Wa dhahira al-qalb min al-wasfi al-madhmum la hasadan la 'ajaban la tasha'um" (The heart [should be] exempt from reprehensible features, with neither jealousy, wondering, nor discouragement).

2. Abdullah Al-Mamun Al Suhrawardy, *The Sayings of Muhammad* (1905; reprint, Whitefish, MT: Kessinger, 2004), p. 53.

3. *Al-Qushayri's Epistle on Sufism,* trans. Alexander Knysh (Reading, UK: Garnet Publishing, 2007) p. 289.

4. In his *Lawā'ih* (Flashes of Light), Jāmī speaks of the instantaneous renewal of the universe: "The universe consists of accidents pertaining to a single substance, which is the Reality underlying all existence. This universe is changed and renewed unceasingly and at every moment and breath" (Jāmī, *Lawā'ih: A Treatise on Sufism,* XXVI, trans. E. H. Whinfield and Muḥammad Qazvīnī [1906; reprint, Whitefish, MT: Kessinger, 2008], p. 42).

5. Martin Lings, *What Is Sufism?* (Berkeley: University of California Press, 1977), p. 82.

6. See, e.g., Frithjof Schuon, *Survey of Metaphysics and Esoterism* (Bloomington, IN: World Wisdom Books, 2000), pp. 75, 20.

7. "Art thou not aware that they roam confusedly through all the valleys [of words and thoughts], [The idiomatic phrase *hama fi widyan* (lit. "he wandered or 'roamed' through valleys") is used, as most of the commentators point out, to describe a confused or aimless—and often self-contradictory—play with words and thoughts. In this context it is meant to stress the difference between the precision of the Qur'an, which is free from all inner contradictions (cf. note on 4:82), and the vagueness often inherent in poetry.]" Muhammad Asad, *The Message of the Qur'ān* (Bristol, UK: Book Foundation, 2003), p. 641n100.

8. Plato *Republic* 3.9.8A–B.

9. "[T]he highest order of poetry will be consciously rooted in Truth. Such poetry can be termed 'the poetry of accomplishment.' Other, lesser forms of poetry may aim . . . to express Truth, without authentically achieving such expression. . . . Below these forms lies what conventionally passes for poetry, some of which may incidentally express Truth, without intending it. Such poetry might be termed the 'poetry of surfaces.'" Ali Lakhani, *The Metaphysics of Poetic Expression* (Vancouver: Sacred Web Publishing, 2008), p. 11.

10. The semantic field of BD' encompasses newness, originality, wonder, magnificence, and uniqueness, and the rhetorical science of 'ilm al-badi' refers to embellishment and adornment by contrast with the sciences of meaning and representation.

11. This aspect of "production" is far more evident in Greek than in Arabic. "[T]he Arabic word for poetry *(shi'r)* is related to the root meaning consciousness and knowledge rather than making as is the case with poiesis," Seyyed Hossein Nasr notes in *Knowledge and the Sacred* (Albany: State University of New York Press, 1989), p. 12.

12. This "embellishment" seems indissociable from Arabic poetry. According to 'Abd al-Qahir the " 'science of figures,' descriptive of the means by which

verbal structure should be 'adorned,' had reached an advanced stage as early as in classical poetics of the 9–11th cc." Vladimir Braginsky, *The Comparative Study of Traditional Asian Literatures: From Reflective Traditionalism to New-Traditionalism* (London: RoutledgeCurzon, 2000), p. 165.

13. *Kitab al-'Umda fi mahasin ash-shi'r wa adabih* (Book on the excellence of the beauties of poetry and letters), in Vicente Cantarino, *Arabic Poetics in the Golden Age* (Leiden: Brill, 1975), pp. 148–149.

14. Lings, *What Is Sufism?* pp. 14–15.

15. In an analogous sense, Jacques Maritain wrote that only the saint is a true "original."

16. Plato *Ion* 534 A–E.

17. Seyyed Hossein Nasr, *Islamic Art and Spirituality* (Albany: State University of New York Press, 1987), p. 87.

18. *Sufi Poems: A Medieval Anthology,* ed. Martin Lings (Cambridge: Islamic Texts Society, 2004), pp. 38–39.

19. Martin Lings, "Preface," in *Sufi Poems,* ed. id., p. viii.

20. "There is an orison wherein God Himself is in a sense the Subject, and that is the pronouncing of a revealed divine name." Frithjof Schuon, *Stations of Wisdom* (Bloomington, IN: World Wisdom, 1995), p. 125.

21. Fatemeh Keshavarz, *Reading Mystical Lyric: The Case of Jalal al-Din Rumi* (Columbia: University of South Carolina Press, 1998), p. 49.

22. Al-Jurjānī identifies *fana'* and *faqr* (poverty) with the "unfathomable black *[sawad]* of the face in the two domains of *mulk* and *malakut,*" i.e., the world of manifestation and that of divine Mystery. What this black is to the visual field, silence is to the auditory realm. As for *baqa',* it is akin, for Ibn al-'Arabī, to the letter *ha* that concludes the Name Allah and "expresses the ultimate synthesis of the unconditioned mystery." 'Alī ibn Muḥammad al-Jurjānī, *Kitāb al-ta'rīfāt* [The Book of Definitions], trans. Maurice Gloton as *Le livre des définitions* (Beirut: Albouraq, 2006), pp. 332, 356.

23. This paradoxical status of the Sufi between absence and presence is expressed by al-Rudhbari: "Sufism is a vigil at the door of the Beloved, even when you are being chased way." Qushayri, *Epistle on Sufism,* p. 290.

24. In *Tarjuman al-Ashwaq,* trans. R.A. Nicholson (London: Theosophical Publishing House, 1978), p. 57, Ibn al-'Arabī makes the point that the outer perception of the Beloved is unneeded, since His reality is to be found in the heart: "Ama yakfihi anni bi-qalbi-hi, yushaidni fi kulli-waqt, amā?" (Is it not enough for him that I am in his heart and that he beholds me at every moment? Is it not enough?). This verse expresses the very mystery of presence in absence.

25. Mahmud Shabistari, *Garden of Mystery (Gulshan-i rāz),* trans. Robert Abdul Hayy Darr (Cambridge: Archetype, 2007), p. 141.

26. "Futuhat, IV," quoted in Claude Addas, *Ibn Arabī et le voyage sans retour* (Paris: Seuil, 1996), p. 87.

27. Quoted in Claude Addas, "The Ship of Stone," *Journal of the Muhyiddin Ibn 'Arabi Society* 19 (1996), www.ibnarabisociety.org/articles/shipofstone.html (accessed June 14, 2010).

28. "Furthermore, the animal's expansion presages, according to Ibn 'Arabi's own remarks, the future of the Shaykh al-Akbar's teachings. This vision

that announces the diffusion of Ibn 'Arabi's work from all appearances falls within the scope of the strictly universal dimension of Ibn 'Arabi's ministry, that is, of the Seal of Muhammadan Sainthood. In the eyes of Muslims, and especially in Ibn 'Arabi's eyes, this characteristic of universality is a privilege (scripturally based on Qur'an 34:28) of the *risala muhammadiyya*, of the mission of the Prophet." Claude Addas, "The Journey of the Heart," *Journal of the Muhyiddin Ibn 'Arabi Society* 19 (1996).

29. Jalal al-Din Rumi, *The Masnavi: Book One*, trans. Jawid Mojaddedi (Oxford: Oxford University Press, 2004), p. 11.

30. Al-Jurjānī, *Kitāb al-ta'rīfāt*, trans. Gloton as *Le livre des définitions*, p. 231.

31. As Claude Addas has demonstrated in "Journey of the Heart" (see n. 28 above), the association of poetry with the Muhammadan Seal and esoteric knowledge in Ibn al-'Arabī, refers to the subtlety of the latter.

32. Massignon contrasts Shushtari and Hallaj, who "would like to shout, as it is, the all so simple coming of the divine touch that has substantially wounded them," with Ibn al-Farid and Ibn al-'Arabī, for whom "the aesthetic concern corrodes the very structure of symbols, to the point of loosening their properly mystical dynamic tension." Louis Massignon. "L'expérience mystique et les modes de stylisation littéraire" (1927), reprinted in id., *Opera minora*, 1: *Islam, culture et société islamiques*, ed. Y. [abbé Youakim] Moubarac (Paris: Presses universitaires de France, 1969), pp. 374–375.

33. "By God, I feel so much love that it seems as though the skies would be rent asunder, the stars fall and the mountains move away if I burdened them with it: such is my experience of love." If I attributed this quotation to Rumi or to Ruzbehan Baqli, no one would be surprised: They are both unanimously acknowledged to be among the most illustrious representatives of the "way of love" that is at the heart of the mystical tradition of Islam. But it is from the *Futuhat*, whose "impassive and icy tone" Massignon denounced, that this cry from an inflamed heart issues. Massignon had read all of it; no doubt he knew this passage, but even if his sight rested on it for a few moments, he probably saw nothing more than a literary device. For him, Ibn al-'Arabī was only a "dry, haughty dialectician and nothing ever succeeded in persuading him to reexamine this opinion which he had held since his youth." Claude Addas, "The Experience and Doctrine of Love in Ibn 'Arabi," translated from the French by Cecilia Twinch on behalf of the Muhyiddin Ibn Arabi Society for the Symposium at Worcester College, Oxford, May 4–6, 2002.

34. Henry Corbin, *En islam iranien*, 1: *Le Shî'isme duodécimain, aspects spirituels et philosophiques* (Paris: Gallimard, 1971), p. 33.

CHAPTER 9

# Innovation in the Visual Arts of Islam

WALTER B. DENNY

A vision of the visual arts common to most cultures in today's world holds that artistic innovation and artistic creation are virtually synonymous. And yet, for most art historians, the defining element of artistic style, as that concept is applied to the art of periods, places, and persons, is that it has characteristics that, although they may evolve over time as the result of innovation of individual artists and artistic movements, also remain distinctive and definable over time. In other words, the very concept of style itself usually posits a relationship with tradition, and the transmission of traditional ways of creating art. Thus a work of art by definition almost always exhibits what we call innovation or originality, but at the same time, by definition, it demonstrates adherence to tradition, because it employs a language of style that it shares with older works of art, along with technique, imagery, and genre, peculiar to an individual, a place, or a period.

Thus the paradox: the very concept of innovation itself requires a tradition from which innovation must then proceed. And in Islamic art, as in every artistic tradition, we measure the degree of originality, impact, and artistic value of innovation by using the traditional past as a yardstick—innovation does not exist without tradition. The pace of artistic innovation (slow or fast) and the nature of innovation (incremental or revolutionary) exhibit the same variety and richness in the various Islamic cultures that they do in all cultures, and thus in this chapter we are not exploring a phenomenon unique to Islamic cultures, but rather one common to all world cultures, that takes place with particular distinguishing characteristics, and within a specific kind of cultural environment, in the various cultures in the Islamic world.

A second problem of definition must also be considered at the outset. The idea that there is an "Islamic" art—an artistic tradition that can be defined within the traditional art-historical concepts of a common style, iconography, media, genres, and aesthetic value—is still a controversial one. Obviously it is an idea to which the author of this chapter subscribes, but in looking at the vast purview of Islamic art across 1,400 years, three continents, and numerous ethnic, dynastic, and linguistic traditions, it is prudent to refer to the art of Islamic cultures, in the plural, rather than subscribing to the simpler but potentially misleading idea of a single Islamic art existing in a single Islamic culture.[1]

This paper will concentrate on a few specific cases demonstrating how artists in various Islamic cultures brought about innovation in technique, style, and genre; the phenomena we observe, however, occur countless times in countless places within the spectrum of cultures encompassed in the Islamic world.

## THE COMPONENTS OF ARTISTIC INNOVATION

In the history of art, innovation may take many forms. One is the development of new styles—new artistic ways of looking at the world embodied in a new set of visual components. In this vein, one might think of the emergence of a new artistic vision of humankind and the human body in the Italian Renaissance, or the startling new vision of epic drama in Persian narrative painting arising in the work of the shadowy Ahmad Musa in fourteenth-century Iran. Another form of innovation is the invention of new genres: the group portrait arises in the urban bourgeois society of seventeenth-century Holland, while fifteenth-century Islamic court artists adapted their sophisticated designs to the ancient medium of the knotted-pile carpet to bring about what we call the "carpet design revolution." Yet another form of artistic innovation arises from new technology leading to new artistic techniques: for example, the invention of industrially-produced pre-mixed oil paints leading to *plein-air* painting in nineteenth-century Europe, or the use of lead flux and enamel pigments to create the famous decorated transparent glass of Ayyubid and Mamluk times. Finally, there are the often inexplicable achievements of individual artists that bring about profound and widespread innovations in art, be it the genius of Bernini in seventeenth-century Rome, or that of Sultan Muhammad in early sixteenth-century Tabriz. These, then, are some of the components that contribute to innovation in the art of Islamic cultures, and that change the course of tradition, while leading to works of art that today show the potential to transcend all conventional boundaries of religion, culture, nationhood, or language in their ability to influence the viewer's mind and heart.

## CODIFICATION AND INNOVATION: ISLAMIC CALLIGRAPHY

The one genre of Islamic art that is found and esteemed in all Islamic societies, and that throughout the history of all Islamic cultures has been honored both by religious authority and secular patronage, is that of calligraphy, specifically the beautiful writing of the Arabic alphabet, as used to render texts primarily in Arabic, but also in other Islamic languages. As the vehicle for manuscripts setting down the spoken word of the Qur'an, calligraphy is associated with the Word of God; in mystical Islamic thought, the *qalam* or calligrapher's pen is a common metaphor for God; from the earliest Islamic times through the twenty-first century, calligraphy has remained both a bulwark of Islamic artistic tradition and an inspiration for innovation in artistic endeavor.[2]

The earliest surviving form of monumental Islamic calligraphy used both for architectural decoration and manuscript texts, is called Kufic, after its supposed origins in Kufa. It appears in 'Abd al-Maliks's late seventh-century inscriptions of the Dome of the Rock in Jerusalem, and in the early manuscripts of the Qur'an from the Abbasid period. Early Kufic is an angular, horizontal script, that later evolved through the innovative practices of Islamic calligraphers into the Maghribi script of the Islamic west, with its long curves below the baseline, and the vertical kufic of the Iranian east, that eventually developed interlacing, and flower or leaf decoration. For manuscripts, the fundamental cursive styles were developed early on, and codified in the famous treatise by ibn Muqla (d. 939), and by the following century the *Aqlama al-Sitta* or six styles—*Naskhi, Thuluth, Muhaqqaq, Reyhani, Tawqi,* and *Riq'a*—were established, with strict rules for their style, size, and proportions, as canonical writing styles, taught and used in texts by professional calligraphers, and incorporated into countless works of art.[3]

Unlike orthodox Islamic theology, in which the period of innovation was deemed to have closed by the eleventh century, Islamic calligraphy, the subject of numerous treatises defining it very precisely, the province

FIGURE 1. Page in Kufic script from a Qur'an manuscript, ink on parchment, Iraq, ninth century C.E. Museum of Fine Arts, Springfield, Massachusetts; 59 MS 84; gift of Roselle Lathrop Shields.

of an educated scribal class with a powerful vested interest in perpetuating tradition, and the vehicle for the inalterable, immutable Word of God, has continued to evolve innovative new forms over the centuries. In the early fifteenth century came *nastaliq* script, today the major vehicle for Persian poetry; in the sixteenth, Ottoman *divani,* the elaborate chancery script of a powerful empire; in the eighteenth *shikasteh* or "broken" script emerged in Iran, an almost abstract art form utilizing tremendous discipline but also an almost random spontaneity. Throughout the centuries, Islamic calligraphic art has manifested what we might call both text-centered and art-centered forms. The rising fame and reputation of individual calligraphers, and the appearance of a collector's market for calligraphic works of art in the eighteenth-century Ottoman empire, turned that epoch into a golden age for calligraphy.[4] Regional variants of the Arabic script have continued to proliferate throughout the Islamic world, from the Maghreb to Xinjang and Indonesia. Today advertising signage throughout the Islamic world shows sometimes startling innovations in calligraphic style, and contemporary artists throughout the Islamic world continue to draw inspiration from ancient calligraphic forms, whether in new media such as oil painting, or older ones such as *ebru,* the art of paper marbling.

FIGURE 2. Page of *shikasteh* calligraphy, ink on paper, Iran, eighteenth century C.E. Museum of Fine Arts, Springfield, Massachusetts; 59 MS 70; gift of Roselle Lathrop Shields.

FIGURE 3. *Shahada* (profession of faith), ink on paper, Kashgar, twenty-first century C.E. Private collection.

FIGURE 4. Advertising signage, Morocco, late twentieth century C.E.

The apparent paradox here is that the very depth of tradition of Islamic calligraphy, its deep cultural embeddedness, its religious sanctity, have all contributed to making it a continual focus of artistic innovation and creativity over the centuries.

What are the reasons for this? First is the ever-present notion in Islamic cultures that within the rules of calligraphy there is always room for the distinctive mode of expression of each individual calligrapher, a notion that strongly supports the idea of originality within the bounds of tradition. Second is the very large number of practitioners of Islamic calligraphy throughout the history of Islamic art. As the preeminent art form of Islam, encouraged by religious authority in almost every epoch, beautiful writing as an act of both art and piety brought the individual practitioner closer to heaven. If such innovations in style are possible in calligraphy—the most traditional, universal, and highly valued of all Islamic art forms—then we should have high expectations for the role of innovation in other areas as well.

## TECHNOLOGICAL INNOVATION: ISLAMIC CERAMICS

The roles of artistic and technological or scientific innovation often converge in the history of art; one has only to think of the advances in the study of anatomy and mathematical perspective in fifteenth-century Italy, or the marriage of technological innovation with art present in much of Islamic architecture, weaponry, glass, inlaid metalwork, or ceramics. The history of ceramics in Islamic lands offers an especially broad panorama of artistic innovation coupled with technological change.

The ceramics of the early Islamic traditions show a wide range of inventiveness coupled with an awareness of the broader world. Excavated ceramics from the most famous period of Abbasid rule in the ninth and tenth centuries C.E. show an enormous range of techniques, but also an attempt on the part of Muslim potters to emulate the fashionable and expensive products of T'ang kilns in China, which were then available in Middle Eastern markets. The challenge and the impetus for innovation in this case was a very open marketplace; as far as we know, ceramic arts were primarily practiced for a middle-class clientele, and the inventiveness shown by potters of the early period appears to be a response to the demands of the marketplace and an attempt to satisfy a clientele that demanded and expected new products, new techniques, and new artistic ideas. The same degree of technical innovation

FIGURE 5. Plate with Kufic inscription, slip on earthenware, eastern Iran, tenth-century C.E. Metropolitan Museum of Art, New York; purchase, Joseph Pulitzer Bequest, 1967 (67.178.2). Image © The Metropolitan Museum of Art.

that we find in the ceramics of Mesopotamia is also seen in the famous early wares of Khurasan and Transoxania produced under Samanid rule in the ninth and tenth centuries C.E. Among the most attractive of these are the kufic epigraphic wares usually painted in black slip on white, whose Arabic messages, generally aphorisms and good wishes, underline the taste and learning of prosperous urban elites of Nishapur and Samarkand during this period of Persian resurgence. In them, the potter's art and command of technology combine with the skill of the calligrapher who creates the epigraphic decoration.[5]

Under the Seljuks and their successors, twelfth- and thirteenth-century Iran saw an especially impressive period of innovation in the ceramic arts, that resulted both from the development of new middle-class urban patronage and from technologies that in turn were evi-

FIGURE 6. Plate with figural decoration, luster on white ware, Iran, thirteenth century C.E. Metropolitan Museum of Art, New York; purchase, Fletcher Fund, 1932 (32.52.2). Image © The Metropolitan Museum of Art.

dently stimulated by changes in artistic style. Although only one major illustrated narrative manuscript in Seljuk style has survived from this period, it is apparent that during this time the relationship between narrative literature and narrative art helped to bring about a flowering of figural art—art that, despite the traditions of Islamic theology to the contrary, prominently displayed human and animal forms in the service of secular and religious narrative. Just as today we rely on Greek vases to tell us the story of classical painting in the age of Pericles, so the decorated ceramics of the Seljuk era in Iran open up to us an entire epoch of painting style, in which contemporary costumes, customs, settings, tastes, and more are vividly depicted. The technique of luster painting on ceramics as developed in the ceramic art of Iran, a complex multifiring process in which a golden-copper pigment that can be very delicately painted on a ceramic surface can closely follow the style of ink and opaque watercolors on paper, is one of the triumphs of Iranian art and technology. Subjects vary from mystical themes taken from Sufi thought to secular narratives and scenes of royal splendor.[6]

Even closer to the style of book painting and wall painting of the time are the works of ceramic art executed in low-fired enamels over the glaze, known as seven-color or *mina'i* wares. Probably used primarily for display and decoration in middle-class homes, these works of art also employed themes from popular Sufi stories, beloved secular narrative poetic texts such as the *Khamseh* of Nizami or the *Shah-nameh* of Firdausi, and the ever-popular scenes of rulers on thrones, hunting, music, dancing, and pairs of lovers gazing raptly into each other's eyes. In a remarkable response of one technology to another, the makers of fine ceramics in twelfth- and thirteenth-century Iran also emulated the technique of reticulated lost-wax bronze casting (especially popular in those days for incense burners in the form of lions) in a group of double-walled reticulated glazed ceramic vessels that today must accounted among the supreme aesthetic and technological achievements of the arts of fire.[7]

One last example of innovation in ceramic art and technology going hand in hand presents us with the solution to an even more impressive challenge: how to create a ceramic art, suitable for building decoration, that can allow a professional artist from a royal design atelier, trained in calligraphy and the arts of the book, to participate directly in the creation of a more permanent, more colorful, and larger-scale work of public art in the same identical style. In order to do this, sixteenth-century Ottoman Turkish master ceramic artists developed a pure white covering for ceramic tiles and vessels that closely approximated the color of paper; they then developed first a blue and then a black pigment that could be applied to ceramics to give the effect of lines made with a reed pen, and a range of brilliant colors that could be fired together under a crystal-clear shiny glaze, an extremely difficult challenge both in its physics and in its chemistry. The resulting Ottoman ceramics of Iznik, closely allied with the royal design atelier in Istanbul, allowed the emergence of radically new painting styles founded in the arts of the book to manifest themselves directly in large-scale public works of architectural decoration. Pounced drawings served as a means of transferring popular motifs and even entire compositions from paper to paper and from one medium to another, and large-scale paper cartoons were used to create the large panels of Iznik tiles with unified overall designs that today grace the interiors of the most famous Ottoman mosques of the sixteenth and seventeenth centuries. In the ceramic art of Ottoman Turkey, we see not only artistic and technical innovation working together but the emergence of innovation in a very short time, with a

FIGURE 7. Bowl with figural decoration, *mina'i* colors on white ware, Iran, thirteenth century C.E. Metropolitan Museum of Art, New York; purchase, Rogers Fund, and gift of the Schiff Foundation, 1957 (57.36.2). Photograph by Walter B. Denny. Image © The Metropolitan Museum of Art.

minimal time lag from conception to final product. Once again, although there is no question that the early genesis of the Ottoman high art ceramics of Iznik relied on court investment and court patronage, it is just as manifest that the huge spate of innovation marking the eventual flowering of Iznik production in the later sixteenth century was also substantially fueled by market forces.[8]

FIGURE 8. Jug with figural decoration, black line under turquoise glaze on reticulated white ware, Iran, thirteenth century C.E.; Metropolitan Museum of Art, New York; purchase, Fletcher Fund, 1932 (32.52.1). Image © The Metropolitan Museum of Art.

Visual Arts of Islam | 155

FIGURE 9. Underglaze-painted tile panel made in Iznik, Mosque of Selim II, Edirne, Turkey, ca. 1572 C.E.

REVIVALISM AND INNOVATION:
ISLAMIC ARCHITECTURE

The achievements and innovations embodied in the various epochs and styles of Islamic architecture are of course well known. From their syncretic beginnings, through the development of what scholars have termed an Islamic classical style, the Islamic architectural traditions demonstrate the same complex interplay between established norms and creative innovation that we see elsewhere in the Islamic arts. The development of specific regional styles—think of the Merinid architecture of the Maghreb and its sister Nasrid style on the other side of the Straits of Gibraltar; the distinctive and radical architectural innovations of the Mamluks in Cairo; the expressive artistry and engineering of the architect Sinan the Great in Ottoman Istanbul; the double-shelled domes and tile-mosaic surfaces of Iranian architecture; the innovative blending of traditional Indian elements and radical Islamic innovation in Fatehpur Sikri—is replete with artistic innovation in both the secular and religious spheres.[9]

There is ample documentation of the innovations in form, decoration, and architectural construction practice that came about in Islamic times. The extraordinary richness of decorative brickwork in Iran, including a magnificent early masterpiece in the Samanid tomb of Bukhara at the turn of the tenth century C.E., was later augmented first by glazed brick, and then as technology progressed, by the highly labor-intensive technique of tile mosaic. In later Islamic times, as bullionist economics molded both state policy and artistic practice, the innovative technique of *cuerda seca* or "dry cord" ceramics, that enabled a number of colors to be fired simultaneously on a single tile, evolved both in Spain and in Iran, at opposite ends of the Islamic world. It is clear that in this case innovation was not necessarily prompted by the concept that "newer is better," as the most prestigious monuments supported by the wealthiest patrons continued to use the more expensive mosaic technique as a matter of artistic preference.

Innovation in architecture may also be seen as a response to the specific needs of the environment. The substantial, expensive, and sometimes seemingly excessive strength of engineering employed by Ottoman architects, and the remarkable innovations both in construction practice and in building design practiced by such Ottoman builders as the great sixteenth-century architect-in-chief Sinan, responded both to the artistic environment—as a challenge to the Byzantine structures of the past—and as a response to the ever-present danger of earthquakes in the Ottoman capital. The penchant of Ottoman builders (and the patrons who paid for their work) for innovation and for what was in those days both a pragmatic and even scientific approach to building, stands in sharp contrast to much of the Iranian building of the fifteenth century, where speed of construction demanded by patrons in a hurry often seems to have resulted in buildings that over time often failed to stand up to the rigors, both seismic and meteorological, of the environment.

FIGURE 10. Tomb of the Samanids, Bukhara, Uzbekistan, ca. 901 C.E.

Coupled with this impressive record of creative innovation, however, is a countervailing tradition of stylistic revivalism, usually reflecting nostalgia for an earlier age. The Saadian monuments of Morocco that in effect mourn the loss of Nasrid Andalusia to the Reconquista, the eighteenth-century classical revival in the Ottoman empire that reflects the nostalgia of the philosopher of history Na'ima for the bygone age of Ottoman conquest and institutional purity, or the twentieth-century neo-Mamluk architecture of Cairo, represent attempts on the part of architects and patrons in an Islamic world under political, economic, and cultural pressure from outside to return to the "pure" styles associated with past political and cultural success.[10]

FIGURE 11. Glazed brick from the Great Mosque of Malatya, Turkey, thirteenth century C.E.

In recent times this tendency has in some times and places—most notably in mosques erected in the Republic of Turkey—often become so prevalent that innovation has been stifled. Those who build gigantic and often artistically sterile concrete replicas of mosque buildings in the style of Süleyman the Magnificent have lost sight of what made that era of Ottoman history so powerful and resplendent—it was of course not the buildings themselves, but the dynamic spirit of innovation and creativity that they embodied. The Islamic world today is full of creative and innovative architects, capable building engineers, and skilled construction labor, and their works are beginning to receive recognition. But in many cases the art of building in the Islamic world lacks true innovation, either by resorting to a show of cosmetic gestures superficially applied to the exteriors of nontraditional buildings, or by demonstrating a blind allegiance to the past. This allegiance has been in some cases fueled by noble if in the end impractical social theories, and in other cases, in more pernicious ways, by using the styles of the past with their intimations of former glories as a kind of escape from the present, or as an expression of megalomaniacal conspicuous consumption as an adjunct to authoritarian politics. Amid a varied and somewhat jumbled architectural landscape, the voices of change and innovation are

FIGURE 12. Tile mosaic from the 'Attarin Madrasa, Fez, Morocco, late thirteenth century C.E.

FIGURE 13. *Cuerda seca* ceramics from the tomb of Mehmed I, Bursa, Turkey, ca. 1421 C.E.

FIGURE 14. Kocatepe Mosque, Ankara, Turkey, late twentieth century C.E.

being heard more and more; the Aga Khan Awards and other stimuli are beginning to result in more and more innovation while simultaneously developing a respect for tradition and fostering a public awareness that innovation within tradition can only occur when we preserve, respect and study the past, rather than copying it superficially.

Ultimately, there will be a place within the cultures of the Islamic world for a plurality of architectures, when the genius and creativity of a Hassan Fathy and a Zaha Hadid are able to develop their creative presence permanently in the Middle East. When that time arrives, Islamic architecture will develop both the influence and the full range of new power and innovative force that by history and lineage it so richly deserves.

CONCLUSION

Three conclusions can be drawn from the preceding analysis of innovation in the visual arts of Islam. First, in the realm of the arts, those epochs in Islamic history universally recognized today as the greatest in terms of creativity in the visual arts have always recognized and encouraged innovation—sometimes in the form of evolution, and sometimes in the form of revolution. Second, innovation in the visual arts in Islamic cultures has almost always resulted from the positive forces of increased patronage, a lively marketplace for luxury objects, the dynamism of new styles, and the development of a public aesthetic, rather than from the restrictions of political and theological demands. Finally, and perhaps most important, it must be recognized that innovation and creativity in Islamic art did not die out in the nineteenth century and are not moribund today in the twenty-first century—something does not cease to exist merely because scholars and the media do not pay attention to it.

NOTES

1. Useful general works reflecting a spectrum of ideas about Islamic art include Richard Ettinghausen, "The Man-Made Setting" in *Islam and the Arab World*, ed. Bernard Lewis (New York: Random House, 1976); Oleg Grabar, *The Formation of Islamic Art* (New Haven, CT: Yale University Press, 1987); and Titus Burckhardt, *Art of Islam: Language and Meaning* (London: World of Islam Festival Publishing, 1976).

2. General studies on Islamic calligraphy include Ernst Kuehnel, *Islamische Schriftkunst* (Islamic Calligraphy) (Graz: Akademische Druck-u. Verlagsanstalt, 1972); Annemarie Schimmel, *Islamic Calligraphy* (Leiden: Adler's Foreign Books, 1970); id., *Calligraphy and Islamic Culture* (New York: New York University Press, 1984); Martin Lings, The *Qur'anic Art of Calligraphy and Illumination* (London: World of Islam Festival Trust, 1976); Anthony Welch, *Calligraphy in the Arts of the Muslim World* (Austin: University of

Texas Press, 1979); and an extremely valuable work, Sheila Blair, *Islamic Calligraphy* (Edinburgh: Edinburgh University Press, 2006).

3. Ibn Muqla's work and the codification of cursive or "round" scripts are discussed most recently in Blair, *Islamic Calligraphy*, chaps. 5 and 6.

4. On eighteenth-century Ottoman calligraphy, see Heath Lowry, "Calligraphy," in *Tulips, Arabesques & Turbans: Decorative Arts from the Ottoman Empire*, ed. Yanni Petsopoulos (Abbeville, NY: Abbeville Press, 1982). Uğur Derman, *Letters in Gold: Ottoman Calligraphy from the Sakıp Sabancı Collection, Istanbul* (New York: Metropolitan Museum of Art, 1998), also has a good deal to say on the subject.

5. On Samanid-epoch epigraphic wares, the classic discussion is Lisa Volov-Golombek, "Plaited Kufic on Samanid Epigraphic Pottery," *Ars Orientalis* 6 (1966): 107–134.

6. For a very complete discussion of Seljuk luster-painted wares, see Oliver Watson, *Persian Lustre Ware* (London: Faber & Faber, 1986).

7. The classic general works on the spectrum of Islamic ceramics remain Arthur Lane's *Early Islamic Pottery* (London: Faber & Faber, 1965) and *Later Islamic Pottery* (2nd ed., London: Faber & Faber, 1971).

8. See Walter Denny, *Iznik: The Artistry of Ottoman Ceramics* (London: Thames & Hudson, 2004), and Nurhan Atasoy and Julian Raby, *Iznik* (London: Thames & Hudson, 1989).

9. A thoughtful and wide-ranging recent general work on Islamic architecture is Robert Hillenbrand, *Islamic Architecture: Form, Function and Meaning* (New York: Columbia University Press, 1994).

10. Revivalism has been the subject of a number of studies: on the Ottoman eighteenth century, see Walter Denny, "Revivalism in Turkish Art: The Hekim Oglu Ali Pasha Mosque in Istanbul," in *Seventh International Congress of Turkish Art*, ed. T. Majda (Warsaw, 1990), pp. 81–88; on the Mamluk Revival style, see Tarek Mohamed Refaat Sakr, *Early Twentieth-Century Islamic Architecture in Cairo* (Cairo: American University in Cairo Press, 1992).

PART III

# Islam in the Modern World

CHAPTER 10

# Liberal/Progressive, Modern, and Modernized Islam

*Muslim Americans and the American State*

SHERMAN A. JACKSON

For some time now the West—the *white* West—has enjoyed a certain "power of definition." In this capacity, it has been able to produce understandings of itself and of others that the latter feel compelled to indulge and either assimilate or refute, but never simply ignore. This is all a part of what I have referred to elsewhere as the problem of the "false universal," that is, the tendency *cum* privilege of speaking as if the shape that one's values and perceptions assume in concrete, specific circumstances are not indebted to historical, cultural, or ideological influences but reflect a transcendent, "natural" order whose validity is obvious to all, save the stupid, the primitive, or the morally depraved.[1]

To be sure, there is nothing essentially new in this analysis. For decades, scholars have inveighed against the excesses of the European Enlightenment. So far, however, the critique of false universals has focused on the problem both *in* and *by* the West. The idea that *non-Westerners* might wield a hegemonic instrument with which to bludgeon others into submitting to the dictates of a "history normalized, internalized and then forgotten as history"[2] has yet to be recognized. Ultimately, this oversight has the effect of placing false universals of non-Western provenance beyond critique. Equally important, it threatens to reduce those who labor under the simultaneous weight of both Western *and* non-Western hegemonies to either a frustrated silence or a "babbling in tongues," as they struggle to find the words to critique either of these regimes without excusing or giving quarter to the other. This is the situation confronting Islam in the West today, where Muslims are called upon to prove, on the one hand, their religion's compatibility with this or that real or ostensible Western norm, *and* to demonstrate, on the other hand, to their Eastern co-religionists that they remain firmly within the fold of Islamic orthodoxy (orthodoxy as owned, defined and monitored, that is, by the Muslim East).

All of this is shorthand for what I like to refer to as "the problem of liminality." The *American Oxford Dictionary* defines "liminal" as "of or relating to a transitional or initial stage of a process; occupying a position at, or on both sides of, a boundary or threshold." The problem of liminality manifests itself in the tendency to speak about Islam across conflicting boundaries, that is, *between* East and West, *between* tradition and modernity, *between* participation and assimilation. The result is often an Islam—or a West, for that matter—that is purely a mental abstraction, un-peopled, un-storied and uninformed by any concrete reality, hovering, as it were, somewhere over the Atlantic, *between* all of these competing mind-sets, histories, and quotidian spaces.

I shall attempt to break out of these liminal spaces and plant my feet firmly in a concrete understanding of both Islam and America. Far from a blind capitulation to the dominant culture in America, however, this move assumes the right, if not the duty, to enter into the competition over the very definition of America itself. At the same time, it assumes that Muslims *in America* are not empty vessels into which some immutable, pre-mixed effluvium called "Islam" is to be poured and expected to quicken into some would-be replica of the Muslim world. On the contrary, Muslim Americans are possessed of agency—real agency; and what Islam in America ultimately becomes will depend on the choices and decisions *they* make.

Having said this much, I should rush to caution against the expectation of the emergence of any monolithic American Islam. And, in this context, I should not hesitate, perhaps, to situate myself within the ideological spectrum of Muslim America. The Muslim community in America is predominantly Sunni, and I shall limit my remarks, therefore, to American Sunnism. At considerable risk of oversimplification, American Sunnism can be roughly divided into three mildly overlapping intellectual groupings: (1) liberals/progressives; (2) modern Islamic movements; and (3) modernized Islamic tradition. In a sense, all of these groupings can be understood in terms of their attitude toward the Muslim intellectual heritage, attitudes that are invariably informed by their understanding and valuation of modern Western culture, thought, and history.

At the obvious risk of gross overgeneralization, Muslim liberals or progressives might be characterized by their tendency to begin with the proposition that Muslim tradition is a problem—perhaps *the* problem— a stumbling block in the way of progress in the modern world. They rightly point to the historical element in classical articulations of Islam and insist that this renders these interpretations *non-normative,* certainly for modern Muslims. They imply that a different historical backdrop could produce and sustain a totally different set of normative understandings of the Qur'an and Sunna. Thus, they insist, modern Western history and interpretive presuppositions should replace those of the premodern classics. This should be joined, in turn, by a renewed commitment to *ijtihad,* that is, direct engagement of the Qur'an and Sunna with absolutely no mediating role played by premodern understandings. This, Muslim liberals and progressives insist, is the way to more life-giving interpretations of Islam that are better suited to the realities and sensibilities of the modern world.[3]

The proponents of modern Islamic movements, on the other hand, also take modern history as their starting point, but this is primarily the modern history of the Muslim world in its largely negative encounter with the West. For them, Muslim tradition is not so much problematic as irrelevant. These movements are essentially Muslim reactions to Western domination and internal Muslim decay in the nineteenth and twentieth centuries. In America, supporters of modern Islamic movements fall roughly into two mildly overlapping categories: "Islamism" (or "political Islam"); and "neofundamentalism." Islamism is represented by such groups as the Muslim Brotherhood *(al-Ikhwan al-Muslimun),* the Islamic Fellowship *(Jama'at-i-Islami),* and the Liberation Party *(Hizb al-Tahrir).* The distinctive feature of these movements is their emphatic insistence on moving beyond simple piety and theological/ juridical casuistry to issues of power and politics. Power is needed to reform modern Muslim society, of course, because power has been (and still is) used to corrupt it. As for the "neofundamentalists," they tend to reject the overtly political agenda of the Islamists and seek instead to reform Muslim society by purifying Muslim beliefs and practices of all of their unsanctioned premodern and modern accretions *(bid'a)* through direct (and often scathing) critique. While "neofundamentalists" place little stock in political violence (they actually tend toward political quietism), they can be quite emotionally and psychologically "violent." In America, the most influential neofundamentalists hail from or are influenced by the Salafi movement.[4]

The third orientation, modernized Islamic traditionalism (or neotraditionalism) is the orientation with which I personally identify, a point I offer only as a check on any tendencies I might have to romanticize this orientation in an effort to elevate it above the others. Rather than beginning with the notion of tradition as the problem, my valuation of the Muslim intellectual heritage begins by investing it with at least three interrelated functions. First, Muslim tradition, not unlike the Greek and Roman heritage for Westerners in general, is an enormous repository of intellectual capital.[5] Second, while the role of Muslim tradition is not to provide cut-and-dried solutions to all modern problems, it can greatly assist modern Muslims in avoiding the trap of prostituting their religion to the latest secular fads, by forcing them to vindicate their conclusions in conversation with their premodern forebears. This can also ensure a place for a number of religious, spiritual, and even epistemological insights (e.g., myth, mystery, the ineffable), which have been largely lost in Western discourse to the purportedly panacean power of reason *('aql)*. As for the final advantage offered by Muslim tradition, this is related, in my view at least, to a particular demographic peculiarity that is specific to American Islam.

Of all the major Western democracies, the United States is unique in that a major segment of its Muslim population consists of native-born, indigenous Americans, specifically Blackamericans. Whereas indigenous (i.e., white) French, German, British, or American Muslims are comparatively few and far between, Islam among Blackamericans has witnessed what I have referred to elsewhere as a "communal conversion."[6] In short, Islam has come to enjoy enough recognition among Blackamericans in general that, in contradistinction to indigenous British, French, German, or white Americans, conversion to Islam among Blackamericans does not constitute an act of cultural or ethnic apostasy. Rather, it is looked upon, certainly within the Blackamerican community itself, as a choice that is wholly consistent with being authentically black—and, by extension, *authentically American!*[7]

Whereas, however, Blackamericans are "freer," in sociocultural terms, to convert to Islam than are white Americans (or indigenous French, German, or British people), this does not translate into parity with their immigrant co-religionists when it comes to religious *authority*. On the contrary, olive skin and Middle Eastern origins routinely substitute for formal training in Qur'an, Sunna, or Islamic law. As a result, Arab and Indo-Pakistani Muslims are *presumed* to be knowledgeable about Islam and thus qualified to speak for the religion, whereas Blackamerican Muslims are presumed to be neither. This has the effect of enabling immigrant Muslims to pass off pre-conscious, secular, and subjective perspectives in the name of Islam without having to validate these in scriptural or traditional terms. Moreover, because these views are not grounded in objective sources to which everyone has equal access, they are routinely placed beyond critique. This empowers immigrant Muslims with an essentially "new Islamic knowledge" over which they preside as owners and beyond which there can effectively be no appeal.[8]

Muslim tradition, meanwhile, effectively challenges this marginal advantage by insisting that all claims about Islam be mediated and negotiated through Islamic sources and a "public reason" that is accessible to all and individually owned by none. In this context, Muslim tradition functions, or at least *can* function, as "The Great Equalizer," inasmuch as it trumps all specific endowments of class, race, gender, culture, or national origins. Moreover, since Muslim tradition tends to privilege process over results, it can—indeed must—accommodate a high degree of pluralism. It is in this context that I see neotraditionalism as the preferred middle road between Muslim liberalism/progressivism and modern Islamic movements.

Contrary to what some may think, however, my difference with Muslim liberalism/progressivism is *not* with their privileging of modern history—even modern *Western* history—over medieval Muslim history. Indeed, on my version of it, neotraditionalism aspires to do the same thing. The problem with Muslim liberalism/progressivism lies, rather, in its tendency to ignore the subjective element in its own articulations and the extent to which this can be as "oppressive" as the unchallenged historical perspectives handed down from the Muslim past. Similarly, there is often a tendency to *compress* modernity into a single, undifferentiated reality and from here to propose a *single solution* for all major modern problems. Thus, for instance, polygamy, to take one of the more prominent examples, is routinely condemned as decadent, unfair, and out of touch with modern sensibilities; and this is presumed to represent the perspective and interests of *all* respectable moderns. Meanwhile, poverty, loneliness and the trials of single motherhood—in America, often poor, semi-educated, single motherhood—are simply swept under the rug as basically none of our business. Similarly, while more than enough time has passed on the Muslim encounter of modernity to render the latter a part of *Muslim* history, nowhere near the amount of effort that goes into sniffing out Islam's "historical accretions" and "viral transmissions" is applied to the construct of modernity. Thus, for example, while Kant and others are all known to have made disparaging remarks about the Negro,[9] there is no attempt to assess the impact of this on Enlightenment thought and what it may be hiding from or bequeathing to us. On the contrary, most liberals/progressives, not only in the Muslim world but in the West as well, appear to remain racially agnostic.

As for modern Islamic movements, again, the problem is not with their taking modern history as the subject of religious contemplation. The problem is rather *whose* modern history and *who* will preside over its interpretation. When proponents of this orientation insist, for example, in unqualified, absolutist terms, that Muslim Americans must, as an Islamic duty, obey the law of the land, how are Blackamerican Muslims to respond, knowing how American law has been deliberately used as an instrument of racial subjugation and how civil disobedience has often functioned as a necessary means of changing unjust laws? Moreover, if the aim of modern Islam's reform effort is to restore Muslim communities to norms and ideals located in the Muslim past, how are we to ensure that the historical imagination of the modern Middle East and South Asia—out of which this ideal past is invariably constructed—is granted no more license than that of modern Muslim Americans? To my mind, the answer to both of these queries lies in Muslim tradition, which eliminates, on the one hand, all nonessential characteristics from the criteria for acquiring religious authority and allows, on the other hand, for a multiplicity of valid views among those in whom religious authority comes to be vested.

Of course, it is precisely the idea of Muslim attachment to tradition that raises the whole notion of a presumed conflict between Islam and modernity, especially Western modernity and even more specifically American modernity. In exploring the question of Islam and Muslims in the American state, I shall attempt a neotraditionalist approach to four main questions: (1) the legitimacy of Muslim residence in non-Muslim democracies; (2) the legitimacy of Muslim loyalty to non-Muslim democracies; (3) the legitimacy of Muslim solidarity with the government and citizens of non-Muslim democracies; and (4) the legitimacy of Muslims sharing common goals with non-Muslims in non-Muslim democracies.

The question of the legitimacy of Muslim residence in non-Muslim polities in many ways informs the value and meaning of the remaining questions. After all, if Muslims are not permitted to *live* in non-Muslim democracies, whatever responses they devise regarding loyalty, solidarity, and the like can only amount to makeshift apologies that are certain to be forgotten as soon as they are powerful or secure enough to dispense with them. This, of course, is precisely what a number of Orientalists (and other critics) have been warning Americans about, especially since 9/11. Almost invariably, however, these critics focus on Muslim *immigrants*. The idea that Islam might recognize a difference between immigrant and indigenous peoples (just as it recognizes, e.g., a difference between a Muslim woman *marrying* a non-Muslim man and a female convert *remaining* married to her non-Muslim husband) is never contemplated. This is a good example of the kind of liminal distortion that I mentioned earlier. But this is not my real concern here; so let me move on.

In her most recent book, *God's Rule*,[10] Professor Patricia Crone of Princeton University leads us to believe that it is religiously *impossible* for Muslims and non-Muslims to co-exist peacefully, especially in non-Muslim lands. According to her, the *dar al-islam / dar al-harb* distinction is a religio-legal *prescription* based purely on the fact that non-Muslims are non-Muslims. Jihad, in her view, is an instrument of what she refers to as "divinely enjoined imperialism." As she put it, jihad is "directed against the infidel, who need not be guilty of any hostility against the Muslims; their very existence is a cause of war."[11] Banned from consideration in all of this is the possibility that the *dar al-harb / dar al-islam* dichotomy may not have been a religio-legal *prescription* but an historically informed *description* born of actual experience. As is well-known, in the premodern world, communities could live as Christians in Cairo, Jews in Jerusalem, and even Zoroastrians in Shiraz, but not as Muslims in Paris, London, or the Chesapeake Bay. In such light, it would make sense to assume that Muslim jurists looked out on this reality and *descriptively* divided the world into *dar al-harb* and *dar al-islam*. For Professor Crone, however, this likelihood appears to remain even beyond the realm of possibility.[12]

As a historical reality, this premodern predicament could change, of course, and with it so could the meaning and utility of the *dar al-harb / dar al-islam* dichotomy. But for Professor Crone, religion—not history—compels Muslims to the conclusion that they can only *honestly* live in lands where they have fulfilled their religious duty to conquer and domesticate the Unbelievers. On this understanding, modern Muslims in the West can only adjust to their reality by relaxing—or disguising—their commitment to "true" Islam.

However irrelevant historical reality may have been for Professor Crone, it was not so for premodern Muslim jurists. This is clear from their legal writings, not only in theory but in actual positive law. A concrete example of this is the famed fifth A.H./eleventh century C.E. Shafi'i jurist al-Mawardi. In al-Mawardi, it is clear that geopolitical reality and not scriptural injunctions determines what is *dar al-harb* and what is *dar al-islam* and that these designations are, again, far more *descriptive* than they are *prescriptive*. In his *al-Hawi al-Kabir,* an eighteen-volume opus on positive law, he defines *dar al-islam* as *any* land in which a Muslim enjoys security and is able to isolate and protect him or herself, even if he or she is unable to promote the religion through persuasion or violence. In fact, al-Mawardi insists that, under such circumstances, Muslims should not migrate from such lands, because, he implies, their doing so would lessen the probability that these lands would be guided to Islam.[13]

Clearly, on this understanding, the designation *dar al-islam* is not limited to lands over which Muslims succeed in expanding their power or authority. As such, the implication that Muslims must "take over" a country before it can be rendered a *dar al-islam* is simply false. But for Professor Crone, al-Mawardi's declaration is all fluff, a sort of tongue-in-cheek theoretical daydream that was never intended to serve as a real basis for action in the world.[14] The real basis of action was, rather, the triumphalist history of the Umayyads and early Abbasids. In the end, the *operative* principle in al-Mawardi's declaration, that is, that a non-Muslim polity like America might technically qualify as a *dar al-islam* without any kind of Muslim takeover, is summarily dismissed, as if this were the clear and only understanding that an honest, nonapologetic reading of al-Mawardi and the classical tradition could yield.

Of course, it might be objected that singling out al-Mawardi, who was a Shafi'i, amounts to stacking the deck, since we know that the real hardliners on this issue were the Malikis.[15] First of all, I see no more justification for taking the Maliki part as the Islamic whole than there would be for taking the Shafi'i part as such. Second, as I have argued elsewhere, the Maliki position was as indebted to historical considerations as was that of al-Mawardi.[16] As such, it too was subject to adjustment based on historical change. In particular, the Maliki concern was explicitly with Muslims "falling under non-Muslim law." By this, however, they did not mean being forced to live by laws that contradicted Islam. This is clearly confirmed by the fact that such major Maliki authorities as Ibn Rushd, "The Grandfather," explicitly allowed Muslims to deal in *riba* (interest) in non-Muslim lands.[17] By "falling under non-Muslim law," the Malikis were simply referring to Muslims *losing their ability to be Muslims*—as actually *happened* in two formerly Maliki-dominated territories: Sicily and Spain. Where such a negative presumption proved to be unfounded, Maliki doctrine emphatically demanded adjustments to the law. In other words, assuming the *actual* facts in the United States, where Muslims have a constitutional *right* to remain Muslims, instead of the ostensibly "permanent facts" of medieval Spain or Sicily, Malikis might be seen as basically agreeing with al-Mawardi.[18]

My point has been simply to suggest that premodern Muslims processed the data of Islam in the very concrete context of historically specific reality as they understood and/or experienced it. To ignore the historical element in their deliberations and thus "transcendentalize" their conclusions as permanent, unchanging laws sent directly down from heaven serve to indulge and produce the kinds of liminal distortions that hamper our ability to come to terms with the dynamic qualities of Islam, past and present.

Having pointed out some of the liminal distortions of non-Muslims, however, I should rush to add that Muslims are also prone to this tendency. This emerges clearly in discussions among Muslim Americans as to whether they can or should accept the U.S. constitutional order. On the one hand, Muslims are often as accepting as anyone else of the rights and protections granted by the Constitution. At the same time, however, as a matter of religious *conscience*, they are often hesitant if not hostile toward acknowledging the actual validity of these rights. This is because such acknowledgement is understood to carry certain theological implications that impinge upon God's sovereignty and authority. This is deeply indebted, however, to certain modern understandings, particularly of the concept of *al-hakimiyah*, or "exclusive rulership," as popularized by the likes of Sayyid Qutb (d. 1966) and Abu al-A'la al-Mawdudi (d. 1979) and assumed to be an extension of the traditional order. According to this doctrine, part of the meaning of the Muslim Testimony of Faith, "There is no god except God," is that God and only God has the authority to confer rights and impose obligations. On this understanding, any Muslim who recognizes the validity of *man-made* law is guilty of attributing ultimate authority to other than God. This is a clear violation of Islamic monotheism *(tawhid)* and an open act of associationism *(shirk),* the gravest and only unforgivable sin in Islam.

Part of the forcefulness of this position is grounded, however, in the liminality of Qutb's and al-Mawdudi's "points of articulation," that is, *between* tradition and modernity and *between* East and West. On the one hand, it is true that the notion of *al-hakimiyah* was unanimously recognized, in substance if not in word, throughout premodern Islam. With the possible exception, however, of certain groups of Kharijites, who were unanimously rejected by the orthodox majority and marginalized as extremists, this notion was *never* understood to mean that *all* "man-made laws" categorically implied a violation of God's rightful monopoly as lawgiver. Indeed, the classical tradition always recognized a certain discretionary power enjoyed by the ruler (as well as judges and other officials) on the basis of which he could issue edicts that were to be obeyed by all.[19] This was, of course, formally institutionalized under the Ottomans in the form of *qanun,* or administrative and adjectival law. But even before the Ottomans, none other than the likes of the reputedly puritanical Ibn Taymiyah would champion the notion of *al-siyasah al-shar'iyah,* "state discretion," as part of an attempt to reinforce the vitality of the religious law. Indeed, his student Ibn Qayyim al-Jawziyah would go so far as to argue that *any* means by which justice is served is to be considered a valid application of *shari'ah,* even if such means should differ from the scriptural deductions contained in the manuals of Islamic law.[20] Thus, for example, Ibn Qayyim insists that if a man mutilates his wife's genitals (and female circumcision was not the issue here), he must either remain married to her *forever,* or, in the event that he should divorce her, he remains financially responsible for her up to the time of her death.[21] Clearly, this was a violation of the letter of Islamic law. But for Ibn Qayyim, this kind of "man-made intervention" was necessary in order to serve justice in the *spirit* of the law.

The point here is not to defend the substance of these interventions but to note the extent to which they challenge the idea that Qutb's and al-Mawdudi's notions of *al-hakimiyah* were simply continuations of Islam in its most authoritative expression. In fact, if I had to guess, I would hazard that their understandings were far more indebted to *modern* Muslim experience where the principle of *siyasah,* or "state-owned discretionary powers," was relied upon, or more properly *abused,* by modern Muslim rulers in their campaign to supplant Islamic law with foreign or locally devised substitutes. It was in this liminal space, in other words, *between* tradition, where human discretion was recognized for its positive functional utility, and modernity, where it was ruthlessly abused by secularizing autocrats, that "man-made" gets conflated with "foreign import," "colonial imposition," or "autocratic fiat" and from here gets turned into a categorical synonym for "intentionally flouting God's law."

Beyond this distortion of premodern precedent through the prism of modern reality, the modern application of the principle of exclusive rulership also appears to be indebted to a liminal oscillation between East and West. From their position as citizens of a modern Muslim state *in the East,* the words of Qutb and al-Mawdudi are presented and understood to have the same application *in the West.* There is no difference, in other words, between a Muslim state failing or refusing to apply Islamic law and a non-Muslim state doing the same. In both cases, the implication is identical: Muslims must not recognize the validity of *any* legal or political order that is not based on *shariʿah*.

It is questionable, however, whether the legitimacy of non-Muslim collectives (such as the ones from which al-Mawardi argued a Muslim "minority" should not emigrate) was ever based solely on whether or not they applied Islamic law.[22] We know, for example, that Muslims negotiated treaties with Crusaders, Mongols, Normans, Spanish Conquistadors, and countless others. That they recognized the legitimacy of these "régimes" is clear from the fact that they recognized the legitimacy of the agreements brokered with them. Of course, one might argue that this was merely a "holding pattern" to be observed only as long as Muslim military weakness afforded no alternative. But such arguments could hardly stand in the face of the Muslim subscription to such principles as "extraterritoriality," reflected in such widely recognized institutions as *aman* (asylum/safe passage) and *imtiyazat* (extraterritorial exemption/capitulations), which explicitly exempted non-Muslims traveling *in Muslim lands* from the laws of Islam, holding them instead to the laws of their native countries.[23] In sum, to argue that it is *shirk* for Muslims to recognize the basic political legitimacy of the American legal-political order, simply because it, as a non-Muslim polity, does not uphold Islamic law, would seem to cast aspersions on some of the most authoritative chapters in premodern Muslim history.[24]

In its own way, this discussion of man-made law and the American constitutional order takes us to the outer precincts of the question of loyalty. The problem of political loyalty begins with the fact that everyone knows that Muslims are in America to stay (at least if they have any say in the matter). On this knowledge, they are often suspected of hiding behind a duplicitous, results-oriented rhetoric that will theoretically concede whatever they need to in order to sustain the conclusion that Islam justifies their staying. If Islam, however, cannot *really* justify Muslim residence in America, any sincere commitment to Islam would seem to breed a fairly nasty strain of double consciousness, according to which Muslims simultaneously struggle *to be* and *not to be* American—to be in order to enjoy the benefits thereof, not to be in order to remain loyal to Islam.

It is here that I would like to introduce—or perhaps reintroduce—a perspective that I think is often crushed under the weight of the modern neologism "Islamic," which tends to convert questions of legitimacy into simple questions of provenance. Indeed, discussions of Islam in the West are often marred by what I consider a false criterion. That criterion typically requires of Muslims that they prove that their tradition or foundational documents are capable of being interpreted in a manner that renders the actual pursuit of, say, democracy or civil rights a religious duty. If Muslims merely declare Islam's ability to *accommodate* democracy or civil rights, they are confronted with the charge that they are not truly committed to either of these because neither is *truly* "Islamic." This, however, in my view, is based on a misunderstanding of Islamic law as it has always existed.

From its inception, Islamic law has often been constituted *not* by translating scripture or tradition into religio-legal institutions but by simply authenticating and reinscribing as Islamic preexisting institutions that were neither dictated nor even inspired by scripture or Muslim extensions thereof. Outside the area of *'ibadat,* or religious observances, this was a basic mode of "legalization," where the move was routinely from the reality on the ground to the parameters imposed by the texts, rather than the other way around. On this approach, for an institution to gain induction into the sanctum of law, it need not be dictated or even inspired by scripture. All it need do is show itself—or be shown—*not* to constitute an irreconcilable contradiction of scripture.

This is clearly what we are witnessing in the development and growth of the "tables of contents" of the early manuals of *fiqh,* where countless disputed situations, institutionalized resolutions, and routine ways of doing things were converted into "Islamic" legal institutions, some in toto, others after adjustment. Much of this occurred in instances where there were no injunctions from the Qur'an or Sunna that required or even exhorted Muslims to develop formal legal institutions, as in the case, for example, of *ihalah* (debt transfers), *wadi'ah* (depositories), *hawalah* (money orders) or even *hirabah* (terrorism). All of this occurred, moreover, during a period when Muslims were numerical *minorities*. As Professor Richard Bulliett of Columbia University demonstrates in his *Conversion to Islam in the Medieval Period,* the central lands of Islam did not become majority-Muslim for centuries after the initial conquests.[25] Yet, the "founders" of the Islamic schools of law—Abu Hanifa, Malik, al-Shafi'i, Ibn Hanbal, even Ja'far al-Sadiq—were all dead before the middle of the third A.H./ninth century C.E.

My point here is simply that many of the habits, customs and "plain old ways of doing things" that were transformed into bona fide, Islamic legal institutions were neither *dictated* by Muslim scripture nor the result of specifically Muslim cultural ingenuity. This raises a point that I have made elsewhere and that I think bears repeating here, namely, that the interpretive theory underlying Islamic law is not a mere exegetical tool whose sole function is to assist would-be interpreters in *extracting* meaning from texts. Rather, Islamic legal theory is just as often called upon to define and impose limits on the extent to which meaning that is discovered or created *outside the text* can be inscribed with Islamic authority and legitimacy.[26] In this light, it becomes clear that the actual *history* of the Muslims, wherever they happened to be, has always informed and contributed to the substance of Islamic law. Indeed, Islamic law has never been *solely* the result of transcendent interpretations of transcendent texts. And provenance has never served as a sole or independent determinant of "Islamicity."

On such an understanding, whether a faithful reading of the Qur'an, Sunna, and schools of law actually *dictate* a commitment to American democracy is not the sole consideration in determining whether the latter may be ultimately sanctioned as "Islamic," at least in the sense of being "acceptable" even if perhaps not ideal. Of course, I do not wish to overstate matters here; the fact that Islam may be able to "Islamicize" American democracy does not necessarily mean that it should. But it is precisely inadequate attention to the reality of how Islamization works that leads many Muslims to see *diwan*s (cabinets), *hajib*s (chamberlains), *madhhab*s (schools of law), and even *ijazah*s (license to teach and or issue legal opinions) as authentically Islamic but democracy, constitutionalism, or political parties as incorrigibly antithetical to Islam. And it is precisely this oversight that leads many non-Muslims to dismiss even the most thoughtful and grounded articulations by Muslims in the West as nothing more than results-oriented, fifth column hypocrisy.

Part of the agnosticism here reverts, again, to the notion that Muslims can only truly embrace an idea or institution if it flows from a spontaneous, faithful reading of Muslim scripture. On this suspicion, it is not enough for Muslims simply to claim that they can *accommodate* a people or institution; they must give assurance of an actual *visceral commitment* to these. Otherwise, or so the insinuation goes, the result will be what some political philosophers have referred to as the "alienated citizen," who "lives within a state, accepts some benefits of social cooperation, and renders the legal duties required of him, but does not seek to share political sovereignty with his compatriots, does not identify with the political system, and resents or is indifferent to the contribution he makes to society's welfare and security."[27]

Let me make a couple of points in addressing this issue. First, assuming as American liberalism does, that Muslims are "free and equal," we should consider *all* the incentives and disincentives, religious *and* nonreligious, they may have for viscerally identifying or not with the "host" polity. Similarly, given that the "host" polity invariably operates from a position of power, instead of implicating Islam as the sole or even primary source of any Muslim alienation, we might want to consider the role of the American state and the differential relationship it has established and sustained with its various constituencies. For the sake of time, let me try to demonstrate my point here with a brief hypothetical case:

> It is ten P.M. You are a Blackamerican Muslim male traveling down a back road in anywhere U.S.A. Your car breaks down and you do not have a cell phone, so you will have to knock on someone's door for help. You get out of your car and come upon a patch of houses. Half of them boast American flags; the other half do not. Which of these houses will you approach?

Whenever I share this scenario with Blackamerican audiences, the overwhelming majority—regardless of class or religious affiliation—emphatically declare that they would approach a house that does *not* have a flag. In such a context, it seems unfair to hold Muslims, let alone Islam, responsible for the kind alienation that might result from such an unlovely reality.

Second, in examining any lack of Muslim enthusiasm for the American state, we might note that traditional Islamic law operated out of a "weak state" tradition, in contradistinction to the "strong state" model of the United States. By "weak state," I am not referring to military or security apparatuses or even to a state's legitimacy. I am referring, rather, to the fact that the premodern Muslim state tended *not* to be the average person's primary focus of loyalty, identity, affinity, or dependence. This relationship between individuals and the state has been described as U-shaped.[28] At the upper-left extremity of this U lies one's primary commitments, for example, to family and tribe. At the upper-right extremity lie their secondary commitments, namely, to religion and perhaps "sect" or "school." The intensity of this secondary commitment is often equal to if not stronger than the primary commitment, especially assuming that no conflict of interest arises between the two. It is simply "secondary" in the sense of having a far greater public as opposed to private resonance. As for the lowest point of an individual's commitment, this is represented by the downward extremity or valley of the U. This is the level of commitment reserved for the state.

By contrast, strong states, like America, tend to function as inverted U's. At the lower-left extremity lies the commitment to family and "tribe," or perhaps, in a modern American context, "race" or ethnic group. At the lower-right extremity lies the commitment to such things as religion, sect, class, or perhaps profession. The greatest level of commitment, however, at least as an ideal, is reserved for the state. This is represented by the uppermost summit of the inverted U.

Much of this difference between weak, premodern and strong modern states is due to differences in economic, security, and other concerns, for example, public education, anti-trust issues, or regulation of the airwaves. Modern, strong-state societies, in other words, tend to look to the state to supervise these, as well as an increasingly expanding array of issues. By contrast, premodern societies, certainly premodern Muslim societies, tended in many ways to view the state almost as a necessary evil. This was neither unanimously nor invariably the case, but, as the late Joseph Schacht perceptively pointed out, Islamic law consciously emerged as an extreme case of "jurists' law," which in many ways developed in conscious *opposition* to the early Muslim state.[29]

This weak-state perspective continues to inform Muslim political culture, thinking, and sensibilities. This has the effect of attenuating, at least as a default, the amount of loyalty a Muslim may feel comfortable giving *any* state, American or other. Of course, some will point to the Muslim world and its various nationalisms as a contradiction of this claim. But here, we must remember that Muslim loyalty to these states is primarily a loyalty to a *cultural identity*, which both precedes and transcends the state itself. To be Egyptian or Indian, in other words—unlike being American—has meaning prior to and above and beyond the Egyptian or Indian state.

Still, given what has been said about the effects of historical change on Islamic legal interpretation, it should be clear that any visceral disincentive to embrace the American state would clearly be open to change. The real issue, however, is whether, and on what basis and to what end Muslims *should* change. If, as Stephen Carter notes, liberal democracy, "begins with the state and asks how religion fits into [its] politics," which in turn, "relegate[s] religion to an inferior position,"[30] why should religiously committed Muslims not withhold their deepest commitments from the state? On the other hand, assuming that Muslims abandon their weak-state perspective, to what extent would America be willing to accommodate the kinds of specific demands that Muslims might make on the strong American state? Would Muslim demands, for example, for full prosecution of fornication and adultery (and we should be reminded that a majority of Blackamerican children are born out of wedlock) be regarded as a legitimate (indeed a reasonable) demand or as an expression of disloyalty and alienation from the mainstream, or worse yet, a fifth-column stealth attempt at the next best thing to "imposing" the dreaded Shari'a?

As for the issue of Muslims sharing common goals with non-Muslims in a non-Muslim democracy, here, I think, once again, our question emerges out of a liminal space, this time *between* immigrant Muslims (as well as their progeny in many instances), on the one hand, and indigenous (read Blackamerican) Muslims, on the other. In fact, it seems to me that such questions often carry a set of racial/ethnic presuppositions disguised as religious difference. Muslims, in other words, are *assumed* to be of a particular race/ethnicity (namely, Eastern) while non-Muslims are assumed to be of another race/ethnicity (namely, white Western). Then, on this filiation, the question essentially becomes, "Can these olive-skinned Easterners and white-skinned Westerners actually share common goals and interests?"

Political correctness aside, this is probably a legitimate and, in the present climate, a very important question. The problem with it, however, is the implicit presumption it carries that to answer it would be to exhaust all possibilities about how *Muslims* and *non-Muslims* might relate to each other in America. There are Muslims in America who do not have olive skin; and there are Americans who are not white. To explore, therefore, the possibilities between stereotypical "Easterners" and "Westerners" would not seem to tell us all that can be known about how Muslims and non-Muslims might relate to each other in America. Let me try to demonstrate my point here by way of a recent (or perhaps not so recent) event involving Blackamerican Muslims and Blackamerican Christians.

Shortly after 9/11, the radio and television personality Tavis Smiley convened a televised conference on the State of Black America in a large Philadelphia church. This conference included top black intellectuals, clergy, activists, politicians, and others from around the country. At one point during one of the panel discussions, the moderator, Charles Ogletree of Harvard Law School, posed a question: What can we do to make Muslims feel more a part of us? Almost before he could complete the question, however, the Reverend Al Sharpton interjected that there was not a person in that room (a church, incidentally) who did not have someone in their lives—whether mother, brother, father, nephew, sister, cousin, uncle, close family friend, or another—who was Muslim. In other words, Sharpton concluded, the Muslims are *already* a part of "us" and "we" should not get so caught up in the mania of the dominant culture that "we" overlook this fact.

My point here is that, while Blackamerican Muslims and Christians recognize their religious differences, they also recognize a historically informed sense of solidarity and shared interests that, however problematically, continues to sustain a sense of common destiny and mutual concerns, at least in sociopolitical terms. Thus, while religion may contribute fundamentally to the enterprise of Muslim-non-Muslim relations, it may make a difference *who* the Muslims and non-Muslims are. And in this context, the role of *history*—once again, concrete, specific history—should not be blithely pushed to the side.

Of course, none of this changes much about how Muslim Americans—Blackamerican, immigrant, white, or other—will be able to negotiate a dignified existence with the dominant culture in America and the American state. American liberalism insists, of course, that, as free and equal citizens, Muslims are perfectly entitled to make whatever demands they see fit and even withhold loyalty and solidarity, as long as they do so on the basis of public reason. In other words, any Muslim demand or petition that did not rely specifically upon the closed, subjective commitment to religion would be eligible for consideration. If Muslims can present their case through the medium of an American "public reason" to which American society as a whole has equal access, there would be no impediments to having their voices heard.

There exist a number of critiques of American (i.e., Rawlsian) liberalism in this regard—from the religious criticisms of Stanley Hauerwas[31] to the calmer analyses of scholars such as Jeffrey Stout.[32] One of my own issues with liberalism's public reason, however, goes back to the 1970s and the (seemingly forgotten) critique of the Harvard law professor Roberto Unger. In 1975, Unger published a book entitled *Knowledge and Politics*,[33] in which he went back to some of the criticisms of the Frankfurt School of Critical Theory and asked about the relationship between power and rationality and whether there can ever be a kind of reasoning that does not seek domination by suppressing or concealing the injustices of which it lives. For Unger, the problem began with liberalism's destruction of the medieval notion of objective, ontological values whose identity could be publicly known with the same immediacy with which we can know a stone or a bird (i.e., because these are the repositories of an objectively identifiable "stone-ness" or "bird-ness").[34] This paved the way for the assertion that all claims to objective values and morals were unavoidably deceptive and naïve. As such, the only way to negotiate public values was through the medium of reason, which *alone* enjoyed the distinction of being objective, *precisely* because it was *distinct* from desire and the world of subjective values and morals.

This, however, according to Unger, was precisely where the problem began. For while reason was "objective" in the sense that it had no desire of its own, it was also ultimately dependent upon desire for whatever direction it actually took. In other words, reason, could not independently judge among competing values but was ultimately dependent upon some prerational desire, value, goal or inclination. As such, while A might be able to convince B of the superiority of A's values, the *real* ground of this prioritization would not be A's reason, which is neutral, but A's desire. Desire, however, as we have seen, is wholly subjective and arbitrary, which is why it cannot make any claims to self-validation. In the end, therefore, it is only because A is a more proficient *reasoner* than B that A ends up being able to force B into acquiescence, despite the fact that there is no *objective* or ontological superiority of A's values over those of B. This, according to Unger, was the problem of domination that liberalism not only failed to resolve, but actually exploited to its benefit.[35]

Now, if the very definition of "Negro" continues to connote "intellectual inferiority" and if part of what makes one "Western" as opposed to "Eastern" is a greater facility or at-homeness in a particular tradition of reasoning, why should Blackamerican or immigrant Muslims accept the requirement that they subject their religious values to a process of vindication that is ultimately stacked against them?[36] Of course, non-

Muslims could ask, as well, why they should accept the values of Muslims simply because they are the values of Muslims. For Unger, the solution to this problem began with what he referred to as the "Theory of Organic Groups,"[37] according to which mutual empathy was generated by a provisional acceptance of others in a manner that provided for the development of increased community, which over time could evolve into shared or at least mutually recognized values. Whether this is possible in the present climate, I am not sure. What I *am* sure of is that predatory reason and rationality will not be of much long-term use in bridging any gaps between Muslims and non-Muslims in America.

Given the power and authority differential between Muslims and non-Muslims in America, I would caution against overlooking the distinction between agreement and acquiescence. I would caution as well against the danger of overlooking reason's ability to oppress *as well as* liberate. These admonitions, however, I would direct not only to the American state and the dominant culture but to those Muslim orientations that might be tempted to exploit the prevailing political circumstances to the unfair disadvantage of an ideological adversary. In the end, we are all susceptible to the urge to try to shape reality in our own image. But we must remember that, beyond its foundational principles, Islam has never constituted a monolith. And there is no reason to seek a monolithic expression of Islam in America today, especially given the enormous—indeed incomparable—diversity within the Muslim American community. Nor is there any need, on the other hand, to pursue a monolithic expression of what it means to be "American." After all, we are speaking of the *United* States of America. And unity, unlike uniformity, invariably presupposes and celebrates diversity and difference.

NOTES

1. For more on this point, see my *Islam and the Blackamerican: Looking Towards the Third Resurrection* (New York: Oxford University Press, 2005), pp. 9–13.

2. Ibid., p. 9.

3. See, e.g., A. Wadud, *Inside the Gender Jihad: Women's Reform in Islam* (Oxford: Oneworld, 2006); A. an-Na'im, *Islam and the Secular State: Negotiating the Future of Shari'a* (Cambridge, MA: Harvard University Press, 2008); M. Fadel, "Public Reason as a Strategy for Principled Reconciliation: The Case of Islamic Law and International Human Rights Law," *Chicago Journal of International Law* 8, 1 (Winter 2007): 1–20. See also, however, some of the essays in *Progressive Muslims: On Justice, Gender and Pluralism,* ed. O. Safi

(Oxford: Oneworld, 2003), where numerous important nuances are depicted. For example, in "In Search of Progressive Islam Beyond 9–11," F. Esack describes Muslim liberalism as "an ideology of and for the bourgeois," "owning the obsession of the powerful as theirs" and "mak[ing] the powerful their own primary subject." By contrast, "Progressive Muslims insisted that the primary subject and focus of their Islam were the 'non-subjects of history'" (*Progressive Muslims*, p. 84).

4. Another, less neatly categorized neofundamentalist movement would be Jama'at al-Tabligh, whose primary focus is on peacefully inviting people to the Faith, specifically to a modern South Asian Islam. Its historical prism, like that of the other movements cited in this section, is primarily the history of the modern Muslim world.

5. It is interesting that some of the most esteemed non-Muslim intellectuals in the West can quote Kant, Hegel, and Locke ad nauseam, and even go all the way back to Plato and Aristotle. This very tendency, however, on the part of Muslim intellectuals in the West (i.e., to draw on premodern Muslim thinkers) is often dismissed as anti-modern, fideistic escapism.

6. See my *Islam and the Blackamerican*, p. 6.

7. We might recall in this context the insight of James Baldwin: "Negroes do not . . . exist in any other [country]." See his *The Fire Next Time* (New York: Dell, 1963), p. 40. To be "Negro," on this understanding, is, ipso facto, to be American.

8. Part of the problem with "Immigrant Islam" is that even where Muslim tradition is not its source, it is vested with an ersatz authority via an inferred association with Muslim tradition. In other words, immigrants are assumed to represent tradition simply by virtue of their hailing from the Muslim world. This adds, of course, a degree of inscrutable authority to Immigrant Islam's "new knowledge." For more on this point, see my *Islam and the Blackamerican*, pp. 12–13.

9. See, e.g., R.A.T. Judy, "Kant and the Negro," *Surfaces* 1, 8 (1991): 7, http://philosophy.eserver.org/judy-kant.pdf (accessed June 16, 2010), quoting Kant: "The Negroes of Africa have by nature no feeling that rises above the trifling. . . . Mr. Hume challenges anyone to cite a single example in which a Negro has shown talents and asserts that among the hundreds of thousands of blacks who are transported elsewhere from their countries, although many have even been set free, still not a single one was ever found who presented anything great in art or science or any other praiseworthy quality, even though among the whites some continually rise aloft from the lowest rabble, and through superior gifts earn respect in the world."

10. Patricia Crone, *God's Rule: Government and Islam* (New York: Columbia University Press, 2004).

11. Ibid., p. 375. One might compare in this context the following standard entry in a classical manual of *fiqh*: "If a Muslim man or woman grants asylum to a non-Muslim individual or inhabitants of a fortress or city, it becomes impermissible for any Muslim to fight them." See Kamal al-Din Muhammad b. 'Abd al-Wahid Ibn al-Humam, *Sharh fath al-qadir*, 10 vols. (2nd ed., Beirut: Dar al-Fikr, n.d.), 5: 462. Of course, this raises the question of why it would be

necessary to grant non-Muslims asylum in the first place. But if religion, as opposed to some more general reason—e.g., presumed hostility—placed upon Muslims an automatic obligation to fight non-Muslims simply *because* they were non-Muslims, such grants of asylum would seem quite anomalous. Elsewhere, following the lead of F. Donner, I have argued that premodern Muslims occupied a world that was characterized by an overall (not necessarily religiously defined) "state of war," according to which not peace but hostility between contrasting communities was the norm. This might explain the need for asylum. See my "Jihad and the Modern World," *Journal of Islamic Law and Culture* 7, 1 (2002): 10–15.

12. Support for the plausibility of this view may be gleaned from the fact that a number of *legal* sources cite Prophetic directives such as the following: "Do not attack the Abyssinians as long as they do not attack you." See Ahmad al-Dusuqi, *Hashiyat al-dusuqi,* 4 vols. (Beirut: Dar al-Fikr, n.d.), 2: 183; Ahmad al-Dardir, *al-Sharh al-kabir* (on the margins of al-Dusuqi), 2: 183. The Abyssinians, of course, though non-Muslims, occupied a positive place in the ancient Muslim psyche, given their role in supporting the Prophet and the early Muslims as the hosts of the "first hijrah."

13. Indeed, speaking of the circumstances in which Muslim "minorities" should not emigrate from but remain in their non-Muslim "host" polities, al-Mawardi writes: "Where a Muslim is able to protect and isolate himself, even if he is not able to proselytize and engage in combat, in such a cases it would be incumbent upon him to remain in this place and not emigrate. For such a place, by the fact that he is able to isolate himself, has become a *dar islam*" (an yaqdira 'ala al-imtina' wa al-i'tizal wa la yaqdira 'ala al-du'a' wa al-qital fa hadha yajibu 'alayhi an yuqima wa la yuhajira li anna darahu qad sarat bi i'tizalihi dara islamin). See *al-Hawi al-kabir,* ed. A.M. Mu'awwad and A.A 'Abd al-Mawjud, 18 vols. (Beirut: Dâr al-Kutub al-'Ilmiyah, 1414 A.H./1994 C.E.), 14: 104.

14. See, e.g., Crone, *God's Rule,* 361

15. See my "Muslims, Islamic Law and the Sociopolitical Reality in the United States," *American Journal of Islamic Social Sciences* 17, 2 (2000): 11–12.

16. Ibid., pp. 14–15.

17. Ibid., p. 13.

18. We might recall in this context a famous question raised by the Maliki, Shihab al-Din al-Qarafi (d. 684 A.H./1285 C.E.):

> What is the correct view regarding those rulings upheld in the school of Malik, al-Shafi'i and the rest, which have been deduced on the basis of habits and customs prevailing at the time these jurists reached these conclusions? When these customs change and the practice comes to indicate the opposite of what it used to, are the legal rulings recorded in the manuals of the jurists rendered defunct, it becoming incumbent to issue new rulings based on the new custom? Or is it to be said, "We are mere followers of the independent, authoritative jurists. It is thus not our place to innovate new rulings, as we lack the qualifications to do so. Therefore, we issue rulings according to what we find in the books handed down on the authority of the independent, authoritative jurists'?"

Al-Qarafi's answer is both clear and emphatic: "Holding to rulings that have been deduced on the basis of custom, even after this custom has changed, is a violation of unanimous consensus and an open display of ignorance of the religion." See Shihab al-Din al-Qarafi, *Kitab al-ihkam fi tamyiz al-fatawa 'an al-ahkam wa tasarrufat al-qadi wa al-imam,* ed. 'Abd al-Fattah Abu Ghuddah (Aleppo: Maktabat al-Matbu'at al-Islamiyah, 1387 A.H./1967 C.E.), p. 231.

19. Indeed, in order to clear up possible confusion on this matter in a premodern context, the Maliki al-Qarafi poses the following rhetorical question: "How can it be said that God has granted anyone the right to impose rules upon people? Does anyone [have the right to] impose rules but God?" Al-Qarafi begins his response by pointing out that God has granted individuals the right to impose obligations and prohibitions upon themselves that He has not imposed via such media as vows *(nadhr)* or *ta'liq,* whereupon a person says, e.g., "If it rains tomorrow I shall make pilgrimage to Mecca" or "I shall divorce my wife," at which time these acts become incumbent upon him by his own, independent imposition. Then al-Qarafi says: "Now, if it is established that God has granted every legally responsible individual, even if s/he is an ignorant layperson, the right to originate obligations in this manner, while there is no necessity for such, it is all the more proper that He grant this right to state officials *[hukkam],* given their knowledge and stature, due to the necessity of averting obstinacy, putting down corruption, extinguishing conflict and terminating disputes." See Shihab al-Din al-Qarafi, *Kitab al-ihkam fi tamyiz ,* pp. 26–28. Of course, al-Qarafi understood such discretionary authority to be for the purpose of supplementing and strengthening the religious law, not as a substitute for or rival to it. One might also note in this context that the entire régime of "nonprescribed punishments" *(ta'zir),* which was widely if not universally recognized by premodern jurists, was essentially a régime of man-made laws inspired, as it were, by Shari'a.

20. See Shams al-Din Abu 'Abd Allah Muhammad b. Abi Bakr Ibn Qayyim al-Jawziya, *al-Turuq al-hukmiyah fi al-siyasah al-shar'iyah,* ed. S. 'Imran (Cairo: Dar al-Hadith), 1423 A.H./2002 C.E.), pp. 10, 18, and passim.

21. See ibid., p. 50. Actually, Ibn Qayyim claims that it was 'Ali b. Abi Talib who handed down this ruling, which Ibn Qayyim emphatically supports, explaining why it is correct.

22. Of course, we should note, for clarity's sake, a fundamental distinction between premodern and modern states. Premodern states, certainly in the Muslim world, did not operate on the principle of legal monism (i.e., a single law of the land uniformly applied across the board); nor did the state by definition exercise a complete monopoly over law. For more on this point, see my "Legal Pluralism Between Islam and the Nation-State: Romantic Medievalism or Pragmatic Modernity?" *Fordham International Law Journal* 30, 1 (2006): 158–176. On this distinction, recognizing the 'legitimacy' of a premodern state might not have the same implications as recognizing the legitimacy of a modern state. On the other hand, modern states, with their constitutional orders, generally extend to their citizens rights and protections that were unknown in the premodern world, an important point in light of such concepts as al-Mawardi's *dar al-islam.*

23. See *Encyclopedia of Islam* (3rd rev. ed., Leiden : Brill, 2007–), *aman* and *imtiyazat*.

24. It should be noted that recognizing the "basic legitimacy" of America as a polity where Muslims can honestly live as Muslims and peacefully co-exist with non-Muslims is not the same as saying that everything about America comports with Muslim ideals or that Muslim Americans, as American citizens, should not work to establish the kind of society that does.

25. See Richard Bulliett, *Conversion to Islam in the Medieval Period: An Essay in Quantitative History* (Cambridge, MA: Harvard University Press, 1979).

26. On this point, see my "Fiction and Formalism: Towards a Functional Analysis of *Usul al-Fiqh*," in *Studies in Islamic Legal Theory*, ed. B. Weiss (Leiden: Brill, 2000), pp. 177–80.

27. Andrew March, "Liberal Citizenship," *Philosophy & Public Affairs* 34, 4. (2006): 383.

28. On this conception of U-shaped and inverted U-shaped states, see S.P. Huntington, *Who Are We? The Challenges to America's National Identity* (New York: Simon & Schuster, 2004), pp. 16–17.

29. Joseph Schacht, *An Introduction to Islamic Law* (Oxford: Clarendon Press, 1964), p. 5.

30. S.L. Carter, *God's Name in Vain: The Wrongs and Rights of Religion in Politics* (New York: Basic Books, 2000), p. 2.

31. See, e.g., Stanley Hauerwas, *A Better Hope: Resources for a Church Confronting Capitalism, Democracy, and Postmodernity* (Grand Rapids, MI: Brazos Press, 2000), 23–34.

32. See Jeffrey Stout, *Democracy and Tradition* (Princeton, NJ: Princeton University Press, 2004), 63–77.

33. Roberto Mangabeira Unger, *Knowledge and Politics* (New York: Free Press, 1975).

34. Ibid., pp. 31ff.

35. Ibid., pp. 43–44.

36. This is a particularly relevant question given Rawlsian public reason's tendency to force us into "un-storied" conversations, where, e.g., on purely "reasonable" grounds there would be no more justification for a Jew to distrust a German then there is for a German to distrust a Jew. In the context of their storied encounter, however, not reason but experience, ineffable as it may be, would seem to justify a difference here. Similarly, the *reasoned* arguments of Blackamericans regarding whatever distrust they might have of, say democracy or the jury-system, may not be convincing. But their story (closed and subjective as it may be) as a subjugated people in a *modern* democracy would seem to add at least some internal consistency here.

37. Unger, *Knowledge and Politics*, 236–95.

CHAPTER 11

# *Hijab* and Choice

## Between Politics and Theology

ZIBA MIR-HOSSEINI

How women dress in public is not only a prominent marker of Muslim identity, it is now one of the most contested issues among Muslims.[1] *Hijab*[2]—defined by classical jurists as a Muslim woman's duty to cover all parts of her body apart from hands and face in public and in the presence of unrelated men[3]—is now regarded as a central Islamic mandate. But what exactly does "cover" mean? Are particular forms of dress prescribed? Must the hair be covered? Who has the right to define the form and limits of covering? Do women themselves have any choice in this? Does the state have the right to define *hijab,* to enforce it, or to ban it?

Since the nineteenth century, these issues have been a major site of ideological struggle between the forces of traditionalism and modernity in the Muslim world. With the resurgence of Islam as a political and spiritual force in the 1960s, they became an arena where Islamist and feminist discourses and rhetoric have clashed head-on. Political Islam and its slogan of "return to Shari'a" turned *hijab* into a symbol of a distinct Muslim identity and a claim to religious authenticity. For Islamists, *hijab* is a religious mandate that defines women's place in society and protects them from being treated as sex objects. For feminists, on the other hand, *hijab* is a symbol of oppression, a patriarchal mandate that denies Muslim women the basic rights to control their own bodies and to choose what to wear.

Until the early 1990s, the debate over *hijab* remained polemical, emotional, and a hostage to identity politics and the legacy of colonialism. There was little dialogue between adherents of the two positions, each side judging the other's position and arguments by its own dogmas and frames of reference. Islamists failed to produce any new or significant juristic arguments, and their policy of imposing *hijab* in countries where they gained power, like Iran and Sudan, were met with women's resistance. At the same time, the ways in which some Muslim women were finding *hijab* empowering, and were making a conscious choice to adopt it, undermined the force of feminist objections. There were also signs of the emergence of a new discourse on *hijab* as a Muslim woman's right, and consensus developed among reformist Muslim thinkers that reflected the following: wearing or not wearing *hijab* is a matter of personal belief and imposing or banning it is a violation of women's human rights. As the language of choice and rights crept in, the terms of the debate began to change. New juristic arguments and positions were advanced.

In this chapter I examine, from a critical feminist perspective, the evolution of debates and juristic positions on *hijab* in Islamic legal tradition. I begin by examining the assumptions that underlie the rulings on *hijab* in classical jurisprudence *(fiqh)*; then, proceed to show how these assumptions have been reproduced, challenged, and redefined in contemporary legal discourses. I do this with reference to Iran, where political Islam had its biggest success in 1979, and which is now one of the primary sites of new juristic arguments and positions on *hijab*. I conclude by exploring the implication of these debates developments for establishing common ground between Islamist and feminist discourses on *hijab*, and for the politics of innovation in Islamic legal tradition.

## *HIJAB* IN CLASSICAL FIQH: "COVERING" OR "CONFINEMENT"

Classical Islamic legal texts—at least the genre that sets out rulings *(ahkam)*, or what we can call "positive law"—contain no explicit rulings on women's dress, nor on how women should appear in public.[4] They do not use the term *hijab*,[5] and they use *sitr* (covering) to discuss the issue of dress for both men and women, but only in two contexts: first, rulings for covering the body during prayers, and secondly, rulings that govern a man's "gaze" at a woman prior to marriage.

The rules are minimal, but clear-cut. During prayer, both men and women must cover their *'awrah,* their private parts; for men, this is the area between knees and navel, but for women it means all parts of the body apart from hands, feet and face. Regarding the "gaze," it is forbidden for men to look at the uncovered body of women to whom he is not closely related—a ban that can be removed when a man wants to contract a marriage and needs to inspect the woman he intends to marry. The rulings on covering during prayer are discussed in the Book of Prayer and are among *'ibadat* (ritual/worship acts), while the rulings on "gaze" come in the Book of Marriage, and fall under *mu'amilat* (social/contractual acts).[6]

There is, however, another notion of *hijab* that remains implicit in these texts: "confinement." This notion rests on two interrelated juristic constructs that cut across *'ibadat* and *mu'amilat,* the two aspects of *fiqh.* The first construct defines a woman's whole body as *'awrah,* a sexual zone, that must be covered both during prayers (before God) and in society (before men). The second construct considers a woman's sexuality to be *fitna,* as a source of danger to public order, and consequently grants men the right to control women's movements.

The rulings related to the first construct are found in the Book of Prayer *(kitab al-salah)* under "covering of private parts" *(sitr al-'awrah),* which remains the only place that requires the covering of specific parts of body. The seminal text on comparative jurisprudence *(Bidayat al-Mujtahid)* by the great jurist and philosopher Ibn Rushd sums up the state of the juristic debates up to his time, the twelfth century C.E., and allows us to glimpse the agreements and disagreements.[7] "The jurists agreed that covering the private parts is an absolute obligation, but they disagreed on whether it is a condition for the validity of prayer? Similarly, they differed about the area of the body, for a woman and a man, that is delineated by the term *'awrah.*"[8] For a woman: "Most of the jurists maintained her entire body constitutes *'awrah,* except for the face and hands. Abu Hanifa maintained that her feet are not a part of the *'awrah.* Abu Bahr ibn 'Abd al-Rahman and Ahmad said that her entire body is *'awrah.*"[9]

Their disagreement:

> is based on the possible interpretation of the words of the Exalted, "And to display of their adornment only that which is apparent," that is whether the exemption relates to defined parts or those parts that she cannot (but help) display? Those who maintained that the intended exemption is only for those parts that she cannot help but display while moving, said that her

entire body is *'awrah,* even her back. They agreed for this on the basis of the general implication of the words of the Exalted, "O Prophet! Tell thy wives and thy daughters and the women of the believers to draw their cloaks close around them. That will make them recognizable and they will not be exposed to harm."[10]

"Those who held that the intended exemption is for what is customarily not covered, that is, the face and the hands, said that these are not included in the *'awrah.* They (further) argued for this on the grounds that a woman does not cover her face during hajj," Ibn Rushd observes.[11]

It is not my intention to enter into a discussion on the theological validity of the "general rule" or whether such a reading of the Qur'anic verse is justified. Such questions have been raised by the emerging feminist scholarship in Islam, which tells us that the theological validity of classical rulings on *hijab* is derived from Qur'anic commentaries rather than Qur'anic prescriptions.[12] Another strand of this scholarship tells us that the further such rulings were from the time of revelation, the more women's presence in public space was constrained; and by the time the *fiqh* schools were consolidated, women's voices in the production of religious knowledge were silenced and they were reduced to sexual beings and placed under the authority of men. These developments were linked to political and socioeconomic factors; in particular, during Abbasid rule with the public presence of female slaves who were treated as sexual commodities and forbidden to cover in order to distinguish them from free women. Significantly, classical jurists considered the *'awrah* of a female slave or servant to be different from that of a free woman; some held it to be the same as that of men, between navel and knees; others argued that it was between chest and knees.[13] Clearly, in deducing the *hijab* ruling, classical jurists were influenced by considerations of status and class rather than by a "divine mandate" for women to cover their hair, as the Islamists now claim.

Women's exclusion from public and political life was reinforced by the way classical jurists defined the marriage contract, in which a man acquires rights over his wife's movement and sexuality. The marriage contract, called *'aqd al-nikah* (contract of coitus), has three elements: the offer *(ijab)* by the woman or her guardian *(wali)*, the acceptance *(qabul)* by the man, and the payment of dower *(mahr)*, a sum of money or any valuable that the husband pays or undertakes to pay to the bride before or after consummation.[14] In discussing marriage and its legal structure, classical jurists often used the analogy of the contract of sale, and they had no qualms about drawing parallels between the two. For instance, this is how Muhaqqiq al-Hilli, the renowned thirteenth-century Shi'a jurist, opens his discussion of marriage: "[I]t has been said that [marriage] is a contract whose object is that of dominion over the vagina *(buz')*, without the right of its possession. It has also been said that it is a verbal contract that first establishes the right to sexual intercourse, that is to say: it is not like buying a female slave when the man acquires the right of intercourse as a consequence of the possession of the slave."[15]

Sidi Khalil, the prominent fourteenth-century Maliki jurist, was equally explicit. "When a woman marries, she sells a part of her person. In the market, one buys merchandise; in marriage, the husband buys the genital arvum mulieris."[16]

The twelfth-century philosopher and jurist Al-Ghazali likewise drew parallels between the status of wives and female slaves, to whose sexual services the husbands or owners were entitled. In his monumental work *Revival of Religious Sciences,* he devoted a book to defining the proper code of conduct in marriage (*Adab al-Nikah,* Etiquette of Marriage), which makes explicit the assumptions in the *fiqh* rulings on marriage. Significantly, he ends the discussion with a section on "Rights of the Husband," which begins: "It is enough to say that marriage is a kind of slavery, for a wife is a slave to her husband. She owes her husband absolute obedience in whatever he may demand of her, where she herself is concerned, as long as no sin is involved."[17]

Interestingly, in this section Ghazali does not invoke any Qur'anic verses but relies on hadith (the sayings of the Prophet) literature to enjoin women to obey their husbands and remain at home.[18]

The Prophet said: "A woman is closest to the face of her Lord when she is inside her house. The prayer she performs in the courtyard of her house is more meritorious than the prayer she performs in the mosque, while her prayer in her apartment is more meritorious than her prayer in the courtyard of her house, and her prayer in her inner chamber is more meritorious than her prayer in her apartment."

That is because it is more private. This is why the Prophet said: "A woman is nakedness, so when she goes out, the devil gets up to look at her. Woman has ten nakednesses. When she gets married, her husband veils one of them, when she dies, the grave veils all ten."[19]

I am not suggesting that classical jurists conceptualized marriage as either a sale or as slavery.[20] Certainly there were significant differences and disagreements about this among the schools, and debates within each, with legal and practical implications for women.[21] Even statements such as those quoted above distinguish between the right of access to the woman's sexual and reproductive faculties (which her husband acquires) and the right over her person (which he does not). Rather, my point is that classical *fiqh* constructed women's sexuality as a commodity that men could acquire either through the marriage contract or by buying female slaves. This construction informs *fiqh* rulings on *hijab*, as does the juristic construction of women's whole body as *'awrah*, a shameful object that must be covered, for which the best means is confinement.

## *HIJAB* IN CONTEMPORARY ISLAMIC LEGAL DISCOURSES

This implicit conception of *hijab* (symbolized by the face veil) became the main focus of criticism and debate in the first wave of Islamic modernist literature, starting with Qāsim Amīn's *Taḥrīr al-mar'ah (The Liberation of Women)* published at the end of the nineteenth century.[22] But *hijab* as confinement was explicitly defended in the twentieth century by Islamic ideologues such as Abul A'la al-Mawdudi in his famous *Purdah*, a text that is now accepted in some Islamist circles as the "Islamic position."[23] Amīn unleashed a debate whose terms continue to be defined by the politics of anti-colonialism and the Muslim world's encounter with modernity, in which *hijab* has been a symbolic battleground. Muslim societies were experiencing profound change, rulers or colonial authorities were taking measures for modernization, secular systems of law and education were expanding and the first girls' schools were established. Muslim reformers such as Jamal al-Din Afghani and Mohammad Abdu were advocating religious reforms, and *fiqh* and its practitioners were losing their intellectual and political clout. As part of modernization policies, some states introduced dress laws, actively encouraging the adoption of European styles of clothing.

These developments were making the notion of *hijab* as confinement increasingly irrelevant to people's experiences and women's aspirations, and gave rise to a new genre of texts, with "*hijab*" in the title or as the main theme or concern. These texts, until recently written exclusively by men, are published by religious publishing houses all over the Muslim world and available in different languages. The stated aims are to shed new light on "the status of women in Islam" or to clarify "misunderstanding about the laws of Islam." Many of the authors, however, are neither jurists *(fuqaha)* nor strictly legal in their reasoning and arguments, which make them more accessible to the general public. While distancing themselves from the *fiqh* notion of *hijab* as confinement, and emphasizing instead the classical rulings on covering, the vast majority of *hijab* texts merely reproduce these rulings; they do not engage with the juristic logic and social and sexual theories and assumptions underlying them. Many of these texts sound like double-talk; one good example in English is Jamal Badawi's *The Muslim Women's Dress According to the Qur'an and Sunnah*.[24] Badawi starts by stressing the importance of the subject of "Muslim women's dress" (he does not use the term *hijab*) to which the "Shari'ah assigns moral, social, and legal dimensions." In the next sentence, he closes the door to rational argument, stating: "One basic requirement to be a true believer according to the Qur'an is to make one's opinions, feelings and inclinations subservient to whatever Allah and his Messenger have decided." Other authors, however, who produce rational arguments for *fiqh* rulings, rely on modern sciences, namely, biology, psychology, and sociology, not classical jurisprudential texts. In some of these, like al-Mawdudi's *Purdah*, *hijab* is less a set of rulings for covering than an organizing principle in society and an ideology for women's subjugation.

This literature, as I have argued elsewhere, should be seen as a response to the changed status of women in society and their new aspirations; it has created its own subject: "Islamic dress" or "*hijab* laws in Islam."[25] A shift in focus in this literature came about simultaneously with the rise of political Islam, when we see the shaping of a new discourse and new juristic positions on *hijab*. To appreciate the social and political contexts in which they emerged, let us take a closer look at the debate in Iran.

COMPETING NOTIONS OF *HIJAB* IN IRAN

In Iran, as elsewhere in the Muslim world, the debate over the two notions of *hijab* emerged at the end of the nineteenth century, as part of a wider debate over modernization and the spread of secular education—developments seen by the religious establishment as a threat to its authority. Though *hijab* was debated during the Constitutional era (1906–11), when the first girls' schools were established, it only became a "problem" in the 1930s, when Reza Shah Pahlavi embarked on a policy of compulsory "unveiling" or *kashf-e hejab,* as part of his program for modernizing and secularizing Iran. The policy reached its peak in 1936 with a law that made wearing of *hijab*—now defined as traditional Iranian attire *(chador)* or its modern version (a large scarf)—an offense, and women who defied it were arrested and their covering forcibly removed. The declared aim was to promote women's rights and their liberation, and the assumption was that in replacing traditional women's dress with Western styles, it would lead to women's increased participation in society. But the banning of the chador and the headscarf brought the confinement of many women and girls from religious and traditional families, since for girls to go to school or women to leave the house without a chador meant—for them—the transgression of a religious mandate.[26]

The unveiling policy caused outrage among the clerics, reflected in *"hijab* treatises" *(rasa'el-e hejabiyeh)*; they make explicit the implicit assumptions that inform *fiqh* rulings on *hijab,* and the intimate links between covering and confinement. They construe women's presence in public space as a negation of sacred laws of Islam, as an alien and harmful innovation *(bid'a),* that was bound to corrupt individuals and destroy the moral fabric of society. In 2001, Rasul Ja'farian, a researcher and cleric, published a collection of these treatises, starting with a 1911 treatise by Fakhr al-Islam, written as a refutation of Qāsim Amīn and ending with Ayatollah Motahhari's 1968 book *The Question of Hijab,* a quasi-modernist text that, as we shall see, became the official position of the Islamic Republic on *hijab.* In between, there were thirty-two other treatises, whose language and defense of *hijab* become more radical after the 1930s. With the exception of Motahhari's text (discussed below), they have a strong anti-modernist stance, largely in reaction to Reza Shah's *kashf-e hejab* policy and to those who had written in its support.[27]

After Reza Shah's abdication in 1941, the compulsory element in the policy of unveiling was abandoned, though its ideology remained intact throughout the Pahlavi era. Between 1941 and 1979 (when the regime collapsed) wearing *hijab* was no longer an offense, but it was a badge of backwardness, a marker of class, and a real hindrance to climbing the social ladder. *Hijab* prejudiced the chances of advancement in work and society not only for working women but also for men, who were increasingly expected to appear at social functions with their wives unveiled. Fashionable hotels and restaurants refused to admit women wearing the chador, and schools and universities actively discouraged it, although the headscarf was tolerated.

Just as the rules and meanings of *hijab* became more subtle and nuanced, so did ways of promoting and identifying it in the emerging

Islamic discourse. By the late 1970s, for many women, *hijab* represented what the Pahlavis had rejected; from a symbol of oppression and a badge of backwardness, it was transformed into act of protest and was made a marker of a new Muslim identity. This was largely achieved in the works of the two main prerevolutionary Islamic ideologues, Ayatollah Morteza Motahhari and Dr. Ali Shari'ati—each tackling the issue from a different perspective.[28]

Hijab *as "Protection"*

In 1962 the Islamic Society of Physicians, one of the professional bodies where Islamic ideology was shaped, started inviting Ayatollah Motahhari as a main speaker to its regular sessions. In March 1968, the society published the selected and edited texts of his lectures as a book, *The Question of Hijab,* which became an instant success; in October, a second edition came out, for which Motahhari wrote a new preface. It remains the most thorough and articulate treatment of *hijab* by a high-ranking cleric, and has gone through over fifty reprints.

In the course of these lectures, Motahhari offers a discursive narrative of *hijab,* its history, its philosophy, its treatment in the Qur'an and hadith, and the rationale for its *fiqh* rulings. He takes issue with both those who see *hijab* as backward and oppressive and with jurists who define it in such a way that it can bring about women's confinement. The true rationale and purpose of *hijab* in Islam, if correctly understood, he argues, is not to exclude women from society but to facilitate their participation; it acts as a safeguard and protects women from being treated as sexual objects.

To argue for this notion of *hijab* as participation, Motahhari reworks the two juristic constructs underpinning the notion of *hijab* as confinement (woman's body as *'awrah* and woman's presence in society as *fitna*). The jurists' view of a woman's body apart from her hands and face as *'awrah,* he contends, sounds offensive only if we adopt the common meaning of the word that denotes the shameful zone of the body. But there is another meaning for the term *'awrah,* which is a defenseless house, and it is in this sense that the idiom must be understood; that is, a woman without *hijab* is defenseless and unprotected.[29] Likewise, Motahhari argues that it is not woman's presence in society that is a danger to the social order, a *fitna,* but rather their "innate desire to show off their beauty," which, if not contained, excites sexual desire in men, who by nature cannot control themselves. That is why Islam, whose laws are in line with "human nature" *(fitra)*, requires women to observe *hijab* and advocates segregation of sexes in society. *Fiqh* rulings on *hijab* are intended to keep the moral order in society intact; they are to protect women against their impulses and their desire to show off their beauty, which can trigger men's aggressive and active sexuality.[30]

Motahhari's notion of *hijab* as protection leaves intact the classical *fiqh* conception of female sexuality as a danger to the social order, but it severs the link between covering and confinement, a link that Pahlavi policies in Iran had reinforced. Being premised on women's participation, the notion of *hijab* as protection invests women with agency and power, which the clerical discourse had denied them. This power, however, is double-edged, because it not only places the burden of society's moral and sexual purity on women by requiring them to observe the *hijab*, but also makes any other mode of clothing a provocation. In a rhetorical statement with which he ended one of his lectures, Motahhari make this crystal clear. "If a woman does not want to be provocative and does not want to appear in public naked [i.e., without *hijab*], then wearing a simple dress that covers all her body and hair is not going to prevent her from outside activity. On the contrary, those women who are obsessed with showing off their beauty, wearing tight clothing, and following different fashions become senseless, inactive individuals, because they must spend all their time in making themselves up."[31]

Hijab *as Protest*

Shari'ati, on the other hand, neither produced a text on *hijab* nor engaged with *fiqh*, whose logic and arguments he considered impotent and irrelevant to his vision of Islam. He broached the topic indirectly and offered a meaning of *hijab* that turned it from a symbol of tradition into a symbol of protest against the Shah's regime and a marker of revolutionary Muslim identity. This he did in the course of two lectures and a seminar in the early 1970s at the Hosseiniyeh Ershad—a religious meeting place that was to become the powerhouse of modernist religious thought.[32] He distinguishes between two types of *hijab*, and between the women who choose or reject them. The first is traditional *hijab*, adopted by women who succumb to religious tradition and the social forces in their milieu. This *hijab*, Shari'ati argues, has no value, because women who wear it have made no conscious choice; they have no awareness; they wear it because their mothers have worn it; and they are likely to abandon it as soon as they start learning about new fashions and frequenting circles where *hijab* is a symbol of backwardness. The second *hijab* is that of those women who are making a conscious choice and re-reclaiming their identity.

With this *hijab,* this generation wants to say to Western colonialism and European culture: "For fifty years, you tried, you schemed to turn me into a pseudo-Westerner; but with this dress I am saying 'NO' to you; I am undoing fifty years of your plotting; [I am saying]: 'You cannot change me!'"... This *[hijab]* has value; this person [who chooses her *hijab*] does not feel inferior to a girl who has never reached such [awareness] or does not value it; she feels superior."[33]

Shari'ati refused to reduce *hijab* to its *fiqh* rulings. Instead, he linked his notion of *hijab* with faith, choice, a quest for returning to find one's true self, and above all, an ideology. Yet these notions are subordinated to his vision of Islam as an ideology for mobilizing the masses and bringing about political change. "[T]he person who has reached the level of ideology [faith] chooses her own life, her way of thinking, her very being, and even her own manner of adornment. She realizes herself. She does not surrender to television, to fashion magazines to make her. In that case she does not even dare to choose the color of her dress [because it may not be in this year's style!] She has returned and is returning fast. To what? To the Islamic dress *[pushesh-e Islami].*"[34]

He certainly had to walk a tightrope to avoid going against *fiqh* rulings on *hijab* and being drawn into a discussion of what form this "Islamic dress" should take, which women choose when they "return."[35] Do women have the right to define the form and limits of their "Islamic dress"? Is it an obligation or a right? It is difficult to know what he intended, as his work contains statements that support both, but a close reading suggests that neither the issue of rights nor that of women's choice were central to his concerns. He imbued them with such a high dose of ideology that his discourse is at best ambivalent and at worst contradictory. All this makes his notion of *hijab* as "protest" as double-edged as Motahhari's notion of *hijab* as "protection."

### Hijab *as Imposition*

Shari'ati died in 1977, and Motahhari was assassinated in 1979, soon after the popular revolution that marked the acme of political Islam. Though it was Shari'ati's notion of *hijab* that inspired many middle-class urban and professional women to take the scarf in the 1970s, it was Motahhari's influence that became the official discourse of the new

Islamic Republic when it started to impose *hijab*. In 1983, a law was passed that made appearing in public without *hijab* an offense against public morality, punishable by the "Islamic" penalty of up to seventy-four lashes.[36] From then on, compulsory *hijab* was defended with such vigor that it became one of the cornerstones of the new Republic, one of those red lines that no one dared to cross. In their Friday sermons, lectures and writings, political clerics often spoke of the making and breaking of the new order in terms of its policy of imposed *hijab*.[37] Yet the ideologues of the Islamic Republic have failed to produce any juristic argument in defense of this policy, nor did any meaningful discussion of the issue emerge until the late 1990s. The vast literature that has appeared on the subject since the revolution simply repeats Motahhari's arguments—sometimes almost verbatim.[38]

Imposition creates resistance, and this simple sociological fact sums up the story of *hijab* in the Islamic Republic, which has become a war of attrition between women and the authorities. Women lost the first battle when women's groups protested in March 1979, after Ayatollah Khomeini went back on what he had promised in Paris, and asked women who worked in government to observe Islamic dress. With the onset of the war with Iraq in 1980 and the ascendancy of the radicals, there could be no more protest; however, by the 1990s it was evident that the Islamic Republic had failed to sell its own ideal of *hijab* to women. The chador, which the official discourse promoted as "the best *hijab*," was becoming associated with fanaticism and state ideology; and what the authorities called "incorrect *hijab*" *(bad-hejabi)*, was becoming more and more widespread. Women were constantly pushing back the limits, especially the younger generation born during or after the Revolution, who had been indoctrinated from childhood to accept *hijab* as a supreme Islamic value.

Meanwhile, a number of dissident thinkers, both lay and clerical, were developing a critique of the Islamic state from within an Islamic framework. Displaying a refreshing pragmatic vigor and a willingness to engage with nonreligious perspectives, they sought a rights-based political order that could open Muslim polities to dissent, tolerance and pluralism, women's rights and civil liberties. Their ideas and writings, which came to be known as "New Religious Thinking" *(no-andishi-ye dini)*, were the mainstay of the popular reformist movement that emerged in the aftermath of the unexpected victory of Mohammad Khatami in the 1997 presidential election. With the opening of political space and the expansion of the discourse of "rights," the discussion of *hijab*, like other issues that had been successfully suppressed since the revolution, inevitably resurfaced. A number of articles appeared in the reformist press questioning the wisdom of the policy of enforcement and pointing out its anachronistic incompatibility with the new discourse advocated by the reformist government.[39]

Hijab *as Choice*

A key moment in the debate was the conference organized by the Heinrich Böll Institute in Berlin in April 2000, where a number of reformists—both secular and religious—were invited from Iran to discuss the prospects for reform. In a panel dealing with women's issues, compulsory *hijab* became the main focus of objections by opposition elements in the audience. The two panelists with a religious perspective—Shahla Sherkat, editor of *Zanan* magazine, and the cleric Hassan Yusefi Eshkevari, an admirer of Shari'ati—had to respond. Both rejected the idea of compulsory *hijab,* and argued that Muslim women should have the choice whether to adopt it or not.

Eshkevari argued that *hijab* and other Qur'anic injunctions pertaining to women are neither fixed nor immutable, but open to change, because they come under the category of social rules *(ahkam-e ejtema'i)*. He produced two jurisprudential arguments in defense of his view. First, when there is a change in the subject *(mouzu')* of a Shari'a ruling, either internally or externally, naturally there will be a need for a different ruling. Since the status of women (the subject of the early Shari'a rulings) has changed drastically, *fiqh* must come up with new rulings to reflect this change. Secondly, the Prophet implemented almost all social rulings of Islam after he formed the Islamic state in Medina. They were part of the laws and customs that already existed in Arabia; "ninety-nine percent of them are *ahkam-e emza'i* (i.e. the Prophet accepted them), not *ahkam-e ta'sisi* (i.e. rulings newly established by Islam)." *Hijab* is among those rulings that the authorities have no right to impose on the believer; people should decide for themselves whether to follow it or not.[40]

Upon his return to Iran, Eshkevari was arrested and charged with apostasy. Tried by the Special Clergy Court, he was sentenced to death, but this was later reduced to seven years in jail. A year later, his co-panelist Shahla Sherkat, in the course of her trial, questioned the religious value of the dress code imposed by the Islamic Republic and called it "official uniform," not "true *hijab*" as mandated by Islam. Convicted of "disturbing the public mind," she was given a suspended sentence of six months' imprisonment and a fine, which was overturned in the Appeal Court.

The genie was now out of the bottle. Following the clampdown on the reformist press that began in spring 2000 and accelerated after the election of hardliner Mahmud Ahmadinejad to the presidency in June 2005, the Internet has become one of the main sites for the *hijab* debates. The material available ranges widely, from personal opinions as to whether the state or religious authorities have the right to enforce *hijab* in the name of Islam to sophisticated juristic arguments as to whether covering of the hair for women can be argued for on the basis of Qur'anic verses and the traditions. Some bloggers have also engaged with the religious authorities as well as reformist clerics and asked for fatwas.[41] In February 2004, in response to a question,[42] Hojjat ol-Eslam Ahmad Qabel, a reformist cleric authorized to deal with religious questions by Grand Ayatollah Montazeri (designated successor of Khomeini but now a dissident), stated that the covering of hair is not obligatory *(vajeb)* but recommended *(mostahab)*. He provided ten arguments for his view, among which were: what is obligatory for both men and women is the covering of *'awrah,* but there is no consensus among the jurists as to what constitutes *'awrah* in women nor whether it includes her hair; and that Qur'anic verses and authentic traditions do not denote obligation but recommendation.[43] In 2005, Mohsen Kadivar, another student of Ayatollah Montazari's and an outspoken reformist cleric, argued against the state's imposition of *hijab* and its failure to make a distinction between sin and crime. Religious texts require both men and women to dress modestly in public but do not mandate any specific form of dress or covering for women. The whole issue of *hijab,* Kadivar argued, comes under the domain of ethical not legal matters; it should be left to Muslim women to choose the form and extent of their covering in accordance with their religious commitment and conscience.[44]

Having lost the public debate over *hijab* as imposition, the hardliners in the Islamic Republic have returned to using the arms of the state by which they imposed it in the 1980s. In April 2007, the police launched an unprecedented aggressive drive to enforce the rule of *hijab* in public spaces. This initiative—named the "Moral Security Plan" *(tarh-e amniyat-e melli)* and involving female police in full chador—was targeted at young women sporting the new fashion of *hijab* which consisted of tight tunics, short trousers, and narrow scarves, whom the authorities call "mannequins." At the time of writing (a year later), the drive had resulted in the arrest of thousands of women, with many hundreds of thousands receiving verbal warnings, but it had already lost its moral authority and brought a rift within the conservative coalition that brought Ahmadinejad to office. Hardliners hailed the new initiative as evidence of the new government's intention to revive the slogans and ideals of the revolution, but the head of the judiciary, Ayatollah Shahrudi, criticized it as leading to the criminalization and alienation of the youth, while members of parliament attacked it as unwise and too harsh.[45]

Despite government attempts to control reporting of the arrests, pictures of girls resisting arrest and being roughly treated by the police circulated throughout the Internet, arousing a great deal of comment both inside Iran and abroad. These comments reveal two consensuses: that *hijab* is a matter of personal belief and imposing it is a violation of women's human rights; and that an imposed *hijab* is not "Islamic" and cannot be defended on religious grounds. In addition to personal views, Women's Field *(Meydan-e Zanan),* one of the web sites through which women activists interact, has started to feature a number of well-documented and informative articles; notably, Nima Namdari's four-part "The Story of Imposition of Hijab"[46] and Nasrin Afzali's "Moral Security: The Plan that was Dormant for Eight Years."[47]

In March 2008 the Tehran chief of police, a key enforcer of the "Moral Security Plan," was arrested for "immoral conduct"; the news leaked that his arrest had been ordered by the head of the judiciary and that there were incriminating videotapes of him and certain women, including one in which he ordered six women to pray naked with him.[48] Whether true or not, such behavior undermines the logic of the "Moral Security" drive, which justifies the arrests of women on the grounds of keeping society safe. This gave rise to a debate in the web sites over the following questions: Who is the real danger to the moral order, women, or a system of values that reduces them to sexual beings? Can imposing *hijab* make society safe? What has gone wrong in the *hijab* debate? Are people turning away from religion? These questions and the answers offered suggest that after three decades, the official discourse of *hijab* as "protection," as developed by Motahhari, has unraveled, and that elements that were latent in Shari'ati's notion of *hijab* as "protest" and "choice" have resurfaced.

## HIJAB DEBATE AND INNOVATION: FROM CONFINEMENT TO CHOICE

The competing concurrent notions of *hijab* that are articulated in Iran are also evident in the rest of Muslim world and in contemporary Islamic legal debate—a debate that is still unfolding. What has this debate to tell us about the notion and politics of innovation in Islamic legal tradition?

First, as we have seen, there is neither clear-cut, coherent set of rules nor a single notion of *hijab,* but rather several contested ones, running the gamut from confinement to choice. These notions rest on different theological, juristic, social, and sexual assumptions and theories, shaped in interaction with sociopolitical and economic forces, and with those who have the power to represent and define the laws based and derived from Islam's sacred texts. *Hijab* became an problem, a legal issue to address, only in the latter part of the nineteenth century when the encounter with modernity and women's increasing presence in public space made classical *fiqh* rulings untenable. In the course of the twentieth century, the tension between "covering" and "confinement," which for many centuries had permeated the discourses on *hijab* in Islamic legal thought, gave way to a different set of tensions: between notions of *hijab* as "protection," "protest," "identity" or "choice." Various elements, in different combinations and at times contradictory, are now invoked, appealed to and enacted upon in different political contexts. A mélange of "protest," "identity," and "choice" have become the main ingredients of what *hijab* means for the vast majority of Muslim women who feel their faith and identity have been undermined, whether this pertains to those living as minorities in the West or those in Muslim countries like Turkey and Tunisia where the state restricts the wearing of *hijab.* But these notions remain theologically undeveloped and subordinated to either traditional or ideological visions of Islam; they therefore become redundant and go into eclipse in traditional settings or under an Islamist regime that attempts to translate classical *fiqh* rulings on gender rights into policy.

The second strand of argument is that political Islam and its gender discourse contain the seeds of their own transformation and, as we have seen in the case of Iran, have provoked women's resistance and the shaping of new juristic arguments and positions premised on a notion of *hijab* as a right and choice for Muslim women. There are two linked processes involved.

The first has to do with the inherent contradiction in political Islam's discourse on *hijab*, which opened the door to its theological contestation. On the one hand, it upholds classical *fiqh* rulings on *hijab*; on the other, it negates and alters the legal theories and juristic logic on which they rest, as well as their consequences. The exclusion of women from social and political participation was both the premise and the consequence of classical *fiqh*, though Islamic ideologues deny this and the mass of *hijab* literature attempts to prove otherwise. In other words, being premised on women's participation, political Islam has emptied classical *fiqh* rulings on *hijab* of their legal logic and coherence, making them empty legal shells. At the same time, the slogan of "return to Shari'a" has brought the *fiqh* texts out of the closet and—unintentionally—exposed their patriarchal ethos to critical scrutiny and public debate; the more Islamists seek to defend classical *fiqh* rulings on *hijab* as God's law, the more apparent are their underlying assumptions about women and sexuality. Juristic constructs such as "women are *'awrah* and their presence in public space is a *fitna*" are so repugnant to modern sensibilities and ethics that no contemporary jurists or Islamic ideologues can afford to acknowledge them openly, let alone to invoke them. All this has paved the way for challenges to the theological validity of *hijab* rulings, even by ideologues such as Hassan al-Turabi in Sudan, who stated in 2006 that: "The Qur'an did not refer to this thing [covering] as *hijab*. This was called *khimar* and was worn over the chest only . . . you keep hearing *hijab*, *hijab*, *hijab*. . . . When the words are distorted, they mislead people."[49] Scholars like Gamal Al-Banna have declared that neither the Qur'an nor the authentic Sunna demand that women cover their hair; the veil is not an Islamic tradition, but pre-Islamic, from the time when Arabs covered their heads and left the upper parts of their chest uncovered. The relevant Qur'anic verses command women to cover their chests, but not necessarily their heads.[50]

The second process has to do with the ways in which political Islam's notion of *hijab*, because it is premised on participation, has proved to be empowering to women, even in situations when the state imposes it, as in Iran. While it undoubtedly has restricted some women, it has emancipated others by legitimizing their presence in the public domain, which has always been male-dominated. Further, state imposition creates resistance, allowing women to challenge and mock its explicit platforms. This has given the traditional expression of women's power of subversion in patriarchal systems a different lease of life, a new political edge, as we have seen in the case of Iran. Likewise, Muslim women who adopt different forms of covering (including, more recently, the face veil) are using *hijab* as a marker of a new identity, as a form of protest, to redefine the terms of their presence in public space. These women defend their choices, either in terms of faith, or by appealing to the feminist critique of the objectification of women's bodies and the post-colonialist critique of the representation of the Islam as the Western "other." They use this modern discourse, not that of classical *fiqh*, to make sense of their experience and articulate their perception of *hijab*.[51] For them, like the Iranian women, the right to choose is central to being a Muslim and a woman. Likewise, the debates over the French ban on wearing *hijab* in school, and the Turkish outlawing of headscarves in government offices and universities, has highlighted the issue of freedom of choice.

It was precisely this combination of faith and choice, private and public, in the discourse of *hijab* as shaped by and practised by Muslim women, that has become problematic, as the debates over the headscarf bans in France and Turkey have revealed.[52] These debates are too complex and multifaceted to enter into here, but one relevant aspect of them is that they reveal the contradictions in secularist feminism as well as its paternalistic and authoritarian tendencies; how its difficult relationship with religion and its claim to speak for all women can negate women's realities and choices. The two core arguments of those feminists who oppose *hijab* are that it is an oppressive practice, and that those who wear it are either duped by a patriarchal religion or are forced into it by their menfolk. Such arguments are, in effect, similar in their premises to those of the Islamists who argue that *hijab* liberates and protects women, that women without *hijab* are "naked" sex objects and slaves of consumer society. Both deny Muslim women agency, the right to choose and to define for themselves the terms of their presence in public space. In the ensuing heated debates, Muslim feminists have come to take a position that constitutes common ground between Islamists and feminists; they insist on women's own right to define the meaning of *hijab* and to enter public space on their own terms, as a matter of both belief and choice.

Finally, the obsession with *hijab* in contemporary discourses (both Western and Islamic), which speaks of its symbolic significance, has in a convoluted way enabled Muslim women to challenge jurisprudential wisdoms and to redefine the terms of their presence in public space.[53] In so doing, they are confronting prevailing notions of *hijab*, giving it a new meaning and symbolic value and provoking the jurists to produce new arguments and positions from within the Islamic legal tradition. That women now have this voice is, in the end, what I consider to be an innovation in Islamic legal thought.

NOTES

1. An earlier version of this paper was published as Ziba Mir-Hosseini, "The Politics and Hermeneutics of Hijab in Iran: From Confinement to Choice," *Muslim World Journal of Human Rights* 4, 1 (2007), available at www.bepress.com/mwjhr/vol4/iss1/art2 (accessed July 30, 2010).

2. *Hijab* has been translated as cover, wrap, curtain, veil, screen, partition. For the difficulty in each of these terms, see Fadwa El Guindi, "Hijab," in *The Oxford Encyclopedia of the Modern Islamic World* (Oxford: Oxford University Press, 1995), 2: 105.

3. A woman's male relatives, known as her *mahram,* include her husband and close members of her family with whom marriage is forbidden, notably father, brother, son, father's and mother's brother, brother's and sister's son, husband's father.

4. For an insightful discussion, see Linda Clark, "Hijab According to Hadith: Text and Interpretation," in *The Muslim Veil in North America: Issues and Debates,* ed. Sajida Alavi, Homa Hoodfar, and Sheila McDonough (Toronto: Women's Press, 2003), pp. 214–286. Clark shows there is little concern in the hadith literature with women's covering and no explicit reference to the covering of hair; there are more hadith on men's dress and covering their *'awrah* than on women's dress.

5. Other terms commonly used today in different countries, such as *parda* (purdah), *chador,* and *burqa,* are not found in classical *fiqh* texts.

6. For these rulings and their rationale, see Murtaza Motahhari, *Mas'aleh-ye Hejab* (The Problem of Veiling) (35th ed., Qom: Entesharat-e Sadra, 1991), pp. 181–183; and Ibn Rushd, *The Distinguished Jurist's Primer (Bidayat al-Mujtahid wa Nihayat al-Muqtasid),* trans. Imran Ahsan Khan Nyazee (Reading, UK: Garnet), vol. 1 (1994), pp. 125–130, and vol. 2 (1996), p. 2.

7. Ibn Rushd's discussion is confined to the four Sunni schools; Motahhari shows that the same issues and style of argumentation are shared by Shi'a jurists, see Motahhari, *Mas'aleh-ye Hejab.*

8. Ibn Rushd, *Distinguished Jurist's Primer,* 1: 125.

9. Ibid., 1: 126.

10. Qur'an 33:59. From *The Glorious Koran,* trans. and ed. Muhammad Marmaduke Pickthall (Boston: Allen & Unwin, 1976), modified.

11. Ibn Rushd, *Distinguished Jurist's Primer,* 1: 126.

12. See, e.g., Barbara Stowasser, "The Hijab: How a Curtain Became an Institution and a Cultural Symbol," in *Humanism, Culture, and Language in the Near East: Studies in Honor of Georg Krotkoff,* ed. Asma Afsaruddin and A. H. Mathias Zahnise (Winona Lake, IN: Eisenbrauns, 1997), pp. 87–104; and El Guindi, "Hijab," in *The Oxford Encyclopedia of the Modern Islamic World,* 2: 147–157. The influence of social forces on the way in which the *hijab*

verses were understood by the commentators al-Tabari and al-Razi is discussed in Soraya Hajjaji-Jarrah, "Women in Qur'anic Commentaries," in *Muslim Veil in North America,* ed. Alvi et al., pp. 146–180. Feminist studies in Islam are too numerous to list here, but see esp. Leila Ahmed, *Women and Gender in Islam: Historical Roots of a Modern Debate* (New Haven, CT: Yale University Press, 1992); Aziza Al-Hibri, "A Study of Islamic Herstory: Or How Did We Get into This Mess," in *Islam and Women,* special issue of *Women's Studies International Forum* 5, 2 (1982): 207–219; Aziza Al-Hibri, "Islam, Law and Custom: Redefining Muslim Women's Rights," *American University Journal of International Law and Policy* 12, (1997): 1–44; Kecia Ali, *Sexual Ethics and Islam: Feminist Reflections on Qur'an, Hadith and Jurisprudence* (Oxford: Oneworld, 2006): 163–89; Asma Barlas, *"Believing Muslim" in Islam: Unreading Patriarchal Interpretations of the Qur'an* (Austin: Texas University Press, 2002); Fatima Mernissi, *Beyond the Veil: Male-Female Dynamics in Muslim Society* (London: Saqi Books, 1985); Amina Wadud, *Qur'an and Woman: Reading the Sacred Text from a Woman's Perspective* (New York: Oxford University Press, 1999); and Amina Wadud, *Inside the Gender Jihad: Woman's Reform in Islam* (Oxford: Oneworld, 2006).

13. For an illuminating discussion and for sources, see Khaled Abou El Fadl, *Speaking in God's Name: Islamic Law, Authority and Women* (Oxford: Oneworld 2001), pp. 255–57, nn. 106 and 107.

14. For more discussion, see Kecia Ali, "Progressive Muslims and Islamic Jurisprudence: The Necessity for Critical Engagement with Marriage and Divorce Law," in *Progressive Muslims: On Justice, Gender, and Pluralism,* ed. Omid Safi (Oxford: Oneworld, 2003), pp. 163–189; id., *Sexual Ethics and Islam: Feminist Reflections on Qur'an, Hadith and Jurisprudence* (Oxford: Oneworld, 2006); Ziba Mir-Hosseini, "The Construction of Gender in Islamic Legal Thought and Strategies for Reform," *Hawwa: Journal of Women in the Middle East and the Islamic World* 1, 1 (2003): 1–28; and id., "Islam and Gender Justice," in *Voices of Islam,* ed. Vincent J. Cornell, vol. 5: *Voices of Change* (Westport, CT: Praeger, 2007), pp. 85–113.

15. Muhaqqiq Hilli, *Sharayi' al-Islam,* trans. A.A. Yazdi, ed. Muhammad Taqi Danish-Pazhuh (Tehran: University of Tehran Press, 1985), 2: 428.

16. F.H. Ruxton, *Māliki Law: A Summary from French Translations of Mukhtasar Sidi Khalil* (London: Luzac, 1916), p. 106. 'Abd al-Qāhir al-Jurjānī (d. 474 A.H./1078 C.E.), another Māliki jurist, defines marriage as "a contract through which the husband acquires exclusive rights over the sexual organs of woman" (quoted by Octave Pesle, *Le Mariage chez les Malékites de l'Afrique du Nord* (Rabat: Moncho, 1936), p. 20.

17. Imam Abu Hamid Al-Ghazali, *The Proper Conduct of Marriage in Islam (Adab an-Nikah), Book Twelve of Ihya 'Ulum ad-Din (Revival of Religious Sciences),* trans. Muhtar Holland (Hollywood, FL: Al-Baz, 1998), p. 89. For another rendering of this passage, see Madelain Farah, *Marriage and Sexuality in Islam: A Translation of Al-Ghazali's Book on the Etiquette of Marriage from the* Ihya (Salt Lake City: University of Utah Press, 1984), p. 120.

18. For critical discussion of these *ahadith,* see El Fadl, *Speaking in God's Name,* pp. 232–247.

19. Al-Ghazali, *Proper Conduct of Marriage in Islam*, pp. 90–91.

20. For similarities in the juristic conceptions of slavery and marriage, see Shaun E. Marmon, "Domestic Slavery in the Mamluk Empire: A Preliminary Sketch," in *Slavery in the Islamic Middle East,* ed. id. (Princeton, NJ: Department of Near Eastern Studies, 1999), pp. 1–24; and John Ralph Willis, "The Ideology of Enslavement in Islam: Introduction," in *Slaves and Slavery in Muslim Africa,* ed. id. (London: Frank Cass, 1985), 1: 1–13.

21. For these disagreements, see Ali, "Progressive Muslims and Islamic Jurisprudence," pp. 70–82; for their impact on rulings related to *mahr* and the ways in which classical jurists discussed them, see Ibn Rushd, *Distinguished Jurist's Primer,* 2: 31–33.

22. Qāsim Amīn's *Taḥrīr al-mar'ah* (1899) remains controversial. For a translation, see *The Liberation of Women; and, The New Woman: Two Documents in the History of Egyptian Feminism,* trans. Samiha Sidhom Peterson (Cairo: American University in Cairo Press, 2000). And see Ahmed, *Women and Gender in Islam,* p. 168.

23. Maulana Abul A'la Maududi, *Purdah and the Status of Women in Islam* (16th ed., Lahore: Islamic Publication, 1998). *Purdah* originally appeared as a series of articles; it was first published as a book in Urdu in 1939, in Arabic in 1962, and in English in 1972, and is now available on many radical Islamist web sites.

24. Jamal Badawi's *The Muslim Women's Dress According to the Qur'an and Sunnah,* first published in 1980, is now available on moderate Muslim web sites.

25. Ziba Mir-Hosseini, *Islam and Gender: The Religious Debate in Contemporary Iran* (Princeton, NJ: Princeton University Press, 1999).

26. For discussion, see Patricia Baker, "Politics of Dress: the Dress Reform Laws of 1920/30s Iran," in *Languages of Dress in the Middle East,* ed. Nancy Lindisfarne-Tapper and Bruce Ingham (London: Curzon, 1997), pp. 178–190; Houchang Chehabi, "The Banning of the Veil and its Consequences," in *The Making of Modern Iran: State and Society under Riza Shah, 1921–1941,* ed. Stephanie Cronin (London: Curzon, 2003), pp. 193–210; Homa Hoodfar, "The Veil in Their Minds and on Our Heads: The Persistence of Colonial Images of Muslim Women," in *Other Circuits: Intersection of Exchange in World Theory and Practice,* ed. David Lloyd and Lisa Lowe (Durham, NC, Duke University Press, 1997), pp. 248–279; and Rasul Ja'farian, *Dastan-e Hejab dar Iran-e Pish az Enqelab* (The Story of Hijab in Pre-Revolutionary Iran), (Tehran: Islamic Revolution Documentation Centre, 2004).

27. Ja'farian gives biographical details for each author, but no critical discussion. His own disapproval of the "unveiling" policy is reflected in his subtitle: "Sixty Years of Scientific Endeavors against the Religious Innovation *(bid'a)* of 'Unveiling'." See Rasul Ja'farian, *Rasa'el-e Hejabiyeh: Shast Sal Talash-e 'Elmi dar barabar-e Bid'at-e Kashf-e Hejab* (Hijab Treatises: Sixty Years of Scientific Endeavors against the Religious Innovation of Unveiling), 2 vols. (Qom: Entesharat Dalil-e Ma, 2001).

28. Motahhari, *Mas'aleh-ye Hejab;* Ali Shari'ati, *Zan* (Woman), in Collected Works, vol. 21 (7th ed., Tehran: Jahanbakhsh Press, 1994).

29. Motahhari, *Mas'aleh-ye Hejab*, p. 244.

30. For further discussion of Motahhari, see Mir-Hosseini, "Islam and Gender Justice," pp. 98–99.

31. Morteza Motahhari, *Pasokh-ha-ye Ostad beh Naqd-ha'i bar Ketab-e Mas'aleh-ye Hejab* (The Master's Response to Criticisms of the Book: The Problem of Veiling) (5th ed., Qom: Enresharat-e Sadra, 1994), p. 204.

32. Ali Shari'ati's first lecture, "Fatima is Fatima," was delivered in April 1971, and the second, "The Expectation of the Age from the Muslim Women," in April 1972; the seminar took place in July 1972.

33. Shari'ati, *Zan*, pp. 274–275. This is from a conversation with a group of followers in 1975, after his release from prison, published later as "Hijab," which clearly suggests how *hijab*, like other Islamic concepts, was for him a tool of political ideology. Ibid., pp. 261–283.

34. Ibid., p. 276; my translation. Bakhtiar's rendering of this passage is a paraphrase that takes away its ambiguity: see Laleh Bakhtiar, *Shariati on Shariati and the Muslim Woman* (Chicago: ABC International Group, 1996), p. 46.

35. Shari'ati, *Zan*, p. 274. For instance, "Once someone asked me about *hijab* (he wanted me to say something against *hijab*, *chador* . . . to give him an excuse to make a fuss and say things against me in the bazaar) . . . I said, '*hijab* is whatever you say it is. I am neither a jurist *[faqih]* nor a cloth merchant, I am a sociologist."

36. Article 102 of the Law of Islamic Punishment.

37. For the treatment of the issue by Ayatollah Azari Qomi, an influential cleric in the 1980s and the early 1990s, see Mir-Hosseini, *Islam and Gender*, pp. 65–67.

38. This literature is too extensive to list here; for examples by clerics who reproduce versions of Motahhari's discourse, see Hossein Habibollahi, *Hijab dar Bihijabi* (Veiling in Unveiling) (Qom: Intisharat Davari, 1994); Ruhollah Hosseinian, *Harim-e Effat* (The Boundary of Modesty) (Tehran: Islamic Propaganda Organization, 1994); and Mehdi Mehrizi, *Asibshenashi-ye Hejab* (The Pathology of Hijab) (Tehran: Javaneh-e Rushd, 2000).

39. See Ziba Mir-Hosseini, "The Conservative and Reformist Conflict over Women's Rights in Iran," *International Journal of Politics, Culture and Society* 16, 1 (Fall 2002): 41–43.

40. For the English text of his speech, see Ziba Mir-Hosseini and Richard Tapper, *Islamic and Democracy in Iran: Eshkevari and the Quest for Reform* (London: I.B. Tauris, 2006), pp. 163–170.

41. In October 2003, for instance, Hossein Khodadad's blog *Hejab dar eslam ejbari nist* (Hijab is Not Compulsory in Islam) was blocked. According to Khodadad, this followed an opinion poll that he conducted through it, in which of 5,600 responses received over ten days, only 4 percent believed that *hijab* was compulsory in Islam; see http://akhbar.gooya.com/politics/archives/017973.php (in Farsi; accessed July 30, 2010). His new blog has also been blocked.

42. This question was asked by Hossein Khodadad and covered in his blog (see preceding note).

43. In July 2005, Hojjat ol-Eslam Ahmad Qabel published an extended version of his argument online, providing juristic reasoning and textual support

for his view that the covering of hair and neck cannot be justified on religious grounds. This received wide coverage on other Farsi web sites. However, Qabel's blog was subsequently taken down.

44. In an interview in January 2005 with Dariush Sajadi on the theme of Islam and Modernity, broadcast by Homa TV (based in the United States and reflecting the views of Iranian reformists); the text of the interview, in five parts, appeared on Farsi web sites. It is now available on Mohsen Kadivar's site: www.kadivar.com (accessed June 17, 2010).

45. For a report in English, see www.payvand.com/news/07may/1033.htm; for a report of reactions in Persian, see www.roozonline.com/archives/2007/04/00 (both accessed June 17, 2010).

46. The last part was posted on April 16, 2008, but the website can no longer be accessed.

47. The website can no longer be accessed.

48. The arrest and the rumors were reported on Iranian web sites, including conservative ones; the Judiciary confirmed the arrest without commenting on the charges; for a sample of coverage, see Omid Memarian, "The Regime's Cover-up for the Naked Commander," *Roozonline*, March 13, 2008.

49. Hassan al-Turabi, interview with Al-Arabiya TV, April 10, 2006.

50. Gamal Al-Banna, *Al-Mar'ah al-Muslimah bayna Tahir al-Qur'an wa Taqyid al-Fuqaha* (The Muslim Woman Between the Qur'an's Freedom and the Limitations of the Jurists) (Cairo: Dar al-Fikr al-Islami, 1988).

51. The literature on contemporary "veiling" is vast; among the most articulate writers on the subject is Katherine Bullock, *Rethinking Muslim Women and the Veil: Challenging Historical and Modern Stereotypes* (Herndon, VA: International Institute of Islamic Thought, 2003).

52. For an incisive discussion of the debate in France, see John R. Bowen, *Why the French Don't Like Headscarves: Islam, the State, and Public Space* (Princeton, NJ: Princeton University Press, 2007). For Turkey, see Nilüfer Göle, *The Forbidden Modern: Civilization and Veiling* (Ann Arbor: University of Michigan Press, 1996), and Elisabeth Özdalga, *The Veiling Issue: Official Secularism and Popular Islam in Modern Turkey* (Richmond, Surrey, UK: Curzon, 1997).

53. See, e.g., Azza M. Karam, "Veiling, Unveiling and Meanings of 'the Veil': Challenging Static Symbolism," *Thamyris* 3, 2 (1996): 219–236.

CHAPTER 12

# Modern Movements in Islam

JOHN O. VOLL

Muslim movements in the modern era provide important examples of innovation in Islamic history. The wide variety of movements itself shows the dynamic diversity of approaches to dealing with modernity and modernization. Over the past century and a half, as modernity itself has changed, Muslim responses to the new modes of modernity indicate the innovative capacity of Muslims. Most frequently, analysts look at innovations in economic, social, and political areas, but the adaptations are also clearly visible in the many religious movements as well. These "religious" movements themselves can be seen as an important synthesis of social, political, and religious elements that points to the emergence of distinctive modes of Islamic expression in a contemporary world of "multiple modernities."[1]

Modern movements in Islam take many different forms. In this diversity, two major types of "modern movements" are identifiable. The first is the set of movements that involve the major conscious efforts in the past century and a half to articulate and develop "Islamic modernism." In this broad movement, an important characteristic is "the self-conscious adoption of 'modern' values—that is, values that authors explicitly associated with the modern world."[2] However, "modernist" activists were not simply modern Muslims, they "also wished to preserve and improve Islamic faith in the modern world."[3] Although "modernist" movements took many different forms, their focus was to maintain an authentic Islam in the contexts of modernity. This venture involves a great diversity of thought and organization over the past century and a half as modernity itself changed and was transformed. In this intellectual-theological dimension, a broad spectrum of intellectuals and activists provide important examples of the processes of innovation in Islam in the modern era.

The second type of "modern movements" in Islam is the set of movements of Muslims that are "modern" in form, regardless of the content of their message and vision. Broad social movements in Muslim societies have developed important new modes of organization that represent important innovative approaches to the institutionalization of major social movements. Some of these new social movement organizations may, in ideology, even be seen as "anti-modern." However, in their organizational forms they exhibit an innovative approach that operates within "modern-style" organizations. This modernizing adaptation may not be conscious in terms of self-definition, but it clearly creates movements that are "modern movements" in form and structure. In many ways, organizational innovation of movements in the Muslim world may be a more important feature of modern Islamic history than the self-conscious development of "modernist" ideologies that change as the content of modernity itself changes over the decades. Often the defining boundary line between "modernist" movements and "modern" movements is very porous or ill-defined, and there is a high degree of interaction between the two different types of movements.

The character of these modernist and modern movements has changed in the past century and a half, reflecting the fundamental changes in "modernity" itself. Perhaps the strongest expression of innovation in Islam in the modern era is this ability of thinkers and organizations to redefine their "modern-ness" as the nature of "modern" itself has been transformed.

## THE CHANGING CHARACTERISTICS OF MODERNITY

One important variable in examining the development of "Islamic modernism" and "modern movements" is the changing nature of modernity itself. In dramatic ways, "modernity" has been transformed and re-transformed in the past two centuries. Two significant lines of change can be identified for purposes of understanding the changing natures of modernity with which innovative intellectuals and groups in the Muslim world were interacting. The first line of change might be described as changing in the structural nature of modernity and in the conceptualization of that nature. This was a transition beginning with a monolithic conceptualization of modernity that changed to a recognition of multiple modernities and then to a globalized sense of modernities. The second line of change involves the changing intellectual content and position of modernity within "modern" societies. This transition was from modernity as a revolutionary force to modernity as mainstream to the emergence of forms that transcend or go beyond the basic content canons of modernity, in what some call a "postmodern" mode.

The first line of change begins by the late nineteenth century. As "modern" societies became an important part of the historical landscape, a relatively monolithic concept of what a modern society was developed, with dominant prototypes being Victorian-industrial England and postrevolutionary France. When additional modern state-societies emerged, as they did in the newly unified Italy and Prussia-Germany, these were viewed as variants of the same model. The culmination of this image of modernity came with the articulation of "modernization theory" by the middle of the twentieth century. As can be seen in the analyses by people like Daniel Lerner,[4] it was possible to identify "modern" as a relatively homogeneous category, and societies and groups could be classified as "traditional," "transitional," or "modern." This monolithic category was basically identified with the forms of society that had developed in western Europe and then North America.

This identification of "the West" with modernity gradually began to seem mistaken during the twentieth century.[5] As societies outside of western Europe engaged in modernization, many aspects of that process did, in fact, involve "Westernization." However, at the same time, many of these societies also maintained a clearly non-European identity that represented some important historical continuities and distinctive cultural characteristics. One of the most important early manifestations of non-Western modernity is in Japan, whose victory over Russia in the Russo-Japanese War of 1904–1905 startled people around the world. By the second half of the twentieth century, it was clear that there were multiple forms that modernity could take. This development opened the way for different conceptualizations of what the cultural-civilizational framework of modernity could be and the recognition of the existence of multiple modernities.

By the beginning of the twenty-first century, still more transformations were reshaping the meaning of "modernity." One of the most important and frequently noted developments in the late twentieth century was the growing importance of globalization. Globalization had been an important feature in the interactions of the major societies of the world for centuries. Geoffrey C. Gunn, for example, speaks of the "first globalization" in the period before modern industrial society, 1500–1800.[6] However, by the beginning of the new millennium, the processes of globalization intensified and, increasingly, "globalization" did not refer to important interactions *between* and *among* different societies around the world. It began also to describe the emergence of new modes of interactions among peoples that transcended and transformed local identities. The profound redefinition of "local" identities and the emergence of global identities shaped by the diversity of local elements around the world create conditions in which contemporary modes of "modernity" involve complex relationships between "global" and "local." Scholars like Roland Robertson identify these processes as "glocalization."[7] Conceptualizations depending upon the existence of clearly separate cultural entities (often given the label "civilizations") that interact misunderstand the transcivilizational dimension of the new "glocal" mode of modernity.

The second line of changing modernity involves the interactions of premodern, modern, and postmodern modes. These developments are parallel to but not identical with the transitions involved in the emergence of "glocal" modernity. Initially, modernity represented a new style of society and thought that emerged in western Europe in the eighteenth and early nineteenth centuries. Potentially it represented a set of revolutionary transformations of all aspects of human life. Although premodern societies were very diverse, they were all faced with significant survival challenges in interacting with the forms of modernity that they faced. These were the societies identified in modernization theory as "traditional." In the narrative of that theory, the "modern age that first became visible in western Europe between the thirteenth and fifteenth centuries and reached the Middle East by the nineteenth and twentieth centuries is thus shattering the traditional community of Islam."[8] Reformers in the Muslim world as well as in the West tended to accept this conceptualization of a monolithic modernity and a monolithic "traditional" society. The transformational reform program instituted by Mustafa Kemal (Atatürk) following World War I is an important example of this conceptualization in practice. In this first phase, the tension and competition was between existing premodern modes and modernity as a revolutionary or transforming challenge. "Modernists" and "modern" movements were competing with and working to change existing premodern patterns. In this context, the anti-modern modes were conservative.

By the twentieth century, in much of the world, modernity was emerging as the dominant mode and pattern of thought and organization. By the middle of the century, the great competitions were not between modern and nonmodern modes but rather, between advocates of different programs and visions of modernity. In the years following World War II, this reached a climax with the global competition between the Soviet Union and the United States and the competing communist and capitalist models of modern society. Similar competitions arose in different regions, with a variety of alternatives being offered, ranging from Pan-African and Pan-Arab visions to rivalries between Soviet, Chinese, and other models of communism. However, these were all "civil wars" within modernity, not opposition to it. Modernity had become the mode of the mainstream of politics and ideology virtually throughout the world.

New critiques of modernity began to be articulated in the second half of the twentieth century. In the emerging debates, some of the critiques came to be identified as "postmodern." In this competition, modernity was mainstream, representing established institutions, and advocates of modernity were thus in a conservative position and their nonmodern opponents represented innovative change. Some of the new postmodern perspective reflected new modes of thought and analysis and other aspects involved new forms of social movement organizations. Mainstream modernity was identified with the type of society created by the Industrial Revolution. In many ways, the prototypical "modern society" was industrial society, and modernization was seen frequently as identified with the industrialization of "traditional" economies and societies. In the middle of the 1960s, scholars like Daniel Bell began to speak of "post-industrial" society in which major structural changes were transforming the nature of society.[9] The broader intellectual and conceptual dimensions of this transformation were identified by many as representing the emergence of a "new 'Post-Modern' world," with analysts like Peter Drucker arguing already in 1957 that at "some unmarked point during the last twenty years we imperceptibly moved out of the Modern Age."[10] This development was not about a particular form of literary criticism; it was a challenge to "modernity" as it had come to be defined in social, economic, political, and religious terms by the middle of the twentieth century.

The era of history beginning in the middle of the twentieth century is, in the words of a major historian of the time, Geoffrey Barraclough, fundamentally a "new period which we call 'contemporary' or 'postmodern'," with "postmodern" marking the recognition that "modern history" was at an end.[11] This postmodernity was and still is built on the foundations created by modernity and is, in many ways, a continuation of the "modern" but in new forms. The emergence of postmodern ideas and structures is closely tied to the development of multiple modernities and the later "glocal" forms of modernity.

The development of "modern movements in Islam" is shaped by these diverse and changing forms of modernity. The intellectual content of Islamic modernisms and the nature of modern Muslim movements and their organizations are part of the continuing transformations of modernity. In this context, it becomes possible to identify in very general terms, four eras of "modern movements in Islam," each relating to the major contemporary mode of modernity with which they were interacting.

The first era is the era of interaction with a monolithically conceived modernity that was identified with western European forms and was a revolutionary challenge to existing conceptualizations and institutions. The second era is a time of developing modes of modernity that were distinctively modern but not necessarily Western in orientation, working for the definition of an Islamic modernity in the emerging global era of multiple modernities. An important part of this was the competition among alternative visions of "Islamic modernity," reflecting the broader global "civil wars" within mainstreamed modernities. The second half of the twentieth century is the time of the complex emergence of postmodern forms. The third era of "modern movements in Islam" reflects the development of movements that are locally and regionally distinctive in a world of increasingly multinational and international developments. In the Muslim world, this involved efforts to redefine basic political and societal units of identity and action in explicitly Islamic terms, rather than working to create Islamic versions of Western and Western-modern forms. By the beginning of the twenty-first century, the fourth era of modernity and of modern movements in Islam is marked by the increasingly strong tendency to go beyond multinational contexts and arenas to transnational and "glocal" modes of thought and organization. In all of these areas, the capacity of Muslim intellectuals and activists to develop new modes of conceptualization and organization reflects a strong tradition of effective innovation in Islam. Key figures in each of these eras provide examples of this innovative dynamism.

## MONOLITHIC MODERNITY AND MODERN ISLAMIC MOVEMENTS

Islamic modernism and modern Muslim movements at the end of the nineteenth century were interacting with Victorian-industrial modernity. These movements were part of the broader spectrum of intellectual trends and organizations that developed in the context of nineteenth-century-style modernity. In this broad spectrum, the place of Islam in framing discourse and providing organizational repertoires varied from little or no impact among extreme Westernizers to being central in the thinking of some intellectuals and activists.

Although some Muslim intellectuals in the nineteenth century dealt with questions of the relationships between Muslim and Western thought in the context of modernity, it was not until the final quarter of the century that major conscious efforts to articulate "Islamic modernism" were made. A number of intellectuals in major Muslim societies participated, but four individuals stand out as the best-known of these "modernists."

Jamal al-Din al-Afghani/al-Asadabadi (1838–1897) is often described as a "precursor" of "a line of ideological modernizers ... who have tried to interpret Islam in new ways to inculcate in Muslims the virtues of reform and self-strengthening."[12] He became identified more with the political vision of creating a Pan-Islamic movement than with religious modernism, but he was a key figure in the emergence of a modernist approach. In this first stage of the articulation of Islamic modernism, he "was addressing people whose primary commitment was to Islamic values, and in saying that modern Western virtues were to be found in Islam he was trying to attain Muslim acceptance of those modern ideas."[13] However, in ways similar to other earlier intellectuals, he was not significantly engaged in the effort to articulate either those "Islamic values" or the "modern Western virtues" in new ways. This effort was most significantly begun in the next generation of scholars in the Muslim world.

Three thinkers provide a sense of the diversity of the modernist effort in the Muslim world at the end of the nineteenth century. Muhammad Abduh (1849–1905), an Egyptian scholar and associate of al-Afghani's, is viewed by many as the true founder of "Islamic modernism." At first he was an activist, working with al-Afghani in a more political arena. However, he returned to Egypt in the era of the beginning of the British occupation and served in a variety of official posts, most notably as the grand mufti of Egypt. He believed that Muslims had fallen drastically behind the West and that this was the result of the medieval historical developments in the Islamic community "whereby the progress of knowledge was arrested."[14] He criticized "the slavish imitation of the ancestors that characterizes the leaders of the religions, with their instinct to hold timidly to tradition-sanctioned ways"[15] and saw no contradiction between Islam correctly understood and modern science.

Sir Sayyid Ahmad Khan (1817–1898), a well-traveled South Asian, was another important figure in the articulation of Islamic modernism. Ahmad Khan argued that modern science, as a way of understanding nature, was not in contradiction to Islam. For him, "Islam is nature and nature is Islam."[16] He established the Mohammedan Anglo-Oriental College in 1875, with a modern curriculum including the sciences. This institution became Aligarh Muslim University (in 1920). It was the core of the Aligarh movement and an intellectual center for Islamic modernism in South Asia.

Ismail Bey Gasprinskii or Gaspirali (1851–1914), a Muslim intellectual in the Russian empire, was a third figure defining a modernist alternative at this time. He is identified as the major articulator of the movement of Muslim renewal called "Jadidism." He told Muslims that because of intellectual stagnation, in terms of science and knowledge, "we are four hundred years behind."[17] He published a journal for Russian Muslims and developed a new educational curriculum to modernize the schools for Muslims within the Russian empire. He advocated close cultural cooperation between Muslims and Russians as the most effective way for Muslims to be a part of the modern world.[18]

Although these early modernists presented a variety of different positions, they were remarkably similar in their general understanding of "modernity." In their thinking, "modern" was viewed in monolithic terms. It was seen as basically identical with "The West" and at the core of modernity was "modern science," also viewed as monolithic. These assumptions shaped the nature of their Islamic modernism. They all started with a faith in the truth of Islam and therefore if Islam were seen to be weak or backward, it was the result of the historic failures of Muslims. The modernists rejected historic traditionalism as being an obstacle to Islamic success and therefore actually counter to Islam. The methodology was the exercise of independent informed analysis *(ijtihad)* of the basic sources of Islam. One result was an absence of a sense of "clash of civilizations" in this modernism. Since modernity was monolithic, the clash was between modernity and conservative traditionalism, not between Islam and the West. This approach illustrates the general characteristic of early modernity in Europe as well as the Muslim world: "the modern" represents the radical change and the anti-modern is conservative tradition.

While Islamic modernism became well-established by the beginning of the twentieth century, "modern movements" were less effectively developing. During the nineteenth century, some modern-style movements developed in the Muslim world, but they were not primarily defined by Islamic concerns. Constitutionalism and groups advocating reforms of governmental structures and similar movements had significance but they represented the beginnings of more secular responses to modernity. Such efforts were basically movements of Westernization with only limited reference to Islam.[19] Movements and movement organizations that were explicitly identifiable as "Islamic" still were not developing in "modern" organizational modes. The most visible and significant Muslim movements in that century were still in organizational terms nonmodern, even though they may have utilized some "modern" technologies. This was especially true of the major jihad organizations that adopted more modern weaponry but were fundamentally nonmodern in their ideology and organizational mode. Important Sufi nonmodern *tariqah* organizational traditions provided the base for jihad movements and movements that came into conflict with the forces of European imperial expansion. Some of the major examples are the Tijaniyyah Tariqah in the jihad movement of al-Hajj Umar Tal in West Africa, the Naqshbandiyyah as a base for the opposition to Russian expansion in the Caucasus, and the Salihiyyah in the Somali jihad of Muhammad Abdullah Hasan. In addition there was the nonmodern framing of ideology and organization in the Mahdist movement in Sudan.

The most "modern" of the explicitly Islamic movements of the late nineteenth century is the Pan-Islamic movement. Al-Afghani played an important role in defining a vision of a worldwide union of Muslim states that could counter the growing global dominance of Europe. This vision also was at least a part of the policies of the Ottoman sultan Abdul Hamid II. In many ways, the Pan-Islamic movement was similar to other macronationalist or Pan- movements that developed in the late nineteenth century, including Pan-Slavism, Pan-Germanism, and Pan-Turkism.[20] However, like the other Pan- movements, Pan-Islam never was able to establish an effective movement organization to mobilize the potential relatively widespread sympathy for the concept. Ultimately, "Islam, rather than Pan-Islam, became an integrative value" in the emerging Muslim nationalist movements and nation-states.[21]

In the first era of "modern movements in Islam," the major innovations were in the development of Islamic modernism as an intellectual and conceptual combination of reconceptualized Islam and monolithic modernity. Early reformers like Rifa'a Rafi al-Tahtawi (1801–1873) in Egypt and Khayr al-Din Pasha (1822–1890) in Tunisia had basically been concerned "to ask whether devout Muslims could accept institutions and ideas of the modern world; they had come to stay, and so much the worse for anyone who did not accept them."[22] However, the writings of Abduh and modernists like him were directed at Muslims who were "men of modern culture and experience who doubted whether Islam, or indeed any revealed religion, was valid as a guide to life."[23] The goal of the Islamic modernist was to articulate Islam as a valid guide to modern life, accepting modernity in its monolithic, Western identity. By the early twentieth century, the writings of Abduh and others provided the intellectual foundations for movements from Java to Morocco. It was the organizations created within these movements that became some of the first Muslim movements that were modern in mode and organization. Up until that time, the organization mode of explicitly Islamic organizations remained relatively nonmodern.

## MODERN ISLAMIC MOVEMENTS AND MULTIPLE MODERNITIES

Islamic modernism and modern Muslim movements were significant elements in Muslim societies around the world during the first two-thirds of the twentieth century. Distinctive modernist intellectual formulations reflected local conditions and the emergence of a global environment in which multiple modernities were recognized as authentic and legitimate. Parallel to these intellectual developments was the emergence of movement organizations that were distinctively modern in structure. However, these movements and modes of Islamic modernism faced the competition of alternative modern ideologies and organizations, especially associated with nationalism, and then later with radical secular ideologies. The "civil war" within modernity was an important part of life in the Muslim world, as it was in other major societies.

In the next generation of modernist thinkers, there was less willingness to define modernity primarily in terms of its Western characteristics. Abduh's student, Rashid Rida (1865–1935), adopted a more restricted vision, distinguishing between copying the West and becoming modern like the West: "Imitating the West will make us dependent on the Europeans forever and eliminate all our hopes to approach and emulate them."[24] A similar approach to Western-style modernity was adopted by a major South Asia modernist, Muhammad Iqbal (1877–1938): "With the reawakening of Islam, therefore, it is necessary to examine, in an independent spirit, what Europe has thought and how far the conclusions reached by her can help us in the revision and, if necessary, reconstruction of theological thought in Islam."[25] Many intellectuals throughout the Muslim world grappled with the challenge of defining an Islamic modernity.

By the mid-century, the major debates were no longer between conservative opponents of modernism and the modernists. Instead, the competition was between more secular visions of society within more nationalist or secularist or leftist positions and those for whom Islam continued to provide important parts of the conceptual repertoire of their modernist programs. One important area reflecting the nature of these debates is the discussion of the rights and responsibilities of women in Islam. This subject had not received much attention in the works of the early modernists. However, Qasim Amin (1863–1908), an Egyptian intellectual in the tradition of Abduh, argued in a famous and controversial book *al-Mar'ah al-Jadidah* (The New Woman), that "Islamic law originally treated men and women equally" and that the patriarchal practices of historic Muslim societies were counter to Islamic teachings.[26] However, most early Islamic modernists paid little attention to gender issues and advocacy for gender equality was primarily by more secular-oriented modernizers.

By the 1960s, in most major Muslim societies, the conservative, non-modern intellectual groups had gone underground or disappeared, while Islamic modernist intellectuals competed relatively unsuccessfully with more secular modernists. In Egypt, for example, before 1952, the more secular nationalist tradition of the Wafd Party competed with liberal nationalists, with the pragmatic political groups associated with the monarchy, and early Islamists in the Muslim Brotherhood. In the era of Nasser, old-style liberal nationalism was replaced by his self-consciously radical Arab socialism, in which modernist Islam played only a minor role.

It is possible, however, to argue that the politics of radical and conservative nationalisms of the 1960s, from Sukarno's Indonesia to Nasser's Egypt and Sekou Touré's Guinea or the more conservative "White Revolution" of the Shah in Iran or the reform programs proposed by King Faysal in Saudi Arabia, all represent a broad spectrum of articulations of forms of Islamic modernism. The classical rationalism of Abduh may not have survived, but Islam was not excluded from the articulation of the modern programs of identity and reform. However, in this new modernism of the mid-twentieth century, Islam was not as central a component as it had been earlier.

As intellectual modernism became less important, the establishment of modern-style Muslim movements and organizations became a major element in the development of modern movements in Islam. While the major innovative responses to modernity in the late nineteenth century were intellectual, during much of the twentieth century, they were organizational. Large Muslim organizations that were basically modern in their structures became a significant part of the social and political landscape throughout much of the Muslim world. While many people speak of what appeared to be the triumph of relatively secular nationalism, the new modern-style, Islamically identified organizations were a major feature of Muslim life throughout the twentieth century. While these organizations may have received some inspiration from premodern Muslim organizational traditions like the Sufi tariqahs, they were basically modern in format and modes of operation and modern (though not always "modernist") in their intellectual formulations.

The best-known examples of these modern organizations are the Muslim Brotherhood in Egypt and the Jama'at-i Islami of South Asia. In organizational structure, these two groups illustrate the effective institutional innovation of Muslims in the contexts of twentieth-century modernity. They were, and continue to be, major participants in the competition for defining the nature of Islamic modernity. They effectively presented a message of committed Islamic activism to the new generations of modern educated Muslims. While some of the old-style scholars *(ulama)* were involved, the leadership for these modern Muslim organizations were not scholars of the old style nor were they Sufi guides like those who had led the jihad groups in the nineteenth century. The result is that these are modern Islamic movement organizations.

The ideological positions of these groups were conscious of modernist intellectual formulations but did not represent advocacy for modernism as such. The ideas of the founders of these two organizations, Hasan al-Banna (1906–1949) in Egypt and Abu al-A'la Mawdudi (1903–1979) in South Asia, were in many ways a bridge between the Islamic modernism of the era of monolithic modernity and the reformulations of modernism in postmodern forms. The debates about gender issues have an interesting place in this intellectual context. Al-Banna and Mawdudi were similar to most of their male contemporaries in giving little priority to gender issues. However, two women made distinctive contributions to the ideological developments of their movements. Zaynab al-Ghazali (1917–2005) established an organization for women that was parallel to the Muslim Brotherhood in Egypt in its modern style, providing an array of social services, publications, and learning opportunities for women, but was theologically conservative on issues of gender. Similarly, Maryam Jameelah (b. 1934) is an American convert to Islam who became closely associated with Mawdudi and emigrated to Pakistan. She is a prolific author, articulately opposing modernist positions on gender equality and a wide range of other issues. She, like Zaynab al-Ghazali, is clearly modern in the technologies of advocacy but anti-modernist in terms of intellectual positions.

Similar organizations developed throughout the Muslim world. Even the most theologically conservative groups have modern-style organizations. One of the best examples of this is the Tablighi Jama'at, which began as a grassroots movement of religious revival (not political assertion) in 1926 in northern India. In the years following World War II, the organization effectively went global, and by the end of the twentieth century, it had millions of supporters and members around the world. In intellectual terms, this is not an Islamic "modernist" group, but it is clearly a modern-style association. Another large organization, primarily in Indonesia, is the Muhammadiya. This association was established in 1912 by someone who had studied in Mecca and became inspired by the modernist teachings of Abduh. This organization, in contrast to the Tablighi Jama'at, is explicitly modernist in its theology as well as very effectively modern in its associational structure. At the beginning of the twenty-first century, it has millions of members and is a major political and religious force in Southeast Asia.

In the era of emerging multiple and competing modernities, Muslims both developed modernist articulations of Islam and movement organizations that are clearly modern in their structures even if they are not modernist is their intellectual formulations. In this second era, Muslims accepted the basic frameworks of modernity and worked to create Islamic versions of those frames of modernity. Globally, the nation and nation-state had emerged as the basic unit of political and social operation and nationalism was a primary framing narrative for identity. Modern Muslim organizations like the Muslim Brotherhood and Jama'at-i Islami, as well as modernist organizations like the Muhammadiyya, worked within the "national" framework. A leading modernist thinker like Iqbal became identified as the father of the idea of a separate Muslim nation-state in South Asia. Islamic modernism and modern movements were an important part of the history of the Muslim world in this era of modernity.

POSTMODERN MODERNITY AND MODERN
MOVEMENTS IN ISLAM

Islamic thinkers and organizations participated in the emergence of postmodern perspectives in the 1960s and later. The influence of modern-style nationalism and positivist rationalisms began to be replaced by efforts to articulate Islamically centered visions and structures that were not necessarily in the previous modern patterns of thought and organization. In political terms, this development is identified with what has come to be called "Political Islam" and the "Islamic Resurgence," while in intellectual terms, Islamic modernism was gradually replaced by new conceptual frameworks that were, at least in some ways, similar to the new conceptual frameworks identified as postmodernism in the West.

During the 1970s, growing popular support for Islamically identified groups and programs throughout the Muslim world created a sense of an "Islamic resurgence." While many of the manifestations of this resurgence were expressed in terms of social activities and intensified piety in personal life, the most visible aspects of the resurgence were political. Political activism was increasingly expressed in Islamic rather than radical secularist or nationalist terms. This new "political" fervor was most visible initially in marginal militant and revolutionary-jihad groups like Takfir wa al-Higrah in Egypt, while the older Muslim "national" organizations like the Muslim Brotherhood and the Jama'at-i Islami moved toward more mainstream political ideological positions.

By the beginning of the 1980s, however, relatively new styles of political Islam were being articulated and provided the bases for the political programs of the Islamic resurgence. The concept of an Islamic state had been part of earlier political programs of Islamic organizations. However, as in the case of the Muslim Brotherhood in Egypt, this had primarily involved working to get Shari'a recognized as a source of law and legislation in independent Muslim nation-states. Even in Pakistan, which had been established as an Islamic state, the issue of defining the actual nature of an Islamic state was a source of constant political tension.

Older established Islamic modernist definitions of an Islamic state were relatively general and could be shaped to fit within the nationalist visions of a modern nation-state. There had been some brief efforts in the 1920s by Islamic modernists to reestablish the caliphate, at least as the basic political ideal. However, the Khilafat Movement in India (1919–1924) was only an effort to preserve the office of caliph in the Ottoman empire rather than a political program defining a modern caliphate. Rashid Rida, Abduh's associate, was probably the most active person in trying to define and then establish a modern caliphate. However, after much effort, the "conclusion was that, however much the Sunni Muslims, himself included, piously wished otherwise, it was impossible to revive the traditional Caliphate, and hence it would be better to devise the nearest alternative to it."[27] The modernist general definition of this alternative was described by Iqbal and echoed later by others in different ways: "The essence of 'tauhid' [divine one-ness] as a working idea is equality, solidarity, and freedom. The State, from the Islamic standpoint, is an endeavor to transform these ideal principles into space-time forces, an aspiration to realize them in a definite human organization."[28]

The new political Islam of the 1980s was much more explicit in its definitions than the earlier modernisms had been. There were calls for the direct implementation of Shari'a, understood as an explicit code of law that was the product of previous centuries of jurisprudential study. An authentically Islamic state was to be different from a modern nation-state in its identification of goals and loyalties. It was to have its foundations in the *ummah*, the community of believers, and not in an ethnically identified "nation." One of the early articulators of this newer nonmodern/postmodern vision was Sayyid Qutb (1906–1966), who noted that the Prophet Muhammad could have led a successful Arab nationalist movement or a successful movement to overthrow the wealthy exploiters of the masses or a major movement of moral reform, but that none of these represented the path he was directed by God to follow, since nationalism, class warfare, or moral reform not based on religious faith all lead to tyranny.[29] Although Qutb did not provide specific descriptions of the society and state that he would accept as "Islamic," it is clear that neither the modern nationalist nor the modern socialist state would meet his standards.

Movements supporting the new visions of political Islam developed in many different parts of the Muslim world and often movement organizations developed that gave concrete form to the aspirations of these movements. In this it is important to remember that broad social movements are the frameworks within which distinctive organizations and mobilizing structures can develop, but the movements and the organizations represent two different dimensions of action.[30] Activists have options in developing mobilization structures for establishing organizations, and they can work within existing structures for political or social mobilization or "they can invent new ones as well as radically alter and creatively combine available ones as they try to achieve their collective purposes."[31] It is in the inventiveness in creating organizational formats that the innovative imagination of Islamic activists of the 1980s is best illustrated.

The most successful movement of political Islam was the Islamic revolution in Iran (1978–1979) that brought about the creation of the Islamic Republic of Iran. The modernizing monarchy of the shahs of Iran, one of the major examples of a basically secular modernizing/ Westernizing regime in the twentieth century, was replaced by a differently conceived political system that accepted modernity and its technology but was built on a distinctive articulation of Islam that is clearly postmodernist. The old concerns of Islamic modernists dealing with whether or not a believing Muslim could also be "modern" or if it would be possible to develop an authentically Islamic modernity were irrelevant to the concerns of those scholars who devised and articulated the new political Islam of the Iranian revolution. The chief intellectual architect of this new political system was Ayatollah Khomeini (1900–1989), who transformed both traditional and modernist Shi'a political thought with his concept of the governance by the legal scholars (*velayat-e faqih*, "governance of the jurisconsultant"), a political system in which the religious-legal scholars were to play the central role in defining the nature of the state. In this vision, "Islamic Government does not correspond to any existing forms of government" whether monarchies or republics.[32] The political system that was established survived a major war with Iraq, the death of Ayatollah Khomeini, and other leadership transitions into the twenty-first century.

In the Sunni world, a wide variety of movements crystallized into activist organizations advocating various forms of an Islamic state and implementation of Shari'a. In Malaysia, a student movement that originally worked for Malay ethnic rights was transformed into an activist political organization, ABIM, led by Anwar Ibrahim. ABIM's vision of an Islamic state was not tied to a conservative understanding of Shari'a as understood through the medieval texts and, instead, emphasized the importance of justice and equity in an Islamic state and society. A similar movement developed in Tunisia and provided the base for the establishment of the Islamic Tendency Movement under the leadership of Rashid Ghannoushi. In the late 1980s, in an effort to become a legal political party in the post-Bourguiba state, Ghannoushi and his colleagues established the Nahdah Party, but the party never received legal recognition and remains illegal. In Sudan, the older Sudanese Muslim Brotherhood (SMB) had long been an advocate of an Islamic Constitution or, at least, constitutional recognition of Shar'ia as a base for the legal system. The most visible leader of the SMB was Hasan al-Turabi, who served in many cabinets from the mid-1960s until the beginning of the twenty-first century. He and his organization supported the implementation of Shari'a in Sudan, as first proclaimed by the military dictator Ja'far al-Numayri in the September Laws of 1983. The 1983 decrees involved a literalist-conservative understanding of the Shari'a that varied from positions taken by Turabi about the need for legal renewal, but that more conservative mode continued in the political system established by a military coup in 1989 and originally supported by Turabi. Each of these movements and their organizations represent a form of political Islam that goes beyond the old political conceptualizations of earlier Islamic modernists. Their diversity also illustrates the innovative capacity of the articulators of postmodernist political Islam.

The high visibility of the movements and organizations of political Islam tended to obscure important intellectual and scholarly developments in the Muslim world during the 1970s and 1980s. During the 1960s, a number of Muslim thinkers began a variety of efforts to develop new modes of articulating Islam that went beyond the earlier modernist critiques of "traditional" Muslim thought and the modernist accommodations to basic knowledge assumptions of modernity. Often now, the critique was of modernism itself and the issues of challenges to modernity as the established mainstream of intellectual life. These new thinkers combined concerns that were specifically Islamic with the broader efforts by intellectuals in all of the emerging multiple modernities to gain new understandings of the new social orders and of "knowledge" itself.

Three Muslim thinkers who studied and worked in France (and elsewhere) during the 1960s present important new analyses that reflect some of the major themes of the innovative rethinking of the time. These are Mohammed Arkoun (b. 1928), of Algerian Berber origin; Hasan Hanafi (b. 1935), an Egyptian; and an Iranian scholar, Ali Shariati (1933–1977). While the thought and careers of each of these three show great diversity, together they provide important examples of the significant new directions of Islamic thought in the second half of the twentieth century. In their thinking and activities, "modernity" is a fact of life to be examined, not a goal to be achieved.

In an era when political and economic thought tended to be dominated by the assumptions of modernization theory and projects for economic development, Arkoun, Hanafi, and Shariati made important contributions to shifting intellectual attention to the question of the nature of knowledge itself. In these efforts they were part of the movements to transform the social sciences.

Arkoun "pushed to the very frontiers of Western social science in an effort to free Islam not just from Western misperceptions and misconceptions but also from the grips of many of its most fervent advocates. In so doing, he put himself on the cutting edge of Islamic discourse, or beyond it."[33] While early Islamic modernists debated the relationship between "reason" and "revelation," Arkoun worked to reconceptualize "reason" itself: "We must abandon the dualist framework of knowledge that pits reason against imagination, history against myth, true against false, good against evil, and reason against faith. We must postulate a plural, changing, welcoming sort of rationality, one consistent with the psychological operations that the Qur'an locates in the heart and that contemporary anthropology attempts to reintroduce under the label of the imaginary."[34]

Hanafi and Shariati also worked to create new methodologies and worldviews for the new understandings of "knowledge" in the world of postmodern thinkers globally. Shariati worked to articulate a philosophy of history and a theory of social change in which Islam was a force for radical social justice and equity.[35] Similarly, Hanafi worked to articulate Islamic thought in a way that would transform it "from a creed into a revolution."[36] While earlier Islamic modernists like Ahmad Khan and others later called for a new *'ilm al-kalam* or theology, Hanafi and Shariati worked to transform *'ilm al-kalam* into a "liberation theology."

By the 1970s and 1980s, this type of approach examining the nature of available knowledge itself opened the way for new thinking on many issues. One major area is gender issues in Islam, a subject that had not been a primary topic for study by modernists or in modern organizations. One leader in this new effort is Fatema Mernissi, a Moroccan sociologist who gained international visibility with her analysis of male-female relations in her study *Beyond the Veil: Male-Female Dynamics in Modern Muslim Society* (1975). This led to a more direct study of Islamic traditions, the life of the Prophet Muhammad, and the inequality of women created by the patriarchalism of male-dominated Muslim society, published as *The Veil and the Male Elite: A Feminist Interpretation of Women's Rights in Islam* (1987). These provided important foundations for the emergence of what some have called "Islamic feminism," involving a transformation of important aspects of the Islamic modernist tradition.

In the works of these Muslim intellectuals and some of their other contemporaries, it is clear that the innovative cutting edge of Islamic thought was now a critique of mainstream modernity rather than continuing the earlier modernist efforts to adopt and adapt to modernity. This development is similar to the changing nature of modern Islamic movements and organizations, which were going beyond the old "modern" canons of political systems based on Western-style nation-states, and working to define Islamic political systems that were, in this political sense, effectively postmodern.

## "GLOCAL" MODERNITY AND MODERN MOVEMENTS IN ISLAM

The world of the twenty-first century is the world of globalized and transformed modernity. All forms of modernism, whether Islamic or Western or any of the other modernisms articulated in the world of multiple modernities, are transcended in significant ways. In this context, even many of the major expressions of postmodernism have a somewhat archaic tone. In particular, globalization has transformed the meanings of distinctive local particularisms, while those new particularisms give new shape and meaning to the global. The result is a world context in which global and local are no longer simply competing polarities but they combine to create processes of "glocalization." In this context, it is possible to view the intellectual equivalents in the twenty-first century of the early Islamic modernists and the organizational equivalents of modern Islamic movements as manifestations of a global rooted cosmopolitanism.[37] It is not possible to provide more than an introduction to a few features of this current phase of the development and evolution of modern movements in Islam.

In terms of movements and movement organizations, like major social movements in societies around the world, social movements and their organizations in the Muslim world are developing in clearly postmodern formats. In broad historical terms, Charles Tilly has speculated that even the very phenomena that have been defined as "social movements" may disappear in the distinctive conditions of the twenty-first century: "*The social movement, as an invented institution, could disappear or mutate into some quite different form of politics.* . . . We must take seriously the possibility that the twenty-first century will destroy social movements as vehicles of popular claim making because the conditions for their survival have dissolved or because new forms of claim making have supplanted them."[38]

Even a quick survey of Muslim activist organizations provides numerous examples of the new forms of claim making that have emerged among the descendents of modern movements in Islam. Movements like the Muslim Brotherhood in Egypt were in the modern format of the activist political party. Observers of the Brotherhood in the early days noted the structural similarities between it and the Communist Party, with carefully coordinated cells and clear centralization of leadership and authority. In the era of political Islam, mainstream organizations like ABIM in Malaysia and al-Nahdah in Tunisia have maintained more "modern" political party structures. However, more radical militant groups have tended, whether consciously or because of circumstances, to adopt forms of modern radical organization developed in the contexts of guerrilla wars by groups like the Viet Cong. In the Muslim world, the best examples are the organizations of the mujahidin in Afghanistan in the war against the Soviet occupation and by the 1990s, the best example is the old centralized structure of al-Qaeda.

By the 1990s, the new global contexts opened the way for the new phase of decentralized electronic networks of activists, creating what could be viewed as the new forms of claim making that are supplanting the old modes of social movement organization. The new structures are networks more than they are organizations. They are the networks of what Marc Sageman calls "leaderless jihad." This new form "has evolved from a structured group of al-Qaeda masterminds, controlling vast resources and issuing commands, to a multitude of informal local groups trying to emulate their predecessors by conceiving and executing operations from the bottom up."[39] One important key to the development of these destructive groups/networks is a remarkably effective and innovative use of the new electronic resources for communication without having to consider limitations of time and space.

It is not only among the terrorist fanatics, however, that the new cosmopolitan, glocal modes of operation have developed. A whole new universe of communication has developed in the emergence of what can be called cyber-Islam.⁴⁰ Interpretations and rulings on questions of Islamic living from around the world are almost immediately available to those with access to the Internet (and that access through local Internet cafes is remarkably widely available). Inspirational religious media stars have thousands, and sometimes millions, of followers. People like the Egyptian preacher Amr Khaled have multinational audiences. His followers are part of the program called Suna' al-Hiyah (Life Makers), which is not a formal centralized organization but rather a network of individuals and groups inspired by his teachings.⁴¹ A similar phenomenon is the success of Abdullah Gynmastiar, "Indonesia's first true megastar Muslim televangelist."⁴² With an audience in the millions, he has become a major figure in the Islamic world of Southeast Asia. In virtually every country or region around the world, there are similar popular figures who are in the forefront of a populist rearticulation of Islamic piety. In a sense, this might be viewed as the pietist Reformation of contemporary Islam.

In intellectual terms, the important efforts at understanding Islam in contemporary terms and in relationship to modernity and its successors continue in the early twenty-first century. The new approaches to knowledge and epistemology set in motion by people like Mohammed Arkoun create new perspectives. While these new lines of thinking involved many different fields, intellectual developments in two areas provide useful introductions to the nature of what must now be considered post-postmodern movements in Islam at the beginning of the twenty-first century. One is the complex question of analytical method for understanding the nature of the basic sources for understanding Islam, and the second involves Islamic responses to the diversity of a world of rooted cosmopolitanism.

Many thinkers throughout the Muslim world are engaged in an effort to articulate a new understanding of the basic intellectual disciplines in the process of understanding the message and meaning of Islam. Gamal al-Banna is engaged in the effort to define a new science of Islamic jurisprudence *(fiqh),* as presented in his three-volume study *Nahwa Fiqh Jadid*.⁴³ In this, he supports the development of new legal hermeneutics for the definition of Shari'a in contemporary terms. In even broader terms, Nasr Abu-Zayd speaks of the need for a general development of "a humanistic hermeneutics," especially in relationship to understanding the Qur'an. Abu-Zayd notes that Arkoun developed important analyses of the Qur'an as text. However, in 2004, Abu-Zayd noted the importance of going beyond this: "I was one of the propagators of the textuality of the Qur'an under the influence of the literary approach initiated by the modern, and still appreciated literary approach. I recently began to realize how dealing with the Qur'an as only a text reduces its status and ignores the fact that it is still functioning as a 'discourse' in everyday life."[44] Abu-Zayd and al-Banna represent an exceptionally important line of intellectual development in contemporary Islamic thought that receives remarkably little attention. Similar analyses of gender issues have continued the transformation of scholarly understanding of gender in Islamic tradition and faith. In the works of Amina Wadud, for example, the foundation of careful textual and contextual analysis provides the foundation for what she called "the gender jihad," which is "a struggle to establish gender justice in Muslim thought and praxis."[45] However, such efforts by these scholars and many others are transforming the whole structure of the intellectual disciplines of Islamic studies.

One of the major features of the Islamic world of the late twentieth century was the growing visibility and importance of Muslim minorities in communities around the world, especially in Western Europe and North America. In global terms, this was part of the increasingly strong incentives to recognize global diversity and to accept more open attitudes of pluralism. The Iranian intellectual 'Abdolkarim Soroush went so far as to put all the world religions on an equal footing in a 1998 essay "Saratha-ye mostaqim" (Straight Paths), "the very title being a sacrilegious pluralization of a fundamental Qur'anic concept."[46]

Scholars have often spoken of distinctive local adaptations that create syntheses of local and cosmopolitan Islamic practice, speaking of "African Islam" or "Malaysian Islam" or many other such local manifestations. However, these localistic particularisms were usually seen as being in tension with standard (sometimes labeled "orthodox") Islam, and as some way representing a popular "dilution" of "true Islam." This assumed the existence of a single, monolithic definition of Islam. However, increasingly, Muslim thinkers have begun to distinguish between "historic" Islamic traditions and cultures that have been the result of human activities and "normative" Islam, which represents the revealed and unchanging message of God—but can be expressed in the many different cultural contexts of believers. One of the early influential scholars who laid foundations for this kind of analysis is Fazlur Rahman, who argued that for the necessary modern transformation of the Islamic intellectual tradition to take place, it was essential "to distinguish clearly between normative Islam and historical Islam."[47] This distinction between cultural particulars and religious universals provides an important foundation for religious acceptance of pluralism in a world of rooted cosmopolitanism and glocalization.

Two contemporary Islamic intellectuals provide important analyses placing the issues of contemporary pluralism in the contexts of the broader reconceptualizations of the basic scholarly disciplines. Tariq Ramadan argues that it is possible for people to be both western Europeans and authentically believing Muslims. In this analysis, he notes that believers have a special obligation to understand the relationship between their particular contexts and the universal message: "it has been possible to differentiate, through reading the scriptural sources, between the universal principles to which the Muslim consciousness must seek to be faithful through the ages and the practice of those principles, which is necessarily relative, at a given moment in human history."[48] In specific terms, this means that it is important "to establish a distinction between the religious principles that define the identity of Muslims and the cultural trappings that those principles necessarily take on according to the societies in which individuals live."[49] Ramadan argues that American and European Muslims have a special opportunity and responsibility in the relationships between Islam and modernity: "Western Muslims will play a decisive role in the evolution of Islam worldwide because of the nature and complexity of the challenges they face, and in this their responsibility is doubly essential. By reflecting on their faith, their principles, and their identity within industrialized, secularized societies, they participate in the reflection the Muslim world must undertake on its relationship with the modern world."[50]

Sherman Jackson, also a contributor to this volume (see chapter 10), presents a similarly challenging agenda and offers an important alternative perspective of ways for believers to live within the diversity of the contemporary world. Among many major themes, he starts with the distinction between the universal-normative and the historic-particular, but he then makes the argument concrete by pointing to the dangers of accepting one universalist-particularist synthesis as being the only definition of the normative heritage. He notes the critical danger of "false universals," by which he means "the phenomenon of history internalized, normalized, and then forgotten as history. This invariably leads to the tendency to speak in universal terms but from a particular cultural, ideological, or historical perspective," and this false universal becomes "a powerful tool of domination."[51]

Whether consciously modernist or simply modern in organizational form, modern movements in Islam have shown a long-term capacity for significant innovation in ways of interacting with the challenges of modernity. As modernity itself has changed in the past century and a half, so too modern movements in Islam have changed. The new modes of conceptualization and movement organization present a picture of remarkable dynamism.

NOTES

1. The term "multiple modernities" is used and defined in a number of places by S.N. Eisenstadt. See, e.g., Eisenstadt, "Multiple Modernities in an Age of Globalization," *Canadian Journal of Sociology / Cahiers canadiens de sociologie* 24, 2 (Spring 1999): 283–295.

2. Charles Kurzman, "Introduction," in *Modernist Islam, 1840–1940: A Sourcebook,* ed. id. (New York: Oxford University Press, 2002), p. 4.

3. Ibid., p. 4.

4. See, e.g., the very influential study, Daniel Lerner, *The Passing of Traditional Society: Modernizing the Middle East.* (New York: Free Press of Glencoe, 1958).

5. See, e.g., the discussion in John Obert Voll, "The Mistaken Identification of 'The West' with 'Modernity,'" *American Journal of Islamic Social Sciences* 13, 1 (Spring 1966): 1–12.

6. Geoffrey C. Gunn, *First Globalization: The Eurasian Exchange, 1500–1800.* (Lanham, MD: Rowman & Littlefield, 2003).

7. See, e.g., Roland Robertson. "Glocalization: Time—Space and Homogeneity—Heterogeneity," in *Global Modernities,* ed. Mike Featherstone, Scott Lash, and Roland Robertson (Thousand Oaks, CA: Sage, 1995), pp. 25–44.

8. Manfred Halpern, *The Politics of Social Change in the Middle East and North Africa* (Princeton, NJ: Princeton University Press, 1963), p. 30.

9. See, e.g., the discussion of the work of the Commission on the Year 2000 led by Daniel Bell and organized by the American Academy of Arts and Sciences in 1965 in "The Post-Industrial Society: The Crisis of Rationality," *Bulletin of the American Academy of Arts and Sciences* 21, 2 (November 1967): 5–15. Bell later published his own conclusions in his book *The Coming of Post-Industrial Society: A Venture in Social Forecasting.* (New York: Basic Books, 1973).

10. Peter F. Drucker, *Landmarks of Tomorrow: A Report on the new "Post-Modern" World* (New York: Harper & Row, 1957), p. xi.

11. Geoffrey Barraclough, *An Introduction to Contemporary History* (Baltimore: Penguin Books, 1967, p. 23.

12. Nikki Keddie, *An Islamic Response to Imperialism: Political and Religious Writings of Sayyid Jamāl ad-Dīn "al-Afghānī* (Berkeley: University of California Press, 1983), p. xiii.
13. Ibid., p. xviii.
14. Muhammad Abduh, *The Theology of Unity,* trans. Ishaq Musa'ad and Kenneth Cragg (London: George Allen & Unwin, 1966), p. 38.
15. Ibid., p. 127.
16. Sayyid Ahmad Khan. "Lecture on Islam," in *Modernist Islam,* ed. Kurzman, p. 296.
17. Ismail Bey Gasprinskii, *Mebadi-yi Temeddün-I Islāmiyan-Rus* (First Steps Toward Civilizing the Russian Muslims), trans. Edward J. Lazzerini in "Turkic Modernism at the Turn of the Twentieth Century: An Insider's View," www.iccrimea.org/gaspirali/modernism.html. (accessed June 17, 2010).
18. See, e.g., Gasprinskii's essay "Russko-Vostochnoe soglashenie," trans. in *Tartars of the Crimea,* ed. Edward Allworth (Durham, NC: Duke University Press, 1988), pp. 202–216.
19. A helpful discussion of this issue as it developed in the Ottoman empire is Niyazi Berkes, *The Development of Secularism in Turkey* (New York: Routledge, 1998).
20. See, e.g., the analysis in Louis L. Snyder, *Macro-Nationalisms: A History of the Pan Movements* (Westport, CT: Greenwood Press, 1984).
21. Jacob M. Landau, *The Politics of Pan-Islam: Ideology and Organization* (Oxford: Clarendon Press, 1990), p. 248.
22. Albert Hourani, *Arabic Thought in the Liberal Age, 1798–1939* (Cambridge: Cambridge University Press, 1983), p. 139.
23. Ibid., p. 139.
24. Rashid Rida quoted in Emad Eldin Shahin, *Through Muslim Eyes: M. Rashīd Ridā and the West* (Herndon, VA: International Institute of Islamic Thought, 1993), p. 50.
25. Allama Muhammad Iqbal, *The Reconstruction of Religious Thought in Islam* (reprint, Lahore: Sh. Muhammad Ashraf, 1968), p. 8.
26. Charles Kurzman, "Modern Thought," in *Encyclopedia of Islam and the Muslim World,* ed. Richard C. Martin (New York: Macmillan, 2004), 2: 470.
27. Hamid Enayat, *Modern Islamic Political Thought* (Austin: University of Texas Press, 1982), p. 76.
28. Iqbal, *Reconstruction,* p. 154.
29. Syed Qutb, *Milestones,* trans. S. Badrul Hasan (Karachi: International Islamic Publishers, 1981), pp. 67–74.
30. See, e.g., the specific comments in Charles Tilly, *Social Movements, 1768–2004* (Boulder, CO: Paradigm, 2004), pp. 48–50, and, more generally, John D. McCarthy, "Constraints and Opportunities in Adopting, Adapting, and Inventing," in *Comparative Perspectives on Social Movements,* ed. Doug McAdam, John D. McCarthy, and Mayer N. Zald (Cambridge: Cambridge University Press, 1996), chap. 6.
31. McCarthy, "Constraints," p. 147.
32. Imam Khomeini, *Islam and Revolution,* trans. Hamid Algar (Berkeley, CA: Mizan Press, 1981), p. 55.

33. Robert D. Lee, "Foreword," in Mohammed Arkoun, *Rethinking Islam: Common Questions, Uncommon Answers* (Boulder, CO: Westview, 1999), p. viii.

34. Arkoun, *Rethinking Islam,* p. 37.

35. See, e.g., Ali Shariati, *On the Sociology of Islam,* trans. Hamid Algar (Berkeley, CA: Mizan Press), 1979.

36. Hasan Hanafi, *Min al-'aqīdah ilā al-thawrah,* 5 vols. (Cairo: Maktabah Madbuli, 1988).

37. This terminology comes from, among other sources, Sidney Tarrow, *The New Transnational Activism* (Cambridge: Cambridge University Press, 2005), and Kwame Anthony Appiah, *Cosmopolitanism: Ethics in a World of Strangers* (New York: Norton, 2006).

38. Tilly, *Social Movements,* p. 153. Italics in the original.

39. Marc Sageman, *Leaderless Jihad: Terror Networks in the Twenty-First Century* (Philadelphia: University of Pennsylvania Press, 2008), p. vii.

40. See the general survey provided in Gary R. Bunt, *Islam in the Digital Age: E-Jihad, Online Fatwas and Cyber Islamic Environments* (London: Pluto Press, 2003).

41. I am grateful to Samuel Harris of Georgetown University for his helpful insights into this movement resulting from his research, especially in Cairo.

42. Julia Day Howell, "Modulations of Active Piety: Professors and Televangelists as Promoters of Indonesian '*Sufisme,*' " in *Expressing Islam: Religious Life and Politics in Indonesia,* ed. Greg Fealy and Sally White (Singapore: Institute of Southeast Asian Studies, 2008), pp. 40–62.

43. Gamāl al-Bannā, *Nahwa Fiqh Jadīd* (Cairo: Dār al-Fikr al-Islāmī, 1995–1999). I am grateful to Ahmed Ibrahim of Georgetown University for his helpful insights into the thought of al-Banna.

44. Nasr Abu Zayd, "Rethinking the Qur'ān: Towards a Humanistic Hermeneutics" (address at conference on "Human Rights and Renewing Religious Discourse," Alexandria, 18–20 April 2005).

45. Amina Wadud, *Inside the Gender Jihad: Women's Reform in Islam* (Oxford: Oneworld, 2006), p. 10.

46. Said Amir Arjomand, "Globalization," in *Encyclopedia of Islam and the Muslim World,* 1: 279.

47. Fazlur Rahman, *Islam & Modernity: Transformation of an Intellectual Tradition* (Chicago: University of Chicago Press, 1982), p. 141.

48. Tariq Ramadan, *Western Muslims and the Future of Islam* (New York: Oxford University Press, 2004), p. 35.

49. Ibid., p. 78.

50. Ibid., pp. 225–226.

51. Sherman A. Jackson, *Islam and the Blackamerican: Looking Toward the Third Resurrection* (New York: Oxford University Press, 2005), p. 9.

# Contributors

NASR ABU-ZAYD (1943–2010) held the Ibn Rushd (Averroës) Chair of Islam and Humanism at the Universiteit voor Humanistiek / University of Humanistics in Utrecht. He received his B.A. in Arabic studies from Cairo University in 1972 and both his M.A. and Ph.D. in Arabic and Islamic studies also from Cairo University. Abu-Zayd was the recipient of several prestigious awards, including the Roosevelt Institute Medal for Freedom of Worship, the Ibn Rushd Prize for Freedom of Thought, and, most recently, the Freedom of Thought Prize awarded by the Muslim Democrats Society in Denmark. Abu-Zayd published fourteen books in Arabic, many of which have been translated into other languages, including Turkish, Bahasa Indonesian, and Persian. His publications in English include *Voice of an Exile* (2004), co-authored with Esther R. Nelson; *Rethinking the Qur'an: Towards a Humanistic Hermeneutics* (2004); and *Reformation of Islamic Thought: A Critical Historical Analysis* (2006).

ADONIS is the pseudonym of the Syrian poet Ali Ahmad Said Asbar. He received his Ph.D. from the University of St. Joseph in Beirut in 1973 and later served as professor of Arabic literature at the Université de la Sorbonne Nouvelle–Paris III. He was also professor of Arab poetry at the Université de Genève. Adonis co-founded and co-edited the literary review *Shi'r* between 1956 and 1964. He was also the founder of the literary review *Afaq* in 1964, a founding member of the Lebanese Writer's Union, and the founder of the literary review *Mawaqif,* for which he served as editor in chief until 1995. A prolific writer, Adonis has published numerous volumes of poetry, prose, translations, and critical essays. Among his earlier works are *Qasā'id Ūla* (First Poems) (1957); *Awrāk Fī l-Rīh* (Leaves in the Wind) (1958); and *Aghani Mihiar ad-Dimashqi* (Songs of Mihyar the Damascene) (1961). The most recent of his poetry publications are *Warraaq Yabii' Kutub al-Noujoum* and *Ihda' Hamlet, Tanachchaq Junoun Ophelia,* which were released in 2007.

MOHAMMED ARKOUN is emeritus professor at the Sorbonne in Paris as well as senior research fellow and member of the board of governors of the Institute of Ismaili Studies in London. He studied at Algiers University and at the Sorbonne in Paris, where he also taught from 1961 to 1992. Arkoun has taught as a visiting professor at UCLA, Princeton University, Temple University, the University of Louvain-la-Neuve, the Pontifical Institute of Arabic Studies in Rome, the University of Amsterdam, and New York University. He also served as a jury member for the Aga Khan Award for Architecture from 1981 to 1998. Arkoun has acted as editor of *ARABICA: Journal of Arabic and Islamic Studies / Revue d'études arabes et islamiques* and is the author of numerous books in French, English, and Arabic, including *Rethinking Islam* (1994), *The Unthought in Contemporary Islamic Thought* (2002; 2nd ed. with the title of *Islam: To Reform or to Subvert?* 2006); *De Manhattan à Bagdad: Au-delà du bien et du mal* (2003); *Humanisme et islam: Combats et propositions* (2006); *L'ABC de l'islam*, and *Getting out of Dogmatic Enclosures* (2007). His shorter studies have appeared in many academic journals and his works have been translated into several languages.

WALTER B. DENNY has taught at the University of Massachusetts Amherst Art History Program since 1970. He has held curatorial positions in Islamic art at the Harvard University Art Museums and the Smith College Museum of Art, and in September 2002 was named Charles Grant Ellis Research Associate in Oriental Carpets at the Textile Museum in Washington, DC, where he was a trustee for six years in the 1980s. He is senior consultant in the Department of Islamic Art, Metropolitan Museum of Art, where he is part of the curatorial team planning the museum's new Islamic galleries, scheduled to open in 2011. His exhibition, with catalogue, of the Ballard collection of Islamic carpets will open at the St. Louis Art Museum in late 2008. Denny's books include *Gardens of Paradise: Turkish Tiles 15th–17th Centuries* (1998), *Anatolian Carpets: Masterpieces from the Museum of Turkish and Islamic Arts, Istanbul* (1999), and, with two co-authors, *Ipek: Ottoman Imperial Silks and Velvets* (2001). His book *Iznik: The Artistry of Ottoman Ceramics* (2004) was translated into French by Christine Piot and Sylvie Barjansky as *Iznik: La céramique turque et l'art ottoman* (2004), and a German translation has also appeared (2005).

NELLY HANNA is a professor of Arabic and Islamic civilizations at the American University in Cairo. She obtained her *doctorat d'État* from the Université de Provence, Aix-en-Provence. Her research has focused on seventeenth- and eighteenth-century history. Hanna was visiting professor at Harvard University in 2001. She is the author of a number of works that deal with economy, society, and culture in Ottoman Egypt, among them *Making Big Money in 1600: The Life and Times of Ismail Abu Taqiya, Egyptian Merchant* (1998), and *In Praise of Books: A Cultural History of Cairo's Middle Class* (2003).

SHERMAN A. JACKSON is professor of Arabic and Islamic studies, visiting professor of law, and professor of Afro-American Studies at the University of Michigan, Ann Arbor. He received his Ph.D. from the University of Pennsylvania in Oriental Studies Islamic Near East in 1991. In 1987–1989, he served as executive director for the Center of Arabic Study Abroad (CASA) in Cairo,

Egypt. Jackson is author of *Islamic Law and the State: The Constitutional Jurisprudence of Shihāb al-Dīn al-Qarāfī* (1996), *On the Boundaries of Theological Tolerance in Islam: Abū Hāmid al-Ghazālī's Faysal al-Tafriqa* (2002), and *Islam and the Blackamerican: Looking Towards the Third Resurrection* (Oxford). He is a member of the U.S.-Muslim World Advisory Committee of the U.S. Institute of Peace, a co-founder of the American Learning Institute for Muslims (ALIM), a former member of the Fiqh Council of North America, past president of the Shari'ah Scholars' Association of North America (SSANA), and a past trustee of the North American Islamic Trust (NAIT). He is featured on the *Washington Post–Newsweek* blog "On Faith" and is listed by Religion Newswriters Foundation's ReligionLink (www.religionlink.com) as among the top ten experts on Islam in America.

MEHRAN KAMRAVA is director of the Center for International and Regional Studies at Georgetown University's School of Foreign Service in Qatar. He is the author of *Revolution in Iran: The Roots of Turmoil* (1990), *The Political History of Modern Iran: From Tribalism to Theocracy* (1992), *Revolutionary Politics* (1992), *Politics and Society in the Developing World* (1993, 2000), *Understanding Comparative Politics: A Framework for Analysis* (1996, 2008), *Democracy in the Balance: Culture and Society in the Middle East* (1998), *Cultural Politics in the Third World* (1999), *The Modern Middle East: A Political History since the First World War* (2005), and *Iran's Intellectual Revolution* (2008), in addition to a number of journal articles. He has also edited *The New Voices of Islam: Rethinking Politics and Modernity* (2006) and is the co-editor of the two-volume work *Iran Today: An Encyclopedia of Life in the Islamic Republic* (2008).

PATRICK LAUDE is professor of French at the Georgetown University School of Foreign Service in Qatar. A former fellow of the Ecole Normale Supérieure in Paris, he has a master's degree in philosophy from the Université Paris-Sorbonne (Paris IV), with certificates in Islamic and Indian philosophy, and a Ph.D. from Indiana University. Laude's scholarly and personal interests lie in the relationship between poetry and contemplative or mystical traditions, as well as in Western representations and interpretations of Islam and Asian religions. He is currently working on a book on Islamic spirituality in twentieth-century French thought and its relevance in the Islamic world. He is the author of nine books, including *Pray Without Ceasing: The Way of the Invocation in World Religion* (2006); *Divine Play, Sacred Laughter and Spiritual Understanding* (2005); *Singing the Way: Insights in Poetry and Spiritual Transformation* (2005); *Frithjof Schuon (1907–1998): Life and Teachings* (2004); *Massignon intérieur* (2001); and *Approches du quiétisme* (1992).

ZIBA MIR-HOSSEINI is a legal anthropologist, specializing in Islamic law, gender, and development. She obtained her B.A. in sociology from Tehran University (1974) and her Ph.D. in social anthropology from the University of Cambridge (1980). She is senior research associate at the London Middle Eastern Institute, SOAS, University of London, and has held numerous research fellowships and visiting professorships. Since 2002, she has been Hauser Global Law Visiting Professor at the School of Law, New York University. Mir-Hosseini's publications include the monographs *Marriage on Trial: A Study of Islamic Family Law in Iran and Morocco* (1993, 2002), *Islam and Gender: The Religious Debate in Contemporary Iran* (1999, 2000), and (with Richard Tapper) *Islam and Democracy in Iran: Eshkevari and the Quest for Reform* (2006). She has also directed (with Kim Longinotto) two award-winning feature-length documentary films on contemporary issues in Iran: *Divorce Iranian Style* (1998) and *Runaway* (2001).

TARIQ RAMADAN is senior research fellow at St Antony's College, Oxford University, Doshisha University (Kyoto, Japan), and the Lokahi Foundation (London). He is also a visiting professor (holding the chair "Identity and Citizenship") at Erasmus University Rotterdam. Through his writings and lectures, Ramadan has contributed substantially to the debate on the issues of Muslims in the West and Islamic revival in the Muslim world. He is active both at the academic and grassroots levels, lecturing extensively throughout the world on social justice and dialogue between civilizations. Ramadan is currently president of the European Muslim Network (EMN) in Brussels. His latest book is *The Messenger: The Meaning of the Life of Muhammad* (2007).

JOHN O. VOLL is professor of Islamic history and associate director of the Prince Alwaleed bin Talal Center for Muslim-Christian Understanding at Georgetown University. He taught Middle Eastern, Islamic, and world history at the University of New Hampshire for thirty years before moving to Georgetown in 1995. Voll graduated from Dartmouth College and received his Ph.D. degree from Harvard University. He has lived in Cairo, Beirut, and Sudan, and has traveled widely in the Muslim world. The second edition of his book *Islam: Continuity and Change in the Modern World* appeared in 1994. He is co-author, with John L. Esposito, of *Islam and Democracy* and *Makers of Contemporary Islam,* and is editor, author, or co-author of seven additional books. He is a past president of the Middle East Studies Association and also of the New England Historical Association. He has served on the boards of directors of the American Council of Learned Societies, the New Hampshire Humanities Council, the New Hampshire Council on World Affairs, the Sudan Studies Association, and the board of the World History Association. In 1991, Voll received a presidential medal in recognition for his scholarship on Islam from President Hosni Mubarak of Egypt. He has published numerous articles and book chapters on modern Islamic, Sudanese, and world history.

# Index

Abbasids, 90, 145, 149, 174, 193
'Abd al-Maliks, 145
Abduh, Muhammad, 9, 195, 219–27
Abdul Hamid II, 221
Abi Dawud Sulaiman bin Al-Aash'ath Al-Sijistani, 1
ABIM, Malaysia, 228, 232
Abu Bahr ibn 'Abd al-Rahman and Ahmad, 192–93
Abu Dhakir, Muhammad Hasan, 92
Abu Hanifa, 100, 179, 192–93
Abu Nawwas, 119
Abu-Zayd, Nasr, 13–14, 17, 98–110, 233–34
Addas, Claude, 136
*adhan* (call to prayer), 4–5
Adonis, 14, 111–24
advertising signage, calligraphic, 146, **148**
Afghani, Jamal al-Din, 9, 195, 219, 221
Afghanistan, mujahidin, 232
Africa. *See* Egypt; Morocco; Sudan; Tunisia; West Africa
Afzali, Nasrin, 204
Aga Khan Awards, 161
"age of *hawashi*," 89
Ahmad b. Hanbal, 107
Ahmadinejad, Mahmud, 203, 204
Ahmad Khan, Sir Sayyid, 220, 230
al-Akbar, 127
'Alavi-Tabar, 'Alireza, 74
al-'Alawi, Sheikh Ahmad, 125

Aligarh Muslim University/Aligarh movement, 220
'Ali Ibn Rashiq, 129
al-Qaeda, 43, 232
American Muslims, 15–16, 168–85, 234–35
Amin, Qasim, 195, 197, 223
"Applied Islamology," 41
Aqajari, Hashem, 61, 64–65, 67–68, 69–70
*'aqidah* (creed), 29, 32–33
*Aqlama al-Sitta* (six styles) calligraphy, 145
Arabic: calligraphy script, 146; colloquial, 13, 86–96; dictionaries, 13, 85–88; Greeks translated through, 41; Latin translations of, 50; poetry, 100–101, 108; Qur'an, 13–14, 26, 98–100, 102, 108, 112–13
Arabism, and translation, 98–100
architecture, Islamic, 6, 155–62, **157**, **158**, **161**
Aristotelianism, 39, 42, 47
Arkoun, Mohammed, 12, 13, 17, 39–57, 229–30, 232
Armin, Mohsen, 66
art: Islamic, 144. *See also* literature; visual arts
Ash'ari theologians, 104, 105
Atatürk (Mustafa Kemal), 216
atheism, 48
Attar's *Mantiq altayr*, 131
autobiographies, al-Maghribi's, 94
Averroës (Ibn Rushd), 6, 175, 192, 193

Avicenna (Ibn Sina), 6
Ayazi, Hojjatoleslam, 68

Bachelard, Gaston, 43–44
Badawi, Jamal, 196
Baghdad, fall of (1258 C.E.), 117, 119
al-Bakri, Muhammad Ibn Abil Surur, 88
al-Banna, Gamal, 205, 233–34
al-Banna, Hasan, 224–25
Baqi, 'Emadeddin, 69, 72
al-Baqillani, Abu-Bakre, 103–4
Barraclough, Geoffrey, 218
Bazargan, 'Abdolali, 62
Bell, Daniel, 217
Berkey, Jonathan, 6
*Bey'at*, 67
*bid'a*, 2–10, 14, 32–33, 129; American Muslims and, 169; dress, 31–32, 197. *See also* innovation
binary thinking, 39–55
Blackamericans: Christians, 183; Muslims, 170–72, 180, 182, 183, 184–85
Bojnourdi, Ayatollah Mohammad Musavi, 67
Bukhara, Samanid tomb, 156, **157**
Bulliett, Richard, 179

Cairo: dictionary of colloquial speech of, 13, 86–96; neo-Mamluk architecture, 157
caliphate: first, 117, 118; modern, 9, 30–31, 120, 227; Umayyad, 119
calligraphy, Islamic, 145–49, **146–48**
Carter, Stephen, 182
Catholicism: divide from other religions, 42–43; exceptionalism, 50–51; nonreligious, 52
ceramics, 149–55, **150, 151, 152, 153**; *cuerda seca* or "dry cord," 156, 160
Chenu, Dominique, 52
Christianity, 39; exceptionalism, 50–51; Islamic divide from, 41–44; nonreligious, 52, 53–54; and Qur'an language, 105–6; reform thinking, 23–24
civil society, democracy and, 68–70
class: clerical, 75–76, 77; scribal, 145–46
Clifford, James, 44
coffee, *bid'a*, 5
coffeehouses, Cairo, 91
colonialism: Western, 40, 117, 221. *See also* postcolonial period
conservatism: Islamic, 1, 2, 6, 7–10, 61–62, 67, 225, 229; traditionalist, 220–21

Constitution, U.S., American Muslims and, 175
consultation (*shura*), 68, 70
context: dictionaries, 88; *ijtihad* and, 71; innovation, 3–6; interpretation and, 27–36
Cook, Michael, 2
Corbin, Henry, 139
cosmopolitanism, global rooted, 231–35
creativity: artistic innovation and, 143, 162; and religious texts, 116–17; Sufi poetry, 129–30, 135, 137
Crone, Patricia, 173–74
cyber-Islam, 232–33

*dar al-harb/dar al-islam* dichotomy, 173–74
decline: literature and, 89–95; "renaissance" as, 119
democracy, 16, 46; Islamic, 34, 60–70, 121; Muslims in non-Muslims polities and, 178–79, 182; West, 16, 54, 65–66
Denny, Walter B., 14–15, 143–63
*dhikr* (remembrance of Origin), 130, 132, 133, 134
dictionaries, 85–88; dialect, 90; "dictionary from below," 13, 92–96; history writing and, 90–91; *Lisan al-'Arabi*, 99, 115; al-Maghribi's, 13, 86, 88–96; and social history, 85–94
"difference," right to protection of, 46–47
*divani* script, Ottoman, 146
Dome of the Rock calligraphy, Jerusalem, 145
Doss, Madiha, 87
dress: both men and women, 31–32, 191–92, 203; women's, 16, 190–212
Drucker, Peter, 217

economies, Islamic, 7–8
'Edalatnezhad, Hojjatoleslam Saeed, 74–75
education: girls' schools, 196–97; modern curriculum, 220
Egypt: Muslim Brotherhood, 224, 225, 226, 232; Takfir wa al-Higrah, 226. *See also* Cairo
elections, political participation by, 67
Eliot, T.S., 129
Enlightenment: false universals, 167; Johnson dictionary, 85–86; racially agnostic, 172; reason, 43–55
Eshkevari, Hassan Yusefi, 202
Europe: exceptionalism, 50–51; Islamic modernists and, 220–21, 222–23; modern state-societies, 215, 216;

Muslims in, 234–35; rational sciences, 6–7, 43–55; trade and competition, 7–8; World War II, 43. *See also* Enlightenment; France

Fakhr al-Islam, 197
false universals, 167–68, 235–36
father, in Islam, 113
Fathy, Hassan, 162
Feiz, 'Alireza, 72
feminists: "Islamic," 231; and women's dress, 16, 190–91, 193, 207
*fiqh* (jurisprudence), 12, 16, 41, 178–79; freedoms, 66; *ijtihad* and, 33, 71–74; *madhabs* (schools of jurisprudential thought), 6; new science of, 233; reform in Iran, 67–77; Shi'a, 13, 62; and women's dress, 191–208
Firuzabadi, 85
Foucault, Michel, 45
France: Muslim thinkers, 229–30; and women's dress, 207
Frankfurt School of Critical Theory, 184
freedoms: Islam, 64, 65–66; opinion, 65–66; religion, 122–24; thought, 65–66; women's dress, 207
fundamentalism, Islamic, 10, 14, 41, 48, 49, 119–20; "neofundamentalists," 169–70. *See also* Islamism
*fusha* language, 90–91

Gadamer, Hans, 52
Gasprinskii/Gaspirali, Ismail Bey, 220
"gaze," man on women, 191, 192
gender issues, 11, 223, 224–25, 230–31, 234. *See also* dress; marriage; women
Ghannoushi, Rashid, 229
Ghaylan of Damascus, 105–6
Al-Ghazali, 24, 194
al-Ghazali, Zaynab, 225
Geertz, Clifford, 44
Girard, René, 52
globalization, modern, 215–16, 231–36
Golden Age, of Arabo-Islamic civilization, 40–41
Goody, Jack, 44
Gouguenheim, Sylvain, 50
government: parliamentary process, 68; religion and, 61–65. *See also* caliphate; democracy; law; politics
Gran, Peter, 91
Gunn, Geoffrey C., 216
Gynmastiar, Abdullah, 233

Hadid, Zaha, 162
*Hadith* (Prophetic tradition), 1, 12, 24–25, 28, 32, 41, 116; and *hijab*, 198; and innovation, 115; and spiritual heart, 126; on women, 194
Hajjarian, Saeed, 68–69, 72, 73
al-Hajj Umar Tal, 221
*al-hakimiyah* (exclusive rulership), 175–76
Hallaj, 131–32, 139
Hanafi, Hasan, 229–30
Hanna, Nelly, 13, 85–97
Hasan, Muhammad Abdullah, 221
Hassan ibn Thabit, 111–12, 128
Hauerwas, Stanley, 183–84
"*hawashi*," "age of," 89
Hayek, Friedrich, 64
heart, Sufi poetry, 125–27, 137
Hegel, G.W.F., 53–54
Heinrich Böll Institute in Berlin, 202
hermeneutics, 59, 233–34; *ijtihad* and, 11, 70–77; legal, 233; and reform, 17, 23–38, 61–77. *See also tafsir* (interpretation)
*hijab* (covering of a Muslim woman's body), 16, 190–212
al-Hilli, Muhaqqiq, 194
historiography, 12, 41, 90–91. *See also* modern period; "mytho-history"; postmodern period; premodern period; social history
Hosseiniyeh Ershad, Iran, 199
Hourani, Albert, 40

'*ibadat* (worship), 32–33
Ibn al-'Arabī, 135–37, 139
Ibn Hanbal, 179
Ibn Mandur, 85
ibn Muqla, 145
Ibn Qayyim al-Jawziyah, 176
Ibn Qutayba, 100–101
Ibn Rushd (Averroës), 6, 175, 192, 193
Ibn Sina (Avicenna), 6
Ibn Taymiyah, 176
Ibrahim, Anwar, 228
*ijtihad* (independent reasoning), 6–12; American Muslims and, 169; and *fiqh* (jurisprudence), 33, 71–74; hermeneutics and, 11, 70–77; Iran, 59, 60, 70–71; reason-centered and tradition-centered, 74–75; reform and, 11, 25, 33–36, 60, 70–74
India: Khilafat Movement, 227; Tablighi Jama'at, 225

innovation, 1–2; artistic components, 144–45; obstacles to, 6–10; Sufi poetry, 129–30, 139; tradition required by, 143–44; visual arts, 14–15, 143–63. *See also bid'a*
intellectual developments, Islamic, 6–12, 23–81, 170, 219–26, 229–36. *See also ulama* (religious scholars)
Internet, 203, 204, 232–33
Iqbal, Muhammad, 223, 225–26, 227
Iran: architecture, 156; calligraphy, 146, **147, 150**; ceramics, 150–51, **150, 151, 152, 153**; Constitution (1979), 59; "Moral Security Plan," 203–4; Pahlavi era, 196, 197–98, 199; reformists, 60, 67–77, 201–4; revolution (1978–79), 58–59, 77, 200–201, 228; Seljuks, 150–51; Shi'ism, 4–5, 13, 58–81, 228; war with Iraq, 58, 59, 201, 228; and women's dress, 16, 191, 196–204
Iraq: fall of Baghdad (1258 C.E.), 117, 119; "just war" vs., 49; war with Iran, 58, 59, 201, 228
*islah*. *See* reform
Islam: in America, 168; "closed official corpora," 41; conservatism, 1, 2, 6, 7–10, 61–62, 67, 225, 229; cyber-Islam, 232–33; electronic communications, 232–33; father in, 113; freedoms, 64, 65–66; "historic" and "normative," 234; instinctive, 112; "institutional fixity," 7, 9; law (Shari'a), 8, 176–82, 191–208, 226–29, 233; "other" in, 117, 121; perceptions of, 15; poetry in, 127–29; political, 169, 190, 191, 196, 200, 205–6, 226–29, 232; religionless, 52–53; timeless, 7, 9, 23; true religion, 42, 43, 53–54, 64; as Western "other," 207. *See also* art; fundamentalism; hermeneutics; intellectual developments; Muslims; Prophet Muhammad; Qur'an; reform; Shi'ism; Sunnism
Islamic Society of Physicians, and women's dress, 198
Islamic Tendency Movement, Tunisia, 229
Islamism: American Muslims, 169–70; and women's dress, 190–91, 207. *See also* fundamentalism; Islam, political; jihad organizations
Ismail, Shah of Iran, 5
Iznik, ceramics, 152–53, **155**

Jabarti, 85
Jackson, Sherman A., 15–16, 167–89, 235–36

al-Ja'd b. Dirham, 105–6
Jadidism, 220
Ja'far al-Sadiq, 179
Ja'farian, Rasul, 197
al-Jahiz, Abu 'Uthman 'Amr b. Bahr, 100
al-Jahni, Ma'bad, 105–6
Jama'at-i Islami, South Asia, 224, 225, 226
Jameelah, Maryam, 225
Japan, non-Western modernity, 215
jihad organizations, 221, 232. *See also* Islamism
*jinn*, 14, 111–12
Johnson, Samuel, 85–86
al-Jubba'i, Abu-Hashim, 102–3
Judaism, 39, 42; Torah, 39, 113, 114
jurisprudence. *See fiqh*
al-Jurjani, 'Abdul-Qahir, 104–5
al-Jurjānī, 'Al&imacr$ ibn Muhammad, 138
justice, God's attribute, 105
"just war," 43, 46, 48, 49

Kadivar, Mohsen, 60, 76, 203
Kamrava, Mehran, 1–20, 58–81
Kant, I., 54, 172
Katir'i, Mostafa, 60
Kazemi, 'Abbas, 71
Kemal, Mustafa (Atatürk), 216
Keshavarz, Fatemeh, 133
Khaled, Amr, 233
Khalil, Sidi, 194
Khatami, Mohammad, 60, 70, 76, 201–2
Khayr al-Din Pasha, 222
Khilafat Movement, India, 227
Khomeini, Ayatollah Ruhollah, 58, 59, 201, 203, 228
Khouri, Ellen, 111
"knowledge," new understandings of, 230
Kufi calligraphy, **145, 146, 150, 150**
Kuran, Timur, 5–6, 8, 9

*laïcité*, 55
Lakhani, Ali, 129
Laude, Patrick, 14, 125–42
law: Islamic (Shari'a), 8, 176–82, 191–208, 226–29, 233; Muslims in non-Muslim countries and, 175–82; Ottoman, 176; positive, 191. *See also fiqh* (jurisprudence)
legitimacy: acceptability and, 67–68; democratic, 66, 67–68; Muslims in non-Muslim polities, 173, 178; predestination for, 105. *See also* law
Lerner, Daniel, 215

Lévi-Strauss, Claude, 44
Levinas, Emmanuel, 52
Lewis, Bernard, 1, 11, 51
"Liberal Age," 40
liberal democracy, 182
liberalism, American, 180, 183–84
liberals/progressives, American Muslims, 168, 169, 171–72
"liberation theology," 230
liminality, problem of, 168, 173, 176–77, 182
Lings, Martin, 127, 130, 132–33
*Lisan al-'Arabi*, 99, 115
literature: Arabic (1600–1800 C.E.), 89–95; and ceramics, 151; and decline, 89–95. *See also* poetry; Qur'an

*madhabs* (schools of jurisprudential thought), 6
al-Maghribi, Yusuf, 13, 86, 88–96
Maghribi script, 145
Mahdist movement, Sudan, 221
Mahmud II, Sultan, 4
Maila, Joseph, 49
al-Makki, 127
Malaysia: ABIM, 228, 232; Islamic state, 228
Malekian, Mostafa, 61, 72
Maliki jurists, 174–75, 179, 194
Mamluks, 85, 157
marriage, men's rights over women, 191, 192, 193–95
Marxist-Communist ideology, collapse of, 46
Marxist positivism, 48
*maslahah* (common good and interest), 25
Massignon, Louis, 139
al-Mawardi, 174
al-Mawdudi, Abu al-A'la, 175, 176, 177, 195, 196, 224–25
Medina, 30–31
Mernissi, Fatema, 230
miracles: by Moses and Jesus, 103; Qur'an, 104
Mir-Hosseini, Ziba, 13, 16, 17, 190–212
modernization/modernity: changing nature of, 214–18; "civil wars" within modernity, 217, 218, 222; freedoms and, 123; globalization and, 215–16, 231–36; "glocal" modernity, 216, 218, 231–36; modernized Islamic traditionalism (or neotraditionalism), 170–72; Mu'awiyam, 118; multiple and competing modernities, 213, 215, 218, 222–26; Muslim movements, 213–38; political, 118; shahs of Iran, 196, 197, 228; sin, 116; and women's dress, 195, 196–97
modern period, 216–18; caliphate, 9, 30–31, 120, 227; industrial society, 217; Islamic intellectual developments, 7–12, 23–38, 44–45, 219–26, 229–36; Muslim movements, 213–38; Muslims in non-Muslim polities, 15–16, 168–85; Ottoman, 89–90; science, 39–55, 220, 230
modesty, 31–32
Mohammedan Anglo-Oriental College, 220
Mojtahed Shabestari, Mohammad, 60, 65, 76
*Le Monde*, 50
monotheism, 41, 114, 175–76
Montazeri, Ayatollah, 73, 75, 203
Morocco: 'Attarin Madrasa tile mosaic, 159; Saadian monuments, 157
mosque architecture, Turkey, 158, *158*, 161
Motahhari, Morteza Ayatollah, 197, 198, 199, 200–201, 204
Mu'adh ibn Jabal, 35–36
Muhammadan Seal, poetry and, 137
Muhammad ibn Idris (ash-Shafi'i), 3, 29–30, 99, 100, 179
Muhammadiya, Southeast Asia, 225
al-Muhibbi, Muhammad Amin, 88
mujahidin, Afghanistan, 232
*Mushaf*, 12
Muslim Brotherhood, Egypt, 224, 225, 226, 232
Muslims: American, 15–16, 168–85, 234–35; France, 229–30; in non-Muslim polities (general), 172–85, 234–35; organizations, 224–29, 232; Russian, 220. *See also* Islam
*al-mutaghayyir* (the changing), 11, 28–33
Mu'tazilites, 102–3, 105–7
"mytho-history," 49, 51
"mytho-ideology," 49–50, 51

al-Nadim, Abdalla, 96
*nahda* ("awakening"), 40
Nahdah Party, Tunisia, 229, 232
*Nahjolbalagheh*, 66
Na'ima, 157
Namdari, Nima, 204
Naqshbandiyyah, 221
Nasr, Seyyed Hossein, 131
*nastaliq* script, 146

nation: modern state-societies, 215, 216; religious, 114, 121, 122–23. *See also* politics
nationalisms: Arabic linked to, 86–87; Islamic state, 226–27; radical and conservative, 223–24
*nazm* (syntax), 104
al-Nazzam, Ibrahim bin Sayyar, 102–3
neotraditionalism, 170–72
"New Religious Thinking," Iran, 201–2
9/11 (September 11, 2001), 43–44, 46, 48, 49, 173, 183
al-Numayri, Ja'far, 229

Ogletree, Charles, 183
organizations: jihad, 221, 232; Muslim, 224–29, 232
Orientalists, and Muslims in non-Muslim polities, 173
originality: artistic, 143; Sufi poetry, 130, 139
Ottomans, 117; Abdul Hamid II, 221; architecture, 156, 157, 158; caliphate, 227; calligraphy, 146; ceramics, 152–53, 155; colloquial Arabic, 87, 90–92; dictionary sources, 86; Ministry of Awqaf (religious endowment), 4; *qanun* (administrative and adjectival law), 176; Sultan Mahmud II, 4; written production, 89

Pahlavi era, Iran, 196, 197–98, 199
painting, ceramics, 151–52
Pakistan, Islamic state, 226
Pan-Islamic movement, 221
parliamentary process, consultation by, 68
Plato, 39, 128, 131
poetry, 14, 113; Arabic, 100–101, 108; *nazm*, 104; "other" in, 117; Persian, 146; Qur'an, 101, 102, 103; renewal in, 114–16; truth in, 111–12, 114–18. *See also* Sufi poetry
political participation: civil society based on, 70; in democracies, 64–68; religious obligation, 66–68; by voting, 67; by women, 197, 198, 199, 206, 207–8
politics: innovation, 5; Islamic resurgence, 226; loyalty, 177–78, 180–81; political Islam, 169, 190, 191, 196, 200, 205–6, 226–29, 232; religion and, 61–70, 117, 118–19, 121–23; and women's dress, 190–91, 196, 200–207. *See also* democracy; law; legitimacy; nation; political participation
polygamy, 171
Pope Benedict XVI, 43, 50
postcolonial period, 40, 41; 9/11 and, 46; women's dress and, 195, 200, 207
"post-industrial" society, 217
postmodern period, 12, 45, 46, 215–18, 224, 226–33
prayer: *adhan* (call to prayer), 4–5; dress during, 191–92; jaculatory *(dhikr Allah),* 133; language, 98, 100, 108; poetry and, 132–33; *salat* (daily prayer), 13–14, 100; Sunna and, 28
predestination, 105, 107
premodern period, 216–17; Islamic tradition, 170; Muslim organizations, 224; Muslims and non-Muslim polities, 173, 176–77, 180–81; Ottoman, 89–90
Prophethood, 24
Prophet Muhammad, 1, 10, 24, 27, 51; *adhan,* 5; *Bey'at,* 67; and *bid'a,* 2–3, 32; conflicts after death of, 118–19; and *islah* (reform), 11, 24–25; Islamic-Christian divide and, 42; and Islamic state, 227; and Medina, 30, 31; and Mu'adh ibn Jabal, 35–36; poet, 111–12; Qur'an language, 98–99, 101, 102, 103, 108, 112–14; revelations, 111–13; *shura,* 68; *sira* (biographies of), 12; Sunna, 28; and *tajdid* (renewal), 24–25; and today's life, 74; and women's dress, 194
Protestantism, nonreligious, 52

Qabel, Ahmad Hojjat ol-Eslam, 74, 76, 203
al-Qadi 'Abd al-Jabbar, 104
al-Qaeda, 43, 232
al-Qasim b. Sallam, Abu-'Ubayd, 99–100
Qur'an: calligraphy in early manuscripts, 145, 146; created, 106–7; discourse, 12, 41–42; eternal, 106–8; freedom, 64, 66; God's speech, 107; *i'jaz* (inimitability), 98, 101–5, 132; immanence of transcendence, 132; interpretation, 26–36; language, 13–14, 26, 98–110, 112–14; on metaphysical origin, 127; mystical poetry compared with, 132–34; originally non-Arabic words, 99–100; on poetry, 128–29, 138; political diversity, 62; political participation, 66; reform and, 11, 26–36, 62, 64, 66; *shura,* 68; translation, 13–14, 98–108; truth in,

111–20; and women's dress, 102, 193, 194, 202, 203, 205; Word of God, 7, 45, 51, 98, 108, 146. *See also* hermeneutics
Qushayri, 127
Qutb, Sayyid, 175, 176, 177, 227

racial/ethnic presuppositions: about Muslims, 182–83. *See also* Blackamericans
Rahman, Fazlur, 234–35
Ramadan, Tariq, 11–13, 17, 23–38, 44, 235
rational sciences, 6–7, 39–55, 230. *See also* reason
reason: "emerging," 47–49; Enlightenment, 43–55; Islamic modernists and, 230; new, 45–46; objectivity, 184. *See also ijtihad* (independent reasoning); rational sciences
reform, 11, 23–38, 61–77; Iran, 60, 67–77, 201–4
Reformation: Christian, 1; in Islam, 13, 77, 233; and Vatican II, 26
religion: atheism, 48; components, 60–61; freedoms, 122–24; pluralism, 64, 171, 234; politics and, 61–70, 117, 118–19, 121–23; return of, 55; revealed truth, 111–24; sciences, 39–55, 72; tolerance, 121–22; true, 42, 43, 49, 51, 53–54, 64. *See also* Christianity; Islam; Judaism; renewal; secularism
"renaissance," 119
renewal (*tajdid*), 11, 14, 24–25, 33–36, 111–24; cultural modernization revolution, 117; defined, 114–16
resurgence, Islamic, 226
"revenge of God," 55
revivalism, architectural style, 157
Reynold, Dwight, 94
Reza Shah Pahlavi, 196, 197
ri'a', in poetry, 138, 139
Ricoeur, Paul, 52
Rida, Rashid, 9, 222–23, 227
Rispler, Vardit, 6
Robertson, Roland, 216
Robson, J., 9–10
Rumi, 133, 137
Al-Rummani, Abu al-Hasan Ali b. 'Isa, 103
Russia, 220, 221

Sageman, Marc, 232
Sahhabi, 'Ezzatollah, 62
Salafism, 9, 30–31, 129, 170
*salat* (daily prayer), 13–14, 100
Salihiyyah, 221
Samanid tomb, Bukhara, 156, **157**
*sarfah*, theory of, 102
Saudi Arabia: Medina, 30–31; Wahhabi, 5–6, 7
Schacht, Joseph, 181
Schuon, Frithjof, 127, 133
science: modern, 39–55, 220, 230; rational, 6–7, 39–55, 230; religious, 39–55, 72; technological innovation in visual arts, 149–55, 156
scribal class, calligraphy by, 145–46
secularism: internal logical contradictions, 61; Iran, 196–97; modernist, 221, 223; and women's dress, 196–97, 207
September 11, 2001, 43–44, 46, 48, 49, 173, 183
Seuil, publisher, 50
sexuality, women's, 192, 193, 194–95, 198–99, 204, 205
Shabistari, Mahmud, *Gulshan-i raz*, 131, 134–35
al-Shafi'i (Muhammad b. Idris), 3, 29–30, 99, 100, 179
Shafi'i jurists, 3, 99, 174, 179
Shahrudi, Ayatollah, 204
Shariati, Ali, 198, 199–200, 202, 204, 229–30
Sharpton, Al, 183
Sherkat, Shahla, 202–3
Shi'ism, 13; *adhan*, 4–5; *ijtihad*, 75; Iran, 4–5, 13, 58–81, 228
*shikasteh* "broken" script, Iran, 146, **147**
al-Shirbini, Yusuf, 88, 92
*shirk*, 138–39, 176, 177
Shoja'izand, Alireza, 65–66
*shura* (consultation), 68, 70
Shushtari, 139
Sinan, 156
Smiley, Tavis, 183
social history, dictionaries and, 85–94
social movements, new forms replacing, 231–32
Somali jihad, 221
Soroush, Abdolkarim, 60, 62, 64, 66, 71, 72, 76, 234
South Asia: Jama'at-i Islami, 224, 225, 226. *See also* Afghanistan; India; Iran; Pakistan

Southeast Asia: Abdullah Gynmastiar, 233; Muhammadiya, 225
Stout, Jeffrey, 183–84
Sudan: Mahdist movement, 221; September Laws (1983), 229; Sudanese Muslim Brotherhood (SMB), 229
Sufi mystical themes, ceramic, 151
Sufi nonmodern *tariqah* organizations, 221, 224
Sufi poetry, 14, 125–42; creation, 129–30, 135, 137; *dhikr,* 130, 132, 133, 134; heart, 125–27, 137; innovation, 129–30, 139; logic, 131–32; *mania,* 131–32; *mantiq,* 131–32; originality, 130, 139; ri'a', 138, 139; *shirk,* 138–39; silence, 133–35
Süleyman the Magnificent, 158
Suna' al-Hiyah (Life Makers), 233
Sunna, 28, 99
Sunnism: *adhan,* 5; American Muslims, 168; eternity of Qur'an, 106; Islamic state, 227, 228
*Surat al-Kahf,* 126–27

Tablighi Jama'at, India, 225
*tafsir* (interpretation), 8, 73. *See also* hermeneutics
Tahmasp, Shah of Iran, 5
al-Tahtawi, Rifa'a Rafi, 222
*tajdid.* *See* renewal
Tajzadeh, Mostafa, 66
Takfir wa al-Higrah, Egypt, 226
*taqlid* (accepting opinions of founders of *madhabs*), 6
*tawhid* (God's absolute unity and uniqueness), 107, 136, 139, 176
technological innovation, visual arts, 149–55, 156
television: *bid'a,* 5–6; State of Black America, 183
terrorists, 232; September 11, 2001, 43–44, 46, 48, 49, 173, 183
*ath-thabit* (the immutable), 11, 28–33
theological studies, 55
"Theory of Organic Groups," 185
Tijaniyyah Tariqah, 221
Tilly, Charles, 231–32
Torah, 39, 113, 114
tradition: American Islam, 170–72; *ijtihad* centered in, 74–75; innovation requiring, 143–44; intellectual capital in, 170
traditionalism: modernists rejecting, 220–21; societies based on, 216

Tunisia: Islamic state, 228–29; Khayr al-Din Pasha, 222; Nahdah Party, 229, 232; women's dress, 205
al-Turabi, Hassan, 205, 229
Turkey: Atatürk, 216; mosque architecture, 158, **158, 161**; tomb of Mehmed I in Bursa, **160**; women's dress, 205, 207

*ulama* (religious scholars): *bid'a,* 4–6, 8; modern Muslim organizations, 224; reform, 23
'Umar Ibn al-Farid, 139
Umayyads, 105, 113, 117, 119, 174
Unger, Roberto, 184–85
*L'Univers historique* (The Historical World), 50
*usul al-din,* 12

Vatican II, 50
Vattimo, Gianni, 52
*Velayat-e Faqih* (supreme jurisconsult), 59, 68
violence: Arab-Islamic history, 118, 121. *See also* wars
visual arts, 14–15, 143–63; architecture, 6, 155–62, **157, 158, 161**; calligraphy, 145–49, **146–48**; ceramics, 149–55, **150, 151, 152, 153**; technological innovation, 149–55, 156
Voll, John O., 16–17, 213–38
voting, political participation by, 67

Wadud, Amina, 234
Wahhabism, 5–6, 7
wars: Arab-Islamic history, 118, 121; "civil wars" within modernity, 217, 218, 222; Iran-Iraq, 58, 59, 201, 228; vs. Iraq, 49; "just," 43, 46, 48, 49; World War II, 43
Weber, Max, 45
West: American Muslims, 15–16, 168–85, 234–35; colonialist, 40, 117, 221; "cultural aggression" *(ghazw fikri),* 40; democracy, 16, 54, 65–66; false universals, 167–68; geopolitical, 50, 51; on history of Islamic thought, 40; Islam as "other," 207; Islam vs., 54; modern Islamic movements and, 218, 219, 220, 221, 222–23; modern state-societies, 215; Muslims in, 15–16, 168–85, 229–30, 234–35; "power of definition," 167–68; and reform of Qur'an, 26, 28; Sufism as

seen in, 128; women's dress as protest vs., 200. *See also* Enlightenment; Europe
West Africa, jihad movement, 221
*What Went Wrong?* (Lewis), 11, 51
*wilaya* (spiritual and temporal authority), in *adhan*, 4–5
women: dress, 16, 190–212; girls' schools, 196–97; rights and responsibilities, 223, 224–25; sexuality, 192, 193, 194–95, 198–99, 204, 205
World War II, 43

Yusofi Eshkevari, Hojjatoleslam Hasan, 60, 61, 64, 67, 74, 76

al-Zabidi, Murtada, 85
Zanjani, Ayatollah 'Abbasali 'Ameed, 66

TEXT
10/13 Sabon

DISPLAY
Sabon (Open Type)

COMPOSITOR
Westchester Book Group

INDEXER
Barbara Roos

PRINTER AND BINDER
IBT Global

www.ingramcontent.com/pod-product-compliance
Lightning Source LLC
Chambersburg PA
CBHW020645230426
43665CB00008B/322